Romantic Days and Nights® in Chicago

FOURTH EDITION

D1251420

Help Us Keep This Guide Up-to-Date

Every effort has been made by the author and editors to make this guide as accurate and useful as possible. However, many things can change after a guide is published—establishments close, phone numbers change, facilities come under new management, and so on.

We would love to hear from you concerning your experiences with this guide and how you feel it could be made better and be kept up-to-date. While we may not be able to respond to all comments and suggestions, we'll take them to heart, and we'll also make certain to share them with the author. Please send your comments and suggestions to the following address:

The Globe Pequot Press
Reader Response/Editorial Department
P.O. Box 480
Guilford, CT 06437

Or you may e-mail us at:

editorial@globe-pequot.com

Thanks for your input,
and happy travels!

ROMANTIC DAYS AND NIGHTS® SERIES

Romantic Days and Nights®

IN CHICAGO

Romantic Diversions in and around the City

FOURTH EDITION

Susan Figliulo

The Globe Pequot Press

GUILFORD, CONNECTICUT

Text design by M. A. Dubé
Interior illustrations by Lana Mullen
Spot art by www.ArtToday.com
Maps by Mary Ballachino

ISBN: 0-7627-2517-6

Manufactured in the United States of America
Fourth Edition/First Printing

With thanks to
all my teachers
and love to my guys

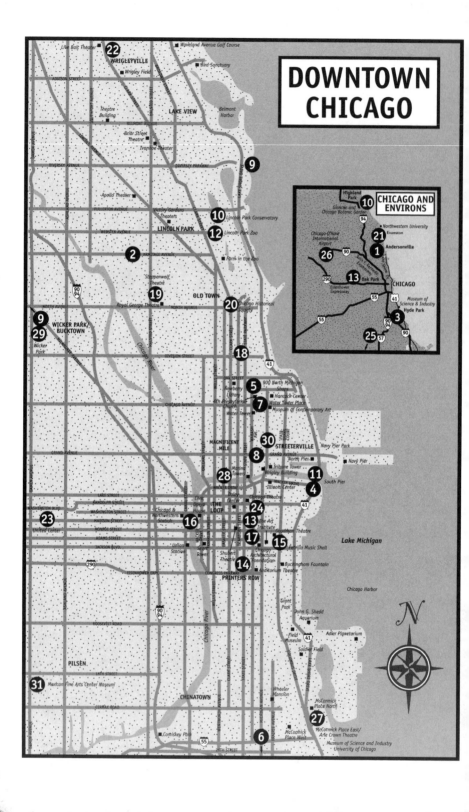

Contents

Acknowledgments — ix

Introduction — xi

Heart of the City

1. Sweet Home Chicago: A Weekend in Andersonville — 3

2. The Good Life on Armitage — 13

3. Hyde Park Honeymoon — 23

4. Fireworks for Two: A Fourth of July Weekend — 31

5. Let it Snow: A Cozy Winter Weekend for Two — 40

6. A Romance with History: African-American Chicago — 46

7. Chicago Christmas à Deux — 52

8. Amore! Chicago Romance Italian-Style — 62

Natural Wonders

9. Adventures in Love: An Outdoor Affair — 69

10. Love in Bloom: A Garden Lovers' Weekend — 75

11. Swept Away: Romantic Lakefront Cruises — 83

12. The Zoo for Two — 92

Arts and Hearts

13. Love Built on Beauty: Architecture in Chicago — 103

14. Words of Love: A Literary Getaway for Lovers — 114

15. Art and Soul: The Art Institute and More — 126

16. Opera Lovers' Tryst — 132

17. The Food of Love: Music in Chicago — 139

18. Shall We Dance? — 147

19. Stages of Romance: A Theater Lovers' Weekend — 154

20. Small Pleasures — 163

The Sporting Life

21. Football Fantasies — 171

22. Wrigleyville Weekend — 178

23. Hoop Lovers' Holiday — 187

24. Romantic Holiday on Ice — 192

Out of this World

25. Stealing Away at Starved Rock — 201

26. Romance and the
Business Traveler:
*How to Savor the
O'Hare Area*   208

27. Un-Conventional:
*A Chance for Romance
at McCormick Place*   214

28. Asian Appreciation
Weekend   220

29. Love in the Hot Zone:
*A Tropics-Inspired
Weekend*   230

30. City Slickers'
Western Weekend   236

31. Hauntingly Romantic:
*Halloween with
Your Honey*   243

INDEXES

General Index   251

Romantic Restaurants   261

Romantic Lodgings   267

Daytime Diversions   268

Evening Diversions   269

About the Author   272

*The prices and rates listed
in this guidebook were confirmed at press time.
We recommend, however, that you call establishments
before traveling to obtain current
information.*

Acknowledgments

FROM THE BOTTOM OF MY HEART, I thank the many people who helped with this book. Anne Basye started the ball rolling; my excellent and congenial editors, Doe Boyle, Laura Strom, Christina Lester, Justine Rathbun, Mimi Egan, and Joan Wheal kept it going with patience, humor, and the occasional nudge. I received all kinds of help, all of it greatly appreciated, from Annie and Mike Chesney, Grace Faustino, Jeff Felshman, Anne Gregory, Diane Hightower, Nicole Hollander, Rick Kogan, Laura Molzahn, Patsy and David Oser, the Riesco family, Mary Shaw, Sue Telingator, Shannon Thor, Hedy Weiss, and the writers. My family was wonderful, especially Stan and Barbara, Carly, Jeanne Bean, my mother, and my sisters. Finally, thanks to Steve Rosswurm for doing whatever he could, even at the last minute, and Barbara Greenman, for her pristine proofreading.

Introduction

ANY CITY WITH A GREAT LAKE IN ITS FRONT YARD has a head start on romance. Chicagoans practically live on the lakefront, especially when they're in love. Even the city's legendary winters don't keep sweethearts from strolling and smooching along Lake Michigan's stretch of up-close natural beauty—miles of it within city limits, and nearly all of it couple-friendly, with walking and biking paths, beaches, boating, and much more.

Along the downtown lakefront, Buckingham Fountain is a favorite spot for lovers to linger in its grand presence. If you're here in spring, summer, or autumn, a visit to the fountain is a must when evening falls and colorful lights enhance the play of water in a magnificently choreographed display.

Let it be noted, too, that scarcely a Chicagoan old enough to neck has missed doing so while parked at Montrose Harbor. We were startled when the city announced plans to return that venerable blacktop to grassy parkland, but Chicago sweethearts are nothing if not resourceful, and excellent necking spots can be found all over town—many of them are mentioned right here in these pages, so you won't have to go looking on your own.

Of course, there's much more to Chicago than water and grass and necking. The City of the Big Shoulders makes you want to lean on a soft shoulder yourself as you take in its wealth of world-class art, architecture, music, museums, theater, and opera. It's also a great sports town, with year-round pro action in basketball, football, ice hockey, and, of course, baseball. (And isn't the Cub fans' perennial cry of "Wait till next year!" just as appropriate when one is disappointed in love?)

Chicago's hotels are cosmopolitan but cozy, its restaurants and clubs sophisticated yet friendly. And because Chicago is known—accurately—as a city of neighborhoods, there are many wonderful ways to get off the tourist path and visit real life in an ethnic enclave, an ivy-covered college "town," or a residential area with something special for the cognoscenti. Exploring with someone you love will give you memories to share forever.

Just a word about the people here: Well, the word is *terrific*. Whether they're lifelong South Side Irish or just in from Central America, Chicagoans find their way here because it's an easy city to love. And a great one to be in love in.

Come and see for yourselves!

The Itineraries

As I was writing this book, I described its romantic weekends and activities to a friend whose life included a newborn, a two-year-old, chaos at work, and a recent move. (Her marriage, at least, is great!) Listening, she sighed and said, "Oh, what fantasies!"

I kept that in mind as I worked, and I offer it to you as you read. As you plan your Chicago interlude, browse through different itineraries and let your fantasies develop, mixing your own interests with the suggestions here to make a getaway that's all your own.

And do remember that when you're in love, money is no object—even if you don't have much. After all, Lake Michigan is the city's single biggest attraction, figuring prominently in itineraries from winter's "Romantic Holiday on Ice" to summer's "Fireworks for Two." And it's free! So is a leisurely ramble through a neighborhood or a just-looking swoop through a posh department store. For every deluxe hotel or four-star restaurant, there's a charming bed-and-breakfast or inexpensive bistro that will be every bit as unforgettable because you've shared it.

Using This Book

All the itineraries here can be used as is, as a sort of romantic road map to an interlude that's intimate, adventurous, challenging, relaxing—whatever you need it to be. At the same time, *please* consider the entire book to be food for your own fantasies.

On the practical side, always call the suggested attractions and establishments to check on dates, prices, and other important information. Every effort has been made to provide accurate information here, but as we all know, things change. Keep in mind that the metro Chicago area telephone system has multiple area codes. Check the telephone directory, or dial 555–1212 (with the applicable area code) for directory assistance to obtain complete information. If you're among the huge number of visitors to Chicago who come on business, surprise! This book has two itineraries just for you, performing the seemingly impossible feat of wresting romance from O'Hare International Airport and McCormick Place. Should you find yourselves with a bit of time away from the business, these and other itineraries offer a zillion ways to enjoy.

If yours is a pleasure trip, note how many itineraries are near each other and think about blending. "Hyde Park Honeymoon," for example, is quite near the locations in "A Romance with History," while the gardens of Lincoln Park detailed in "Love in Bloom" are only yards from the delightful day in "The Zoo for Two" and a few blocks from the charming shops in "The Good Life on Armitage" and the Midwest Buddhist Temple in "Asian Appreciation Weekend." Even some far-flung itineraries can be combined: The Oak Park landmarks in "Love Built on Beauty" aren't far from Brookfield Zoo, in "The Zoo for Two."

Finally: Don't *ever* give up on a place you'd love to visit because it seems beyond your means. Hotels are always offering discounts and special rates. (As my friend, fashion writer and woman-about-town Lisbeth Levine, sniffs: "*Nobody* pays rack rate!") Half-price tickets for practically everything in town are available on the day of the show at Hot Tix booths. (See "Stages of Romance" for details.) And many restaurants offer special early dinner menus with lower prices. Even at an expensive restaurant, a dinner of appetizers may be affordable, and the bill could be downright moderate if you go for lunch instead of dinner. And speaking of restaurant prices: When you see "inexpensive," "moderate," or "expensive" here, it indicates an approximate price range for appetizer, entree, and dessert but excludes drinks, tax, and tip. "Inexpensive" means less than $20 per person, "moderate" between $20 and $40 per, and "expensive" more than $40.

Speaking of inexpensive, the budget icon (look for the piggy bank in the margins) indicates less expensive hotel, restaurant, and entertainment alternatives.

Remember, then, always to ask about special arrangements. There's no one more special than you and your sweetheart.

GETTING HERE AND GETTING AROUND

The gigantic O'Hare International Airport brings thousands of travelers to Chicago daily—and leaving can be easier than arriving. Domestic and international terminals are linked to the Chicago Transit Authority (CTA) rapid transit train that reaches downtown in about thirty-five minutes for just $1.50 per person. Maps are abundant and clearly marked if you need to make connections (free!) from there.

To go directly to a hotel downtown or in the North Shore or Oak Brook suburbs, consider the Continental Airport Express van service. One way downtown is $14.75 (round-trip, $25.50). If you prefer a taxi, the ride downtown takes about thirty minutes (or much longer in rush hour) and costs about $30. The two of you can take advantage of the shared-ride program, which allows a flat rate of $13 per passenger.

Midway Airport (5700 South Cicero Avenue; 773–838–0600) is a smaller airport whose three terminals meet in a central lobby. Here, too, CTA rapid-transit trains can get you downtown in about half an hour for $1.50. Continental Air Transport van service is $10.50 to downtown, $19.00 round-trip; trip length, again, varies with traffic, but twenty minutes to downtown is possible.

Chicago also is Amtrak's hub, with about fifty trains arriving and departing daily from Union Station (210 South Canal Street; 312–655–2385). Cabs are readily available at both the upper- and lower-level exits from the station.

Public transportation in the city is easy via CTA rapid-transit, subway, and elevated trains—all of which are commonly and collectively referred to as "the El." Bus service honeycombs the city and reaches anywhere the El doesn't. Bus or El rides cost $1.50, transfers get you from bus to train or vice versa, and from bus to bus, for an extra 25 cents, and there are a few surcharges for going into the suburbs. The system is reasonably well kept and reasonably safe, especially if you're traveling during the day and other people are around. The CTA, for my money, is the best bargain in town.

Most Romantic Places in Chicago

Most Romantic Lodgings

Windy City Inn, Chicago
Fish out of Water, Chicago
Drake Hotel, Chicago
Starved Rock State Park Lodge, Starved Rock
Wheeler Mansion, Chicago

Most Romantic Restaurants

Ambria, Chicago
Geja's Cafe, Chicago
Restaurant on the Park, Art Institute, Chicago
La Bocca della Verita, Chicago
Tallgrass, Lockport

Best Places to Steal a Kiss

Lakeside, outside the southeast entrance to the east building at **McCormick Place**

On the north- or southeast side of the **Michigan Avenue bridge**

While watching a fireworks display from **Grant Park**

On the steps of the **Art Institute**

At the top of the world (more or less) on **Sears Tower**

Best Places to Go Glamorous

Opening night at **Lyric Opera,** Chicago

Dancing at the **Pump Room,** Chicago

A concert by the Chicago Symphony at **Symphony Center,** Chicago

High tea at the **Four Seasons Hotel,** Chicago

A big show at the **Auditorium Theatre,** Chicago

Secret Gardens

Japanese Garden, Wooded Island, Chicago

Merrick Rose Garden, Evanston

Northshore Sculpture Garden, Skokie

Shakespeare Garden, Northwestern University, Evanston

Lincoln Park Conservatory, Chicago

Heart
of the City

Sweet Home Chicago
A WEEKEND IN ANDERSONVILLE

CHICAGO HAS ALWAYS BEEN KNOWN as a city of neighborhoods, and this little gem is one of the sweetest. It's in the northern part of the Edgewater area, and though it's less than a mile in from Lake Michigan's shore, Andersonville has escaped the high-rent hustle of many lakefront areas. This is a genuine neighborhood, friendly and unassuming, not a bit snobbish or suspicious about strangers.

Andersonville was first settled by Swedes, and you'll find a distinctly Scandinavian flavor along its main avenue, North Clark Street. But don't be fooled by this blue-eyed, blond exterior; Andersonville's heart is vibrantly multiethnic and proudly tolerant, which helps explain how, through more than a century of change and growth, Andersonville has kept a homey, down-to-earth feeling that's as cozy and romantic as snuggling by the fireplace.

PRACTICAL NOTES: This three-day itinerary assumes a long weekend, but feel free to tailor it to your availability. Any time of year is pleasant in Andersonville, although obviously a day at the beach works only during the summer. That's when the local bed-and-breakfast fills weeks in advance, so be sure to call well before your visit.

Getting around in Andersonville mostly consists of walking, though we've noted the places where you'll want to grab a cab. In general, the neighborhood is safe, and cabs are needed only at night for distances too long to walk.

Romance AT A GLANCE

◆ Make a charming neighborhood your own for the weekend in **Andersonville**, home of the **Swedish American Museum** (5211 North Clark Street; 773–728–8111).

◆ Travel the globe in a coffeehouse at **Kopi, a Travelers' Cafe** (5317 North Clark Street; 773–989–5674); sample Swedish specialties at **Ann Sather** (5207 North Clark Street; 773–271–6677).

◆ Revel in the pleasures of the lakefront—most of them free!—with swimming, sunbathing, fishing, and golf at **Lincoln Park.**

◆ Ramble through the past at **Rosehill Cemetery** (5800 North Ravenswood Avenue; 773–561–5940); plan your future next to a cozy fire at the **Fireside Restaurant** (5739 North Ravenswood Avenue; 773–878–5942).

DAY ONE: morning/afternoon

Begin your Andersonville visit by settling in at **The Inn on Early** (1241 West Early Avenue; 773–334–4666; www.innonearly.com). Located on a side street in this gentrifying but still diverse neighborhood, The Inn on Early is as unpretentious as it is cozy. (Instant evidence: the pretty NO WHINING plaque hanging in the foyer.) From its lovingly tended backyard garden to the piano in the living room to the double Jacuzzi in the Manhattan Room's master bath, you'll appreciate the inn's winning mix of comfortable accommodations and down-to-earth hospitality. (The daily continental breakfast doesn't hurt, either.) "We like to consider our guests as part of the family," says your hostess, and it must work; the "family" includes quite a few repeat visitors. The Inn on Early books well in advance during busy periods (spring graduation at nearby Loyola University is one), so call as far in advance as you can. And be pleasantly surprised at rates that start at just $95 a night.

BREAKFAST

Some guests choose to start their Andersonville day the way many residents do: with a serious breakfast at **Ann Sather** (5207 North Clark Street; 773–271–6677), a charming, inexpensive restaurant that only looks as if it has been a neighborhood fixture for years. Its upper story is quieter than the bustling ground floor, but both offer window tables that are fun for people-watching. When ordering, heed the one inviolable rule at Ann's, which is never to skip the cinnamon rolls. These sweet, yeasty favorites are the sort of thing a Chicagoan might bring a homesick friend stuck out of town. And try the Scandinavian specialties, such as lingonberry pancakes, and mild, meaty potato sausage (think boudin blanc). The kitchen can work up a carryout lunch, too; or choose your own from **Wikstrom's** deli (5247 North Clark Street; 773-878-0601).

Summer weekends in Andersonville mean taking time to stretch out at **Kathy Osterman Beach,** a sandy slice of heaven that, inexplicably, is crowded only on the hottest days. Arrive early nonetheless to stake out your spot. The beach is east and north of Andersonville, starting at Hollywood Avenue, where Lake Shore Drive turns into Sheridan Road. Smart beachgoers beat the parking squeeze by taking a cab.

Not a beach day? Then stroll through the northern stretch of **Lincoln Park,** from around Foster Avenue as far south as you care to go. Joggers, bicyclists, tai chi practitioners, and other

That Posh Pink Building

Perhaps you've noticed the huge pink stucco building on the corner of Sheridan Road and Bryn Mawr Avenue at Andersonville's northeast tip. It's the **Edgewater Beach Apartments,** fraternal twin to the old **Edgewater Beach Hotel.** This lavish resortlike outpost was among the world's grandest hotels in the 1920s and 1930s, with a private beach, outdoor dancing under the stars, and seaplane service to the Loop. You can visit a charming reminder of its glory days in the apartment building, where **Anna Held Flower Shop** (5555 North Sheridan Road; 773-561-1940) holds stunning blooms and a tiny ice-cream parlor.

pleasure seekers will be there, too, enjoying this quiet area that's truly open to all and considered not a bit dangerous. As you walk south, keep an eye out for a small hill topped by shrubbery and trees. This is a federally protected bird sanctuary, and if you've brought binoculars, you can sit and watch carefully for any rara avis.

A bit farther south is Montrose Harbor, complete with a bait shop to service the pier's fishing enthusiasts. These could include you, of course, so plan accordingly if you or your sweetheart might feel the urge to cast a line. You can even arrange your own fishing expedition, including everything from boat to bait, through the shop; call (773) 271-2838 for information.

Golfers adore the lakeside challenge of the nine-hole, par thirty-six **Sidney Marovitz Golf Course,** a little south of Montrose Harbor at Waveland Avenue. It's one of the Chicago Park District's toughest courses, but if you and your partner are up to snuff, get tee-time reservations by calling (312) 245-0909.

DAY ONE: evening

DINNER

After a day outdoors, head to one of Andersonville's many moderately priced restaurants. At the very chic, BYOB **Tomboy** (5402 North Clark Street; 773-907-0636), the menu is eclectic and the atmosphere is friendly—but the noise can rival any in New York, so come early and take the cozy table near the window for good people-watching at a tolerable decibel level.

Italian restaurants represent the old and new in Andersonville. The chic **La Donna** (5146 North Clark Street; 773-561-9400) offers a sophisticated menu with attractively spare decor (get a table in back). Or go retro at **Calo** (5343 North Clark Street; 773-271-7725), a culinary time capsule that looks like a set for a Martin Scorsese movie. But don't watch for "goodfellas"; these are just neighborhood people who want noodles, not nouvelle. There's pizza, too, and always fish on Friday. Ask for a booth where you can linger over an after-dinner drink—or step right next door to sip in high style at Calo's trendy little sister, **La Finestra** (5341 North Clark Street; 773-334-4525), which attracts the fashionable folks who prefer Florentine to Siciliana.

Andersonville being a residential area, later nightlife in the neighborhood tends to be quiet. North of the area, in Rogers Park, is a funky, friendly coffeehouse, **No Exit** (6970 North Glenwood Avenue; 773-743-3355), where there's often live music and always caffeine to fuel conversation. (*Hint:* Cab or drive there; the bus means a long wait at night.) Or step across the street to a bona fide Chicago institution, **Heartland Cafe** (7000 North Glenwood Avenue; 773-465-8005; www.heartlandcafe.com), where the '60s never stopped and the buffalo burger consists of just that. (Naturally, the kitchen is also very much vegetarian- and vegan-friendly.) Outdoors, getting a table in the front area guarantees that life's rich pageant will entertain you until closing. Indoors, you can browse the alternative-minded General Store for anything from hemp handbags to socialist magazines. Or just get a table and sit for hours, taking in live music, poetry readings, and the intense discussions around you. For a more adventurous atmosphere, the two of you can check out the scene to the south of Andersonville at **Big Chicks** (5024 North Sheridan Road; 773-728-5511). Weekends are packed with an incredibly eclectic clientele of gays, artists, and other people who appreciate a *lot* of diversity.

DAY TWO: morning

After sampling the goodies from the **Swedish Bakery** (5348 North Clark Street; 773-561-8919), stroll a block south to visit the small but proud **Swedish American Museum** (5211 North Clark Street; 773-728-8111; www.samac.org), which hosts traveling exhibits and is a treasury of anecdotal information about the neighborhood's early days. The gift shop boasts a good supply of Scandinavian-themed books and souvenirs.

Browsing along Clark Street, you'll find plenty of little shops with unique identities and merchandise to match. Book lovers lose hours at **Women & Children First** (5233 North Clark Street; 773-769-9299; www.womenandchildrenfirst.com), where the staff of friendly feminists stock fascinating books, periodicals, music, and literary paraphernalia. A large area is devoted to books and music for kids, and any staffer can offer educated suggestions on an age-appropriate gift for

your favorite small fry. Comfy chairs and a civilized air make it manda-
tory to linger and read. As you leave, don't miss the countertop baskets
of lapel buttons sporting the latest politically correct messages.

Next door, at **Studio 90** (5239 North Clark Street; 773-
878-0097), designing owners Angela Turley and Jill Hilgenberg create women's fashions that offer a wardrobe's worth of possibilities;
likewise a great selection of unusual jewelry and accessories, some
of which could even make a good unisex gift.

Across the street and also chock-full of intriguing finds is **Los
Manos Gallery** (5220 North Clark Street; 773-728-8910), where
the work is cutting edge yet, in the spirit of the neighborhood,
unpretentious and very much an alternative to the downtown scene.
And don't miss the possibilities in the three-level **Landmark of
Andersonville** (5301 North Clark Street; 773-728-5301), which
holds several little shops offering everything from delicate linens to
picture frames. Be sure to check out **While You Wait** for maternity
gear—including rentable clothes for special occasions—and
Gourmet Cabinet for kitchen gear and gift items.

LUNCH

If a day of slow-paced browsing isn't everyone's idea of an
excellent time, take a lunch break at **Kopi, a Travelers' Cafe**
(5317 North Clark Street; 773-989-5674). From the wall of postcards at its entrance to the tiny boutique in back, Kopi is a coffeehouse with a personality—one that likes globe-trotting and
dropping a line to the folks back home. *Kopi* is an Indonesian word
for "coffee," and behind the counter's upper walls, a neat lineup of
clocks tells the time in various parts of the world.

Kopi has plenty of tables for two, but the best place to linger is
right in front. Remove your shoes, step up to the elevated area at
your right, and snuggle in among the pillows at these near-the-floor
tables. This hangout for the neighborhood's artistic types is one of
those places where you'll fall silent while eavesdropping on the next
table's fascinating discussion. Coffee is the menu's most serious
subject—and the barrels in front are full of take-out beans—but the
salad and focaccia entrees are good, and the rich desserts are made
for sharing. Be sure to check out the boutique; it's where I got the
best little black dress ever, in travel-perfect crinkly rayon.

DAY TWO: afternoon

As you explore Clark Street, ramble toward the neighborhood's north end, with its sudden stretch of green at **Gethsemane Garden Center** (5739 North Clark Street; 773–878–5915). This sprawling gardeners' haven offers everything from herbs in tiny pots to ready-to-plant trees, and browsing together is fun even if you don't buy. Watch out for puddles underfoot, and be prepared for a crowd if the weather is at all nice. Chicago's motto may be *urbs in horto*— "city in a garden"—but weather-dependent gardeners go by *carpe diem*—"seize the day."

Back south on Clark Street, check out performance times at the **Griffin Theatre** (5404 North Clark Street; 773–769–2228). This is one of the younger companies in Chicago's famed theater community, and its productions of *All the Way Home, And Neither Have I Wings to Fly,* and others have won critical acclaim. Its humble home is nothing to brag about, but nothing to apologize for, either; such makeshift origins preceded glory for Steppenwolf and other local companies.

A more offbeat production is at the **Neo-Futurarium** (5153 North Ashland Avenue; 773–275–5255), just west of Clark at Foster Avenue. In its home above the venerable Nelson Funeral Home, this company has made a late-night cult hit of *Too Much Light Makes the Baby Go Blind*, a constantly

Hot Properties

When the weather's friendly, wander with your sweetheart through the residential neighborhood just east of Clark Street. It's called Lakewood-Balmoral and is one of the city's hottest real estate areas, with blocks of century-old homes and two- or three-flats. Many are beautifully restored and home to members of the very tony Saddle & Cycle Club, which lies just west of the lake on Foster Avenue and is one of the city's most exclusive private clubs. But you don't have to be a member to stroll arm in arm along Lakewood-Balmoral's well-tended blocks and dream of the day when you and your honey might move into one of these Victorian jewels.

evolving collection of short pieces. It's the kind of eccentric show that Chicagoans love to discover and support with word of mouth, so if you and your beloved are at all interested in the theater, give it a whirl.

And speaking of giving a whirl, consider a different form of amusement farther south on Andersonville's main strip. A plain exterior and dingy interior disguise the colorful history of **USA Rainbow Roller Center** (4836 North Clark Street; 773–271–5668). Rainbow has been just about everything a big old barn of a building could be, from old-time movie palace to ice rink to psychedelic haven (where Led Zeppelin performed on its first American tour) to speakeasy—complete with underground escape tunnels exiting in the cemetery across the street. Today Rainbow is a favorite for skating and blading alike, offering open skating on weekends both early in the day (which is the least crowded but more family-oriented time) and late at night after the children have gone to bed; call to check on open-skating times.

No skates? No problem: Strap on rental in-lines or traditional roller skates and glide away with your good sport of a sweetheart. Listen for couples-only songs; the music is loud, but the atmosphere's undeniable—although the noisy, overlit arcade in the rear is best avoided. When you're ready to rest, choose a booth just beyond the skating area. Snacks are strictly of the hot-dogs-and-nachos variety, but this is a roller rink.

DAY TWO: evening

DINNER

After a workout on wheels, you'll probably be ready to think about dinner—and there's nothing better than Middle Eastern for healthful, slightly exotic fare. Several Middle Eastern restaurants are among the neighborhood's best for dinner. The largest is **Reza's** (5255 North Clark Street; 773–561–1898), where the decor is loftish, the menu is Mediterranean, and kabobs are a familiar choice of entree. A table for two along one of the sandblasted-brick walls will let you linger over tea long after the baklava's finished. Turkish fare is on the menu at the upscale **Cousins** (5203 North Clark Street; 773–334–4553), where a window table is the nicest. At **Kan**

Zaman (5204 North Clark Street; 773–506–0191), ask for the front area where seating is on comfy floor pillows, which will let you relax while enjoying a mix-and-match menu prepared with your choice of seafood or meat. All three restaurants are located an easy stroll from the Griffin and the Neo-Futurarium theaters, and all three are moderate in price.

DAY THREE: morning

BREAKFAST

 Head for the neighborhood's western border and **Pauline's** (1754 West Balmoral; 773–561–8573). This quintessential diner serves up a breakfast that can't be beat, from plenty of hot coffee to authentic hash browns, all for about seven bucks per person. And the atmosphere's thicker than the vinyl tablecloths. Pauline's major influences include Elvis, Marilyn, jukebox culture, and the Chicago Cubs. Each booth holds magazines to browse, once you've sampled the visual feast of vintage photos and advertising that covers every inch of flat surface. (Pauline's is swell for lunch, too.)

An offbeat but genuinely pleasant way to pass the morning is with a long walk through one of the neighborhood's landmarks, **Rosehill Cemetery** (5800 North Ravenswood Avenue; 773–561–5940). I've walked Rosehill hundreds of times and always appreciate the serenity in its acres of lush greenery, glittering ponds, and well-tended pathways. Some markers show dates reaching back to the eighteenth century, but there are far more memorials here from the nineteenth century; and if you happen to come on Memorial Day weekend, Rosehill sponsors a program saluting its many veterans of the nation's wars.

As you ramble the grounds, be sure to notice the cemetery's silent treasures. At its entrance are neat rows of tombstones commemorating some of the Illinois soldiers who died in the Civil War. Just to the north is a touching monument to Chicago's firefighters, its statue surrounded by a knee-high border that, if you look closely, turns out to be a length of hose. Farther in is a lovely marble statue of Frances M. Pearce and her infant daughter, who died of tuberculosis in 1854. Coming upon this glass-enclosed statue, atop its 5-foot-high pedestal, has been described as finding the sleeping Snow White; mother and baby lie together as if napping, their eyes closed, the mother's hand resting over her child's.

Through the cemetery, other statuary and large, ornate mausoleums salute moneyed families, including that of Charles Hull, whose Hull House was Jane Addams's most famous settlement house. A newer Asian area is all colorful ribbons and tombstone inscriptions in characters of other languages. Perversely, wandering through this place of remembrance can make you and your loved one rejoice in being alive and together.

LUNCH

When you've walked enough, head back to the cemetery's east entrance and stop for lunch across the street at the **Fireside Restaurant** (5739 North Ravenswood Avenue; 773–878–5942). This unpretentious spot offers an enclosed garden area if you're up for more of the great outdoors; if you'd rather warm up, head for the eponymous fireplace. Booths along one wall are cozy, too. The menu is inexpensive to moderate, its items standard but well prepared—burgers, chicken, salads, and some nice entrees, if you're really here for an early dinner. The owner is usually present and eager to please.

The Good Life on Armitage

L IVING THE GOOD LIFE ON ARMITAGE—even if only for a weekend—is a time and place for dreaming about the future together. Here's hoping it's as bright as the gleaming restorations and trendy businesses you'll enjoy here. You may be surprised to learn that it wasn't always thus. Back in the 1960s, the side streets east and west of North Halsted Street were where the young and impoverished came to find their first apartments in two-flats, brownstones, and frame cottages dating from the turn of the twentieth century. In the time-honored Chicago tradition of regarding major streets as impregnable borders, West Armitage Avenue became a sort of "dividing line" separating these hippie-era apartment dwellers from the territory of the notorious Cabrini-Green housing project, a few blocks south.

What a difference forty years makes. Today Cabrini-Green is mostly memory, and those old buildings north of Armitage, now handsomely restored, commonly fetch seven figures. Many are still residences, but many others have been transformed into chic little shops, restaurants, and bars. And the people in them are, uh, no longer hippies. Nor, however, are they the Gold Coast crowd; even though there's plenty of money in this area, its apartments remain affordable for young career types who keep its style distinctly Lincoln Park, not Water Tower. Spend a weekend exploring the park and a mile or so of West Armitage, and you'll feel pretty darn stylish yourselves.

PRACTICAL NOTES: Expect to plan months in advance for reservations at Charlie Trotter's and weeks ahead for a Park West

♦ Dine in splendor at one of the world's finest restaurants, **Charlie Trotter's** (816 West Armitage Avenue; 773-248-6228).

♦ Shop till you drop at trendy boutiques and chic salons lining **Armitage Avenue.**

♦ Spend a day smelling the roses at the **Lincoln Park Zoological Gardens** (Cannon Drive, from North Avenue to Fullerton Avenue; 312-742-2000) and exploring local lore at the **Chicago Historical Society** (North Clark Street and West North Avenue; 312-642-4600).

♦ Dip into fondue at the restaurant that's often called the single most romantic spot in town: **Geja's Cafe** (340 West Armitage Avenue; 773-281-9101).

show. Any time of year is fine for this getaway—but no matter when you choose to do it, bring your Christmas and birthday gift lists. You're going to get a *lot* done.

DAY ONE: evening

On a quiet, tree-lined street that seems incongruous so near downtown, you'll find just the kind of place people have in mind when they think of a bed-and-breakfast. **Sutter House** (booked through Bed & Breakfast Chicago, 800-375-7084; www.bed-breakfast-chicago.com) is the lovingly kept Victorian home of a friendly family whose garden apartment will be your home away from home this weekend. From its charming nineteenth-century exterior, complete with bay windows and a welcoming red door, to the thoughtful amenities in the guest apartment (including a private telephone line), Sutter House combines the comforts of home with the privacy a couple needs.

Or choose from a dozen other possibilities in the area booked through Bed & Breakfast Chicago. Several have private patios with gardens that offer respite after a hard day of flashing plastic, and all are homey, welcoming places to hang your hats.

Once you're settled in your weekend home, venture forth for an evening on the town. Both the evenings suggested here will require some planning well in advance, because you're going to see two very different shows on your two evenings—one a food extravaganza at Charlie Trotter's renowned restaurant, the other a show-business performance at the snazzy Park West.

DINNER

In one fan's words, if other restaurants are airplanes, **Charlie Trotter's** (816 West Armitage Avenue; 773–248–6228; www.charlietrotters.com) is the space shuttle. Trotter is a bespectacled chef who is influenced by everything and inspired by. . .well, some call it genius, some call it obsession, but nobody goes away hungry. Or bored.

The menu changes constantly, and Trotter's sole concession to simplification is to offer set menus each evening. The multicourse degustation, which is available in a regular version ($115 per person) or vegetable ($110), will guarantee you a sample of everything the chef has on his mind at the moment, prepared with only the very finest, very freshest ingredients. The food is complex, often prepared with incredibly painstaking work, and often results in many unexpected flavors. But don't be intimidated—this isn't a food-appreciation class, and the food is never weird or off-putting. Come with an open mind, ready to let your palate be educated, and arrive on time—seating begins at 5:30 P.M. Friday and Saturday, 6:00 P.M. Tuesday, Wednesday, and Thursday. (The restaurant is closed on Sunday and Monday.)

You can opt for a table right in the kitchen, if you want to see how it all comes together. The kitchen table, which books months in advance, is $175 per person, with a minimum of four and a maximum of six. (Well, bring friends!) And, if the prices take your breath away, consider that dinner here is the entire evening. It's also one of the nation's premier restaurants, so there is some bragging value here, too. Charlie Trotter's is truly the place to take someone you want to impress.

DAY TWO: morning/afternoon

After a lazy cup of coffee from your bed-and-breakfast kitchen, you're ready to wander west. Today is shopping day, to be spent dipping into the many shops that line several blocks of Armitage west of Halsted Street (at 800 west). As you travel west on Armitage, you'll pass a few blocks of residences and Lincoln Park High School, once a divey hangout but now a spruced-up magnet school that draws good students from all over town.

BRUNCH

The little storefront shops along this stretch tend to come and go, but one that endures is **HeartBeat** (707 West Armitage Avenue; 773-664-3278). Step up, step in, and be surrounded by hearts. Everything in this delightful boutique is marked with hearts, and that makes it the perfect place to start shopping for everyone you love. Stationery, accessories, gifts and goodies: You name it and this heart-happy place has it. (And do we have to ask what the gift wrap looks like?)

As you emerge, decide whether to start your shopping on the south or the north side of Armitage. Working along the south side from east to west, you'll start at **Cynthia Rowley** (808 West Armitage Avenue; 773-528-6160), the hometown shop where local girl Rowley, a darling of the fashion world and author of *Swell*, offers her creations. Dresses, multipiece outfits, and accessories are available for a totally personal look that the store's clerks will be happy to help you assemble.

The walk-up storefront at 826 West Armitage Avenue is home to the deliriously numerous, rigorously organized holdings of **Mayet Bead Design** (773-868-0580). This tiny treasure trove offers a bounty of buttons and beads, plus a wealth of ideas for using all this raw material to create your own personal finery. Why not take home some semiprecious stones and lacy ribbon to craft a picture frame for a photo of the two of you?

Peek in to survey the floral finery at **Fischer** (852 West Armitage Avenue; 773-248-1900), and you might just pick up a posy for your sweetheart. Across the street, **Studio 910** (910 West Armitage Avenue; 773-929-2400) is a gift-and-goodies boutique where one-of-a-kind accessories are displayed along with equally distinctive women's clothing. With its exquisite selection of "occasion" dresses, Studio 910 is a must for the snappy dresser. The staff is friendly, chatty, and helpful.

Down at **Urban Gardener** (1006 West Armitage; 773-477-2070), a converted three-floor town house now holds absolutely everything the gardener could need, want, or fantasize about. Tools, pots, seeds, bulbs, and all the rest of a gardener's equipment are here, along with gorgeous baskets, wreaths of dried flowers and greenery, stationery, soaps, linens, spectacular outdoor furniture, and more. If the two of you are thinking of life in tandem, planting something together is a step in the right direction.

You'll notice that Armitage Avenue seems to end just west of Urban Gardener. Actually, it's just curving a bit to the south, but this does mark the end of the street's shopping strip. So cross the street and head back east, starting at **Faded Rose** (1017 West Armitage Avenue; 773-281-8161), where beautiful slipcovers transform furniture into a Shabby Chic lifestyle statement. Next door, at **Tabula Tua** (1015 West Armitage Avenue; 773-525-3500), you'll find all sorts of goodies to set your table—some amusing, some exquisite—and cookbooks to help you whip up a gourmet meal. This is a good spot to search out mom-type presents (for your mom or your mate's).

One of the street's nicest shops is **Frivolity** (1013 West Armitage Avenue; 773-327-8900; www.frivolitychicago.com), where you'll find a socially conscious selection of Tribute 21 plates (created by celebs to benefit UNESCO) arranged on the house carpenter's custom-crafted cabinetry (and he's available to the store's clientele, too). Beautiful things here include bejeweled doorknobs (billed as "house jewelry"), tiny clocks, unusual picture frames, velvety overstuffed chairs, and a look that overall is sleek, yet cozy and whimsical. The gift alert goes out here for your terrific boss, that terminally hip teen cousin—most of all, for each other.

If you're both sufficiently self-indulgent—or is it simply self-preserving?—you can relax under the soothing ministrations of hair, nail, and skin-care experts at **Salon 1800** (1011 West Armitage Avenue; 773-929-6010). Schedule his-and-hers massages ($80 for an hour, $50 for half an hour) or even a "day spa" session to primp as long as you like. Relaxing "body-mask" wraps are $70; facials are about $80; and hair procedures, which vary according to the stylist, range from about $35 to about $55.

If one of you isn't in the mood for the full salon treatment, you can take a good book to the neighborhood's own **Coffee & Tea Exchange** (833 West Armitage Avenue; 773-929-6730) or the always cordial **Starbucks** (1001 West Armitage Avenue; 773-528-1340) nearby.

LUNCH

Hungry? There's something that's sure to hit the spot at **Metropolis** (924 West Armitage Avenue; 773–868–9000), where barbecue or rotisserie-roasted chicken vie with pastas, pizzas, and, of course, plenty of sandwiches for the lunch bunch. Prices are very reasonable, especially for this fashionable area—about $8.00 or less for most selections. Several eat-in tables are available, but if the day is pleasant, take your lunch outdoors and stake out a sidewalk bench from which to watch the passing parade while you eat.

Back on the street: How about a shiny aluminum checkbook cover? With an address book to match? These sleek accessories, and lots more in jewelry and art, are at **Ancient Echoes** (1022A West Armitage Avenue; 773–880–1003). Smaller than some stores on the street, Ancient Echoes makes up for its size with a carefully selected range of merchandise, including a line of furniture so smooth, they're calling it "the essence of furniture."

Just beyond the Armitage El stop, you'll see everything from overalls to trekking gear in the windows of **Active Endeavors** (935 West Armitage Avenue; 773–281–8100; www.activeendeavors.com). Several storefronts are bursting with Active Endeavors' sporting gear and chic necessities for the vigorous set. This is the place to rent your in-line skates to whiz around the neighborhood (which can be pretty crowded, so rent helmet and pads, too). There's also a big bulletin board with information on many sports groups around town; it's where to look for tips on pursuing a sport the two of you might want to try together.

Another sort of clearinghouse for enthusiasts is the **Old Town School of Folk Music** (909 West Armitage Avenue; 773–525– 7793), whose long traditions and loving musicians are steeped not only in the protest strain of folk music but also in that of many ethnic groups. Celtic music is a particular favorite, and African music has a large coterie of fans as well. Instruments, lessons, sheet music, recorded music, and a huge dose of camaraderie are all available at the school, which is often the first destination of visitors to Chicago from all over the world. (Check here on performance schedules at the school's second site, farther north on Lincoln Avenue.)

The comforts of home—from tea cozies to tons of scented soaps—are featured at **Findables** (907 West Armitage Avenue; 773-348-0674). The freeze-dried flower arrangements are pretty, and the hats are fun. Amusing hats also are everywhere at **Isis on Armitage** (823 West Armitage Avenue; 773-665-7290), where you'll also find fab accessories and women's clothing in nonmodel sizes—a welcome admission of diversity in an area that sometimes seems to be populated exclusively by fitness buffs.

By now—loaded down with packages and all shopped out—you're ready to taxi back to your bed-and-breakfast before an evening out. Happily, the rest of the day does not require spending any time on your feet.

DAY TWO: evening

DINNER

First things first, and that means dinner. One of the most romantic restaurants is conveniently located in the immediate area. Stepping into **Geja's Cafe** (340 West Armitage Avenue; 773-281-9101) is like entering a protected area for the endangered species of die-hard romantics. Everything here—secluded alcoves, classical guitar music, dim lighting—is planned to enhance an intimate evening for the two of you. That also goes for the food, which is fondue and salad (so you won't waste much time trying to make decisions). There's no better way to share a meal—and a deliciously sensual

Ax the Ex

All this shopping puts a person in the mood for finding a jokey gift, doesn't it? You'll have to travel south of Armitage to get a great one, but it's definitely worth the trip to make your sweetheart very happy—or at least to give both of you a good laugh. Get your hands on that photo he or she treasures, except for its glaring inclusion of the ex. Take the picture to **Gamma Photo Labs** (314 West Superior Street; 312-337-0022), where just about every photographer I know goes for retouching that is second to none. Ask the Gamma folks to rectify this unfortunate photographic situation by artfully obliterating the offending mug. And if you'd like to replace it with your own likeness, well, why not?

experience—than by huddling over a hot pot in which to dip a dinner's worth of tender morsels: bread in fragrant melted cheese to start, meat or chicken in seasoned oil as an entree, and fruit or cake in smooth, luscious chocolate for dessert. Geja's prices are moderate—about $80 for the two of you—and wines are available by the glass; note that the next stop on your agenda, Park West, is likely to have a drink minimum, so you may want to imbibe more moderately here, but at the same time, do allow yourselves plenty of time to linger.

When your fondue *est fini*, head over to **Park West** (322 West Armitage Avenue; 773-929-5959). Naturally, you've done your homework and called well ahead to find a show you and your companion will both enjoy here. The club's streamlined, black-and-silver decor tells you that Park West aspires to be the kind of swanky nightclub Fred and Ginger graced. For the most part, it's successful in attaining that ideal, with good sightlines, a nice balcony, and clean washrooms. Depending on the show, a dance floor may be cleared in front, near the stage. Oh, and the bar makes a fine cocktail, too.

Perhaps the best thing about Park West, though, is its booking policy, which is the very definition of eclectic. This snug stage has held practically everyone who's anyone, from Judy Collins to Henry Rollins. I've seen Tom Paxton, Cheap Trick, Steve Earl, Talking Heads, and Laurie Anderson here, to name a few.

There is a drawback to an evening at Park West: Its no-reservations seating policy could leave you farther from the stage than you want to be. If your priority is getting the best view of the show, arrive early and, as soon as the doors open, claim a couple of stools along the bar area that faces toward the stage. The view also is excellent from the booths, but no one ever seems to know just how you can be *sure* of getting one of those. It's worthwhile to broach the subject with one of the club's many security types, but don't promise your date anything you can't be sure to deliver. Keep in mind that there isn't a truly bad seat in the house—and those rickety little tables for two are kind of cute.

After an evening of dinner and a show, you may want to stroll the neighborhood. There are plenty of bars if you're looking for a nightcap—and if your sweet tooth suddenly acts up, stop in at **Ben**

Classic Chicago Couples:
Kogan and Osgood

Well, let's call them a classic Chicago duo. Rick Kogan is the writer, Charles Osgood is the photographer, and all of us are the beneficiaries of their partnership at the Chicago Tribune Magazine, *which carries their weekly column* Sidewalks. *The column got its start a few years ago, with the dangerously gimmicky idea of visiting one ward each week, and the completely ungimmicky result, with evocative pictures and vivid prose, took readers to corners of the city they'd never have seen on their own.*

When they'd done all fifty wards, the guys just kept looking, into the suburbs as well as around town, and they never run out of places to go and people to meet. Whether they're slurping gelati in Little Italy, chronicling an old-timer's war stories, or exploring the state of contemporary magic with local practitioners, Kogan and Osgood bring the city alive in all its humanity.

Kogan has been at it his entire life—growing up in Old Town, writing for the old Chicago Daily News *and the* Chicago Sun-Times *before the* Tribune— *and his lean, graceful prose is just right for the city that works and doesn't get all mushy about it. He even does radio:* Sunday Papers, *live at 6:30 A.M. every week. How the former Dr. Nightlife manages to be fresh and funny at that hour is a question perhaps best left to speculation. What's certain is that nobody writes quite so much from the heart about our hometown.*

& **Jerry's Ice Cream Parlor** (338 West Armitage Avenue; 773–281–5152) for a scoop or two to share. You can head back west to **Uffa** (1008 West Armitage Avenue; 773–665–4410), where the downstairs bar is a best-kept secret. Or see if you can get an outdoor table at **Tarantino's** (1112 West Armitage Avenue; 773–871–2929), where the kitchen might just whip up two more of the daily risotto or fish specials.

DAY THREE: morning/afternoon

Here's a low-key finish to a fabulous weekend that will occupy as much or as little time as you care to spend. After coffee in your bed-and-breakfast kitchen, stroll across Clark Street to wander through **Lincoln Park Zoological Gardens** (Cannon Drive, from North Avenue to Fullerton Avenue; 312–742–2000; www.lpzoo.org). More than thirty-five acres of zoo, conservatory, and parkland are open from 9:00 A.M. to 4:30 P.M. daily, free of charge. At the south end of this stretch is the **Chicago Historical Society** (North Clark Street at West North Avenue; 312–642–4600; www.chicagohistory.org), which is open from 9:30 A.M. to 4:30 P.M. daily except Sunday, when hours are noon to 5:00 P.M. Admission is a reasonable $5.00 per person (Mondays are free). Be sure to look at exhibits on the American Revolution and the Civil War, as well as the delightful cases of Chicago memorabilia that include full uniforms from beloved members of each of the city's major sports teams. The museum also owns a famous costume collection built largely from local socialites' couture donations. The holdings are more Jackie O than Secondhand Rose, and they're definitely museum-quality, so if you're at all interested in fashion, check out whatever is on display.

LUNCH

For lunch stop in at the museum's own **Big Shoulders Cafe** (312–587–7766), where the gateway to the old Chicago Stockyards now lives. The cafe is operated by local restaurateur Jerome Kliejunas and is one of the best museum food-service facilities around; just ask guests at one of the parties held here on many an after-hours evening. Daily specials are always worth a try, Sunday brunch is dandy, and prices are very reasonable—a $20 lunch for two is very doable.

Or cross North Avenue to the **Village Arts Theater** (1548 North Clark Avenue; 312–642–2403), a multiscreen movie house that gets the best titles and offers popular weeend late-night shows, too. It's a great place to catch something you wanted to see—and the early shows are the least expensive at just $4.00 each.

ITINERARY 3
Three days and two nights

Hyde Park Honeymoon

HEN HARRY MET SALLY, it happened here—on the gloriously Gothic campus of the University of Chicago. Their first encounter, you'll recall, set the tone for the relationship: opinionated, brainy, verbal, a tad aggressive; definitely a pairing of differences, if not complete opposites. Totally Hyde Park. And just as Meg Ryan's presence filled the restaurant where she and Billy Crystal discussed sex, so does the University of Chicago fill its lakefront neighborhood. For better or worse, the university's overwhelming presence makes Hyde Park something of a college town.

But let's be fair. There is more to Hyde Park than hyperintellectualization. There's the Museum of Science and Industry, a fabulous entertainment that also tickles the intellect. There's the lovely Jackson Park lagoon. And there's the fact that this community has made racial integration work for nearly half a century. Totally Hyde Park. Come on down and see for yourselves.

PRACTICAL NOTES: You'll want to do some planning for a Hyde Park weekend. For information on entertainment or educational programs that the university opens to the public, call (773) 702-9729 or visit www.mab1.uchicago.edu. This is the Major Activities Board, which programs popular music and the like. The Council of University Programming (773-702-0433) arranges other, more esoteric events. (And you haven't seen esoteric till you've been to Hyde Park.) If you're music lovers, call (773) 702-8068 (or visit

◆ *Settle yourselves in the historic Prairie Avenue district at the **Wheeler Mansion** (2020 South Calumet Avenue; 312–945–2020), a stunning century-old landmark that's now a bed-and-breakfast.*

◆ *Dig into Southern cooking at **Dixie Kitchen & Bait Shop** (5225 South Harper Avenue; 773–363–4943).*

◆ *Change your pace at the **Baby Doll Polka Club** (6102 South Central Avenue; 773–582–9706).*

◆ *Visit the incredible **Museum of Science and Industry** (Fifty-seventh Street and Lake Shore Drive; 773–684–1414); stroll the adjacent **Jackson Park lagoon** area and **Promontory Point.***

◆ *See a classy bit of theater at **Court Theater** (5536 South Ellis Street; 773–753–4472).*

◆ *Roam the **University of Chicago campus,** with a stop at **Rockefeller Memorial Chapel** (5850 South Woodlawn Avenue; 773–702–2100).*

www.chicagopresents.uchicago.edu) for a schedule from the **Chicago Presents Chamber Music and Early Music Series,** which sponsors about twenty concerts during its October-to-May season. Tickets are $30 ($11 with a student ID), and seating is reserved.

DAY ONE: evening

For all its charm, Hyde Park is short on romantic accommodations. Happily, however, just a few miles (or a quick cab ride) to the north, there's romance aplenty in one of the city's premier bed-and-breakfast houses. Actually, *house* isn't enough word for the eleven sumptuous rooms of the **Wheeler Mansion** (2020 South Calumet Avenue; 312–945–2020), which was built in 1870 and thus predates the Great Chicago Fire. Located in the landmark Prairie Avenue Historic District, the Wheeler Mansion has been restored to its original splendor and simultaneously converted to its present use as a boutique hotel—not much of a stretch, really, from its original role as a grand home in one of the city's first really fashionable neighborhoods. Modern guests love the Wheeler Mansion's landscaped grounds, fireplace-centric great room, gourmet breakfasts, and, above all, its beau-

tifully furnished, exquisitely comfortable rooms (whose rates start at
$225 per night) and suites (from $265). This friendly place even
offers rental bikes for folks who want to tour the lakefront, which is
all of 2 blocks away, and the kitchen will gladly pack up a picnic, too.

The reasonable prospect of pedaling south to your Hyde Park
destinations makes this a good point at which to tackle the delicate
subject of safety, ever an issue in this area. While there's lots of new
construction here, some very rough areas are close by. But Hyde
Parkers believe their neighborhood is no more dangerous than any
other city neighborhood, and I'm inclined to agree. Keep in mind,
though, that Hyde Parkers (and I) are longtime urban residents
whose antennae never go down. Get yours up, especially after dark.
Don't stray from well-lighted streets where others are out and about
and you should be fine.

While you still have some daylight, get out and explore the center of the community—the **University of Chicago campus,** 175 acres
of impressive architecture and greenery that's home to scads of schol-
ars, including quite a few Nobel Prize winners. The solidly Oxbridge
basis for the campus's design and classical-looking limestone buildings (by Henry Ives Cobb) gives a unified feeling to much of the campus, and its twentieth-century buildings are by such giants as Ludwig
Mies van der Rohe (the School of Social Services Administration
Building, 969 East Sixtieth Street) and Eero Saarinen (Laird Bell Law
Quadrangle, 800 block of East Sixtieth Street, and Woodward Court
residence hall, 5825 South Woodlawn). Many buildings have lovely
courtyards where you can linger.

DINNER

When you get hungry, go north and east of the campus to a lively spot
that's a great local favorite. **Dixie Kitchen & Bait Shop** (5225 South
Harper Avenue, in Harper Court; 773–363–4943; www.dixiekitchenbait.
com) serves up fabulous soul food and southern specialties in a setting that looks like a northerner's idea of southern living. But there's
no quarrel with the food, which includes jambalaya, gumbo, catfish
blackened or fried, and all the right sides: black-eyed peas, coleslaw,
collard greens, and johnnycakes. Come hungry and don't leave till
you try the pecan pie. Prices are moderate—you may even be able to
hold dinner for both of you to under $50, especially if you go easy
on that Dixie beer.

Your evening's entertainment may well be on campus (see Practical Notes, earlier in this chapter, for how to get information on what's happening). If you want to keep it low-cost, check out what's playing at **Documentary Films,** better known simply as Doc. This student group has been choosing and running film programs for more than thirty years. Sometimes it's totally weird, sometimes it's the greats—but for $4.00, give it a try. Call (773) 702–8575 for information and decide for yourselves.

Maybe you're feeling, well, frisky. So hop in the car or cab and drive west, west, west toward Midway Airport till you reach Central Avenue. Two blocks south is the **Baby Doll Polka Club** (6102 South Central Avenue; 773–582–9706). Open seven days a week, the Baby Doll offers live bands on Saturday and Sunday evenings for people of the polka persuasion. And there isn't even a cover charge for this wacky, wonderful way to dance up a storm. At fortysomething, the Baby Doll is a South Side institution so hip, so out-there, you're certain to be the first ones you know to go.

DAY TWO: morning/afternoon

Head out early to take in the best of the **Museum of Science and Industry** (Fifty-seventh Street and Lake Shore Drive; 773–684–1414; www.msichicago.org), which includes old kid favorites like the giant walk-through heart and the baby chicks' hatchery, and goes right up to "AIDS: The War Within" and a smashing Omnimax movie theater where any current feature is a don't-miss. Also catch the World War II–era U-505 submarine; the working coal mine (although if you know anything about mining, don't look for authenticity); Yesterday's Main Street, where you can have your picture taken in century-old duds; and the Whispering Gallery, where you'll have the chance to whisper sweet nothings to each other from an incredible distance.

Admission to the museum costs $9.00 (Thursday is the free day), and it's open from 9:30 A.M. to 5:30 P.M. daily. You could easily spend the entire day, except for the unfortunate dining situation—a no-win choice between vending machines and fast food. One delightful exception has been here forever and qualifies as part of the museum: the old-fashioned, wood-furnished Finnigan's Ice Cream Parlor, which I can never resist. An ice-cream soda isn't *that* much of a compromise to your diet, especially if you sip one with two straws, like a couple of kids in a 1940s movie.

LUNCH

 If you're ready to leave the museum around noon-time, have lunch across the street at **Piccolo Mondo** (in the Windermere, 1642 East Fifty-sixth Street; 312–643–1106). This beloved spot features salads and lighter fare, as well as the Chicago original, chicken Vesuvio. There's a selection of pasta, even spaghetti and meatballs, and prices are moderate—maybe $15 each for dinner, even less for lunch.

Or make your way farther south, to **Jackson Harbor Grill**, (6401 South Coast Guard Drive; 773–288–4442), where during the season—mid-April to mid-September—you can eat on a balcony right over the water. Lunch and dinner bring an array of southern-accented seafood specialties, such as barbecue-grilled salmon with cheese grits and chef Troy Price's version of that five-letter word for heaven, gumbo. Prices are at the low end of moderate; there's a full bar, and when you're finished, you can spend some downtime at the **Jackson**

Hitched in Hyde Park

One of the most wonderful weddings I ever attended was a Hyde Park event. The bride was Bye-lorussian, the groom Japanese; both were artists, and the ceremony took place in the Unitarian church. The reception was held in a slightly shabby but still fine old hotel, where the food was great and the dancing was even better, thanks to the couple's slightly shocking decision to have a jukebox instead of a boring grown-up band. As we all danced the night away, we saluted this fearless pair's faith in themselves, their individualism, and their love and marriage.

Park Lagoon (west of Jackson Harbor, officially, 6401 South Stony Island Boulevard). At this rural oasis you'll see people fishing right behind the museum and, on its far-east **Wooded Island,** find one of the city's finest spots for bird-watching.

You can easily spend hours at the lagoon and the island. Be sure to look for the famous monk parakeets that have lived here for years, even though they're completely unsuited to the climate. They manage by wintering at the steam vents of a nearby building and moving to the area of the island when weather permits.

On the way back north, you might want to cross Lake Shore Drive near the museum so that you can stroll the beach around **Promontory Point.** It offers a wonderful view of the city's skyline that you won't see anywhere else.

DINNER

As you return to civilization, you'll want to stop back at your B&B before the evening's entertainment. A good choice for dinner is **Orly's** (1660 East Fifty-fifth Street; 773–643–5500), where the menu is perhaps best perused while sipping what the house calls "a mean margarita." Prices are moderate, and dinner is served from 5:00 to 10:00 P.M. nightly. Another possibility is **La Petite Folie** (1504 East Fifty-fifth Street; 773–493–1394), a bit of Paris in a parking lot. Actually it's a small shopping center and any parking at all is a big plus in this car-choked neighborhood. You'll forget everything but each other once you're inside, nibbling on foie gras while choosing from a menu

The Bridges of Cook County

Go to the lovely Japanese garden on **Wooded Island** *and lose yourself in its serenity. Built for the 1893 Columbian Exposition (which took place in the neighborhood) and abandoned during World War II, the garden has been restored by Chicago's sister city, Osaka, and now features a pavilion, a sparkling waterfall, and a lovely bridge whose arch is meant to suggest the curve of the moon. Another nearby bridge is just as attractive: three stone arches overlook the harbor and the old Coast Guard auxiliary patrol, just south of a broad lawn-bowling green. You'll never believe you're still in the city!*

that's a French hit parade. What with the charming atmosphere, moderate prices, and friendly service, it's easy to see why you'll need reservations for a weekend dinner at this beloved spot.

After dinner, head over to a stimulating evening at **Court Theater** (5535 South Ellis Street; 773-753-4472; www.courttheater.org). An institution in the city as well as the neighborhood, Court provides theater for the demandingly intellectual locals, and it is therefore a good bet for one of the better shows around town at any given time during the theater season. Court sticks to the classics, from Euripides to Tom Stoppard, and often presents works you're not likely to see elsewhere. *Note:* If this makes Court sound stuffy, it's not. A Molière farce here is guaranteed yucks, and even a somber production is a pleasure in its reliable quality. So go. But be sure to call well in advance, because weekend shows often sell out early. Curtain is at 8:00 P.M.

After the show, you can indulge in a quintessential U. of C. pastime by hitting the **Woodlawn Tap and Liquor Store** (1172 East Fifty-fifth Street; 773-643-5516) for a drink and a discussion. But, for heaven's sake, don't refer to the place as anything but Jimmy's. As much a Hyde Park institution as the university itself, Jimmy's is a student hangout where the discourse is as serious as the drinking.

DAY THREE: morning/afternoon

Sunday morning seems like the perfect time to visit one of the campus's highlights, **Rockefeller Memorial Chapel** (5850 South Woodlawn Avenue; 773-702-2100). When John D. put up the money for the campus, he specified that its chapel be—always—the tallest building on campus. And so it is. You can see for yourselves from 8:00 A.M. to 4:00 P.M. daily, except when religious services take precedence. These times may vary, so do be sure to call before visiting.

BRUNCH

For a weekend brunch, try yet another Hyde Park tradition. Brunch at **Medici's Pan Pizza** (1327 East Fifty-seventh Street; 773-667-7394) need not involve pizza. A menu replete with breakfast favorites gives you more than enough possibilities without having to decide between a thick or thin crust. It's inexpensive,

too—you both should be able to leave well fed for around $20.
Saturday or Sunday brunch is also a delight at the previously mentioned Orly's, which offers a dessert-and-pastry bar, selection of
entrees, and a luscious orange-strawberry drink, all for $9.95.

After brunch, pay a visit to the **David and Alfred Smart Museum of
Art** (5550 South Greenwood Avenue; 773–702–0200; www.smart
museum.uchicago.edu), a lovely gallery that showcases the university's collections—which means you can see ancient Greek vases,
modern sculpture by Henry Moore, works by Matisse and Degas,
and lots more, including twentieth-century creations as diverse as
Frank Lloyd Wright's austere furniture and Ed Paschke's neon-like
paintings. The museum also mounts special exhibits, so be sure to
find out about these in advance. Best of all, it's free. The Smart
Museum is closed on Monday; Tuesday through Friday it's open
from 10:00 A.M. to 4:00 P.M. (until 9:00 P.M. Thursday), and weekends from noon to 6:00 P.M.

You're not far from another gem of a small museum, the
Oriental Institute Museum (1155 East Fifty-eighth Street;
773–702–9514; www.oi.uchicago.edu). Looking spectacular after a
complete makeover, the institute showcases impressive collections
from the Middle East that span the centuries from 5000 B.C. to the
eighth century A.D. See if this exotic atmosphere—its centerpiece a
17-foot-tall statue of King Tut himself—doesn't make you feel like
flagging down a magic carpet on the way out. The Oriental Institute
Museum is open daily except Monday; its hours vary enough to suggest calling ahead, but admission is always free.

FOR MORE ROMANCE

If you happen to be in Hyde Park on a Monday evening, make it
your business to be at Fifty-seventh Street and University Avenue,
where **Mitchell Tower** holds a set of ten bells rung in changes each
week. Not to be confused with the songs typically played on church
bells, changes are complex patterns that are a marvel to hear—a
spine-tingling audio experience you'll be glad you shared.

Fireworks for Two
A FOURTH OF JULY WEEKEND

NOT MANY YEARS AGO, Chicago's Fourth of July celebration consisted of a classical-music concert in which the Grant Park Symphony performed, among other works, Tchaikovsky's 1812 Overture. The booming cannons that highlight the piece were coordinated with the aural and visual "boom" of fireworks exploding over the lake. It was a spectacular finish to a glorious day spent picnicking and playing in what Chicagoans modestly believe is the world's nicest front yard.

Today the picnicking and playing and music and fireworks have grown to epic proportions. Nobody packs a sandwich anymore; now, there's Taste of Chicago, a massive food fest in Grant Park, which starts a week or so before the Fourth of July and continues through the holiday. The Taste, as it's known, offers bargain-priced samples from the menus of dozens of local restaurants, including some of the very best. Music and contests and countless other amusements surround the feast, which naturally attracts huge crowds and thus may not seem conducive to romance.

But still, the Taste is *such* a well-known Chicago tradition. And wouldn't it be a shame to miss the fireworks and the concert, too? Sure it would. Here's how to join in while creating your own fireworks on this festive holiday.

PRACTICAL NOTES: The city's fireworks display is usually held on July 3. Dates of the Taste vary with where the Fourth falls in the week. Usually, the Taste lasts ten days, including the two weekends before and after the Fourth. Be sure to check well in advance before you start scheduling.

$\mathcal{R}$omance
AT A GLANCE

◆ Check into the posh **Swissotel** *(323 East Wacker Drive; 312–565–0565) and scope out your vantage point for the weekend's fireworks display.*

◆ *Stroll the gardenlike banks of the Chicago River, stopping to smooch at one of the city's most romantic spots—on the **Michigan Avenue bridge** (North Michigan Avenue at the river).*

◆ *Play it smart at the **Taste of Chicago** (Grant Park, between Washington Street and Jackson Boulevard) by going early in the morning or during the postlunch-predinner lull, good times for maximum enjoyment and minimum mob scene.*

◆ *Pop the cork and sit back in your hotel room to toast your own romantic fireworks while watching the city's Fourth of July extravaganza.*

◆ *Go underground to explore the site of many movies' slam-bang car chases: **Lower Wacker Drive** (parallel to the river).*

DAY ONE: afternoon/evening

Swissotel (323 East Wacker Drive; 312–565–0565; www.swisso tel-chicago.com) is just the place from which to base your fabulous Fourth. It's located on what downtowners call the New East Side, an area that includes the Navy Pier and North Pier entertainment complexes; lots of hotel, office, and apartment buildings; and the massive Illinois Center trio of buildings. In this prosperous area, the hotel that is closest to the lake itself and also offers a good view is—you guessed it—Swissotel. This means you'll have a great seat for the Fourth fireworks display, which is launched well out over the lake. The idea is to enjoy the show without having to cope with the crush of humanity.

Therefore, when you book your room (and the further in advance, the better), ask for one with a lake view. Of course, you won't be the only ones with this idea, so realize that "you can request, but we don't guarantee a lake view," says Swissotel public-relations representative Nicole Jachimiak.

Will you want to go, even without a guarantee? *Mais oui!* You'd be caviling to find any Swissotel room with a bad view. Some look out toward the endlessly fascinating cityscape, including a good vantage point from which to watch Taste of Chicago. Others look toward the glittering expanse of North Michigan Avenue, where you'll spot the landmark John Hancock Building among the towers. And if your room's view fails to satisfy, notice that you would have a great view of the fireworks just by standing in the hall where you'd wait for the elevators.

Swissotel's rooms are spacious and comfortable, recently redecorated in a soothing slate blue. Most offer a minibar, and all have fabulously comfy chairs in which to relax while you appreciate that view. Baths have one of my favorite features, a separate shower and tub, plus hair dryers. The health club has a pool and whirlpool, plenty of exercise machines, a separate weight-lifting room, a sauna, and more of that terrific view. Massages, manicures, pedicures, and facials are available as well.

The hotel offers several weekend packages, one of which includes two passes to the health club. At about $239 a night, it's an option well worth considering. The basic weekend rate is about $259 per night, which excludes the health club but does provide the services of a helpful (multilingual, even) front-desk concierge. Ask him or her about getting you

The Bridges of Cook County

Don't miss this chance to linger on another landmark, the Michigan Avenue bridge. In a recent "best of" issue, Chicago magazine praised this span as the very best place to feel like you're in Chicago. The magazine specifies sunset, on the west side of the bridge, but there's magic here anytime. Examine the historic scenes depicted on the bridge's four pylons; watch the sight-seeing boats and pleasure craft along the river. You might even see their blue-collar counterpart, a grimy, hard-working barge steaming down- or upriver. As you linger on this bridge, if you can resist the urge to hold hands and kiss, it's time to reconsider your relationship.

tickets to the Taste, which you'll need to exchange for food. (There's no admission or entertainment charge; all you need is the food tickets, but you don't want to stand in line on the scene for these.)

Once you've settled into your room, go right back out to enjoy the preholiday afternoon. If the weather cooperates—and anything but a driving thunderstorm counts as good weather during a Chicago summer—give yourselves an hour or two to wander North Michigan Avenue and the beautiful banks of the Chicago River.

The easiest way to get to the river is to descend the stairway just outside the hotel, then walk a block west on Lower Wacker Drive to Columbus Drive. Cross Wacker heading north, and you'll find yourselves at the river. Below is the south bank, which is undeveloped and grassy, perfect for a stroll or for just sitting. Across the Columbus Drive bridge is a lovely river walk decorated with flowers, trees, and benches for relaxing. If you walk a block east and go upstairs, you'll find yourselves just east of **Pioneer Court,** where fountains and beautiful landscaping invite passersby to linger.

Pioneer Court looks onto Michigan Avenue and, across the street, the landmark **Wrigley Building.** The court adjoins another Chicago landmark, **Tribune Tower,** home of the redoubtable *Chicago Tribune* newspaper and its corporate sibling, WGN Radio, whose call letters stand for the slogan the *Trib* once proclaimed across the top of its front page—"World's Greatest Newspaper." Modesty remains a foreign concept to this civic pillar, whose other local holdings include a television station (WGN–TV, of course) and the Chicago Cubs. Right across Michigan, just beyond the Wrigley Building, lies the **Chicago Sun-Times Building,** home of the Trib's scrappy rival, so you can see why each paper refers to the other as "across the street" (as in "We scooped across the street!").

But I digress—from the bustling yet delightful atmosphere of Pioneer Court, where steps away, a lineup of Good Humor trucks is waiting to serve you. They're parked just off the **Michigan Avenue bridge,** which definitely deserves your attention.

DINNER

When hunger strikes, you're quite close to **Shaw's Crab House** (21 East Hubbard Street; 312–527–2722), a couple of blocks west and north of the bridge. (Note that if you walk west, past the *Sun-Times* and IBM buildings, you'll need to descend a staircase to street level.) Shaw's has some of the best seafood in town, with oysters and crab cakes as good appetizers and all sorts of wonderful ways to enjoy shrimp. Nonshellfish choices are always whatever's freshest, and you can't go wrong with a side of au gratin potatoes. Even the wine list is arranged according to what goes with which seafood. Dinner will run about $90 for the pair of you here and is available seven days a week till 10:00 P.M. in the romantic dining room as well as in the more informal bar area.

If you'd rather head back toward the hotel, consider stopping a block to the west at the Fairmont Hotel, 200 North Columbus Drive. Here, at the elegant **Aria** (312–444–9494), you can watch as daylight dims and the lights of Navy Pier begin to twinkle. (Again, mention your wish for a good view when you make your reservation.) Dinner is served from 5:30 to 10:00 P.M. daily, and entree prices range from about $25 to about $35 for the restaurant's eclectic cuisine. But now that you're here, consider being adventurous enough to try one of the more exotic options around: tenderloin of buffalo. These farm-raised critters provide a hearty, flavorful meat that doesn't taste like chicken—and it's definitely something to tell the folks back home about.

Care for a drink after dinner? The Fairmont's **Metropole Lounge** is comfortably sophisticated and sometimes books cabaret artists whose songs offer just the polished ending you want for the evening. Also, just west of Swissotel is **Big** (in the Hyatt Regency Chicago, 151 East Wacker Drive; 312–565–1234). True, it's the world's largest stand-up bar—but you can sit down if you want to. And there are literally hundreds of selections to sip or mix into just about any cocktail you dream up.

If you're still wide awake and looking to party, you'll find ample opportunity on another Chicago institution, **Rush Street.** This Near North strip has long been home to lovers of nightlife, and the current crop of clubs carries on the tradition well. (It's near yet another nightlife institution, **Division Street,** where singles still swing.) Check out **Gibsons Steak House** (1028 North Rush Street; 312–266–8999), where sports and media celebs often go for whopping big martinis, steaks, and the buzz of hyper-trendy atmosphere. It's in the former home of the old Mister Kelly's nightclub and is hugely popular (therefore, not exactly intimate) among people who have outgrown singles bars. Also beloved by a similar clientele—and somewhat less noisy, especially when pianist Nick Russo is at work—is **Jilly's** (1007 North Rush Street; 312-664-1001). This sophisticated spot, named for Frank Sinatra's late friend Jilly Rizzo, is a home away from home for fans of the Rat Pack lifestyle. Indeed, the idea here appears to be total preparation for a spur-of-the-moment visit from the Chairman of the Celestial Board: a good-looking bar, plenty to drink, a model train in operation (Sinatra was a train fan), and plenty of people ready to party. Again, not exactly a quiet spot for two, but a fun place all the same.

DAY TWO: morning/afternoon

Take your pick of two good ways to start the day: an appetite-whetting workout at Swissotel or an early attack on the **Taste of Chicago** before it's too crowded. You may want to do the Taste first, because when it gets crowded, it's *really* crowded. On the other hand, the postlunch, predinner lull also can be relatively calm. It's your call.

Scope out the Taste before setting foot in Grant Park by asking your concierge for a guide to the food booths and choosing the ones you want to sample. The mix of restaurants always includes more than enough purveyors of pizza, burgers, corn on the cob, and ribs, so be selective, and be sure to visit the top-of-the-line gourmet pavilion, where each day a different fine-dining restaurant takes the spotlight.

At the same time, leave some room for spontaneity. Even with a list of good intentions, you'll want to allow yourselves to be distracted. In addition to the food, food, food, the Taste offers top-notch musical entertainment, an art fair, cooking demonstrations, and all manner of other fun. You might as well buy a pair of corny Taste of Chicago T-shirts, too; the longer you're in town, the more you'll notice that everyone has one.

Some Tasters like to collect several samples and head for the lake, where you can find a quiet patch of grass to relax with your food and your honey. Here, too, stage and street musicians will serenade you as the sights, smells, and sounds of the city's biggest festival drift your way.

When you've had enough Tasteing, head back to your posh, quiet room—or grab a cab to a local institution, **Waveland Bowl** (3700 North Western Avenue; 773-472-5902; www.waveland bowl.com). Located about 20 minutes from the Loop, at the northwest tip of the Roscoe Village neighborhood, Waveland is open 24 hours a day, 365 days a year, and with everyone else downtown at the Taste, you're sure to score a lane. A recent renovation has left Waveland as spiffy as any 24/7 joint can be, and its bargain prices are unbeatable: Games go for as little as $1.00 on weekday mornings, prime weekend nights top out at $6.00, and shoe rental is only $4.00. Just be sure to call before you go; Waveland is beloved for its potentially raucous Cosmic Bowl birthday parties.

DINNER

After finishing your golf outing, relax with a drink on the adjacent patio or head back to Swissotel to meditate on where you'll have dinner. You may want to stay in-house and dine at **The Palm** (312-616-1000), the Chicago outpost of the famous steak-house chain. The steaks here are stunning and the atmosphere studly. It's not cheap (side dishes, especially, can add up), but you're likely to emerge feeling that you got what you paid for.

Possibly, however, a major dinner isn't quite what you want after a belly-busting day at Taste of Chicago. In that case, stop downstairs at **Currents,** where quiet rules and leather booths offer lovers blissful solitude in which to order from a menu of sun-kissed Mediterranean fare. Or take a short cab ride to Navy Pier, where **Riva** (700 East Grand Avenue; 312-644-7482) features steak, seafood, pastas, and more of that great lakefront view. It's on the second floor of Navy Pier, and, though the Pier is certain to be crowded, Riva is just as certain to maintain a quiet elegance in which you can enjoy good food and a great vantage point from which to watch a vibrant city at play. Dinner entrees are moderately priced and are served from 4:00 to 8:30 P.M. daily.

Nine P.M. is about nightfall and the latest you'll want to get back to your room and catch every bit of the fireworks display. Check with the concierge about which radio or television station will simulcast the fireworks, so you can listen to the music as you watch. And don't forget to have a bottle of bubbly—domestic, of course—on hand to toast the birthday of the U.S.A.

DAY THREE: morning/afternoon

BRUNCH

Why not make the most of your proximity to the lake by getting right on it? The *Odyssey* (312-321-7600) offers a shipshape Sunday brunch that cruises Lake Michigan from noon to 2:00 P.M. Passengers enjoy a live jazz band while cruising and a lavish buffet that includes lots of cold and hot salads, fresh fruits, baked treats, and an entree. The cruise costs $60.72 per person, and boarding begins at 11:00 A.M. from Navy Pier. (More details about *Odyssey* cruises appear in the subsequent chapter "Swept Away: Romantic Lakefront Cruises.")

When you return—or, if you're feeling intrepid, even instead of the cruise—explore the scene of many a movie chase along **Lower Wacker Drive.** Running literally right underneath Wacker Drive, Lower Wacker was the brilliant idea of nineteenth-century architect Daniel Burnham, who recognized the need for a downtown "truck route" long before gridlock became an urban curse. Sidewalks are nonexistent along some parts of this winding, eerily green-lit stretch of road, but you can walk along much of it; commuters do it all the time, and you never hear about anyone getting hurt. Beware of traffic, though; it's something of a local sport to drive very briskly along Lower Wacker. That doesn't seem to deter a few homeless people who camp here, though it can be nerve-racking when regular drivers, not action-movie daredevils, are behind the wheel.

As you make your way, notice the many little staircases leading to the surface and the way Lower Wacker hugs the river. If you get hungry, or want to make the pilgrimage many visitors won't leave town without, stop at **Billy Goat Tavern** (430 North Michigan Avenue; 312-222-1525), home of the "cheezborger,

cheezborger" made famous on *Saturday Night Live* and still a popular spot among the newspaper and advertising folk who work nearby. No health food at the Goat, but those burgers are darn good.

Be sure to pause on the *lower* Michigan Avenue bridge, where you can kiss again, right under the spot where you did the same thing the other day. It's a perfect way to say "Happy Fourth" in the city with the great front yard—and a pretty cool basement, too.

FOR MORE ROMANCE

Chicago has *another* fireworks festival every year. It's called **Venetian Night,** and it takes place in late July. If the Fourth of July doesn't work for you, consider taking the itinerary for this chapter (sans the Taste) and applying it to Venetian Night, which also features a virtual flotilla of private boats that take to the lake for the occasion. Even folks who lack a private yacht can enjoy the fireworks from right on the water by boarding a **Mercury cruise** (312-332-1353; www.mercuryskylinecruiseline.com). Go to the southeast corner of the Michigan Avenue bridge–on the lower level, at water's edge—to join the regularly scheduled Summer Sunset Cruise, which spends a leisurely couple of hours touring the lakefront. Most nights, Buckingham Fountain's are the brightest highlights, but on Venetian Night, you'll have the best vantage point from which to oooh and aaah at the fireworks. Cruise tickets (a very reasonable $17) go on sale at the dock ticket office an hour before departure, and the dazzle, of course, is free.

Just weeks later, the city puts on yet another lakefront extravaganza, the **Air & Water Show,** a noisy but awesome display of military prowess and civilian stunts. You might consider hopping a cruise for this event, too, but Mercury's Diane Uczen points out that boats are kept so far from the action that you're better off ashore. She recommends staking out a spot on **Oak Street Beach** (Oak Street to North Avenue at the lakefront), where the noise is deafening but the thrill is undeniable.

Let It Snow

A COZY WINTER WEEKEND FOR TWO

IF YOU'VE EVER EXPERIENCED A CHICAGO WINTER, you know why midwesterners seem to be obsessed with the weather. What a delicious fantasy, during these cold and cruel winters, to imagine a whole weekend with your beloved during which you never set foot outdoors.

Here's how to make the fantasy come true in a luxurious way. It isn't cheap, but this is a case of getting what you pay for.

DAY ONE: evening

The season doesn't matter once you enter the posh 900 North Michigan building, at the northern end of the city's Magnificent Mile. Inside 900 North, the atmosphere of gracious civility counters whatever miseries nature is inflicting on the unfortunate masses outdoors.

To get to the **Four Seasons Hotel** (312–280–8800; www. fourseasons.com), you'll use the building's side entrance at 120 East Delaware Avenue. There, a greeter will direct you to the elevators that whisk you to the hotel (it starts on the seventh floor, giving new meaning to the phrase "heaven on seven").

Marble floors, gleaming dark wood, and massive flower arrangements give the Four Seasons its upper-crust look, but what's really special is the blend of friendliness and professionalism you'll discover in the staff. And, given the hotel's high level of service and the fact that you aren't planning to leave the premises, you'll see a lot of the staff during your weekend.

◆ *Indulge yourselves with two ultra-comfy nights at the posh **Four Seasons Hotel** (900 North Michigan; 312–280–8800), plus room-service breakfast and afternoon tea.*
◆ *Dine in high-end splendor at **Seasons** (in the hotel; 312–649–2349), one of the city's very finest restaurants—and one of the most romantic.*
◆ *Pamper yourselves with fitness luxuries at the Four Seasons: the latest workout equipment, a gorgeous indoor pool, a personal trainer, or a relaxing massage. Then surprise your sweetie with room-service ice-cream.*
◆ *Linger over an elaborate Sunday brunch at Seasons, then cushion your reentry to the real world by stepping into a horse-drawn carriage summoned by the doorman.*

Once you've checked in, it would be hard to resist taking some time to appreciate your deluxe accommodations. Even if you don't pop for a suite, a Four Seasons room for two offers a king-size bed with an elegant armoire to house the television set, plus a wonderfully spacious bathroom and, from every window, a stunning view of the city. Suites give you even more space, of course, with French doors separating bedroom from sitting room. Weekend room rates begin at $295 a night—but it's a once-in-a-lifetime extravaganza, right?

If you're celebrating, the hotel can arrange to have flowers and champagne in your room when you arrive. When you're ready to step out, you might enjoy sipping a predinner drink in the lobby—not a single long hall, but a comfortable warren of sitting areas, all furnished with inviting chairs and handy tables to facilitate a lingering chat.

DINNER

Dinner awaits downstairs at **Seasons** (312–649–2349), a perennial on the top-ten lists of local critics that also made the cut for *Food & Wine* magazine's collection of the most romantic restaurants. The room itself is lovely, its cool pastel color scheme punctuated with more big flowers and underscored with dignified wood paneling. There's a small army of white-coated staff providing service that never misses a beat against a backdrop of tinkling crystal, crisp white linen, delicate bone china, and glamorously hushed conversation.

The menu offers plenty of variety, including the pleasant surprise of more than one vegetarian option (about $26). Fish and meat are about equally represented ($30 to $42). One unusual touch is an opener of essig, an aperitif wine vinegar that's fashionable among the food cognoscenti.

In surroundings this luxurious, it's easy to make an evening of dinner, perhaps with coffee or an after-dinner drink in the lobby, where a jazz trio performs on Saturday evenings. If you're so inclined, the nearby bar allows smoking, including cigars. (When I visited, a patron couldn't tell me enthusiastically enough just how much he appreciated this accommodation.)

DAY TWO: morning/afternoon

Start your day with a leisurely breakfast from room service, or just head directly into another swirl of self-indulgence. The Four Seasons recently created a spa program, offering its own facial, massage, and body treatments to make you feel as rich as the caviar you'll be served—with champagne, of course—after a "Perle de Caviar Facial." (It's caviar extract, and they swear it doesn't smell.) The elixir paraffin body wrap promises better circulation and realigned energy meridians, and even the relatively brief "body polish," using crushed pearls and lavender, has a luscious appeal.

Of course, the usual health-club accouterments are here, too: Stairmasters, Lifecycles, Nautilus equipment, and more, all ready to plug into the hotel's personal portable stereos. Some machines offer television monitors. If you need extra motivation, turn yourself over to the hotel's personal trainer, who will design a workout program and help you learn to implement it at home. The daily newspapers are here, as well as a welcoming tray with coffee, juice, and fruit. The hotel's indoor swimming pool looks positively California-ish under a beautiful skylight (it was used in the movie *Home Alone 2*), and the level of service is such that you can even borrow workout clothing or a disposable swimsuit if you've forgotten your own. Saunas and steam rooms separate men from women, but you can get back together to lounge poolside.

When you're as fit as you can stand to get, shower and get down (via elevator, of course) to some power shopping in the 900 North

Michigan building. Tenants include **Bloomingdale's** (312–440-4460)— hours in itself—and **Gucci** (312-664-5504), as well as unusual boutiques to browse. Guests at the Four Seasons receive a "900 Card," which offers discounts at participating merchants in the building (although you're probably already in the "if you have to ask, you can't afford it" zone.)

LUNCH

Back upstairs, the Four Seasons serves up a relative bargain at lunchtime, with the cafe's Mediterranean Table (or, on Fridays, Asian Table) setting forth an all-you-can-eat spread for about $15.50 per person. Soup, salad, sandwiches, pizzas, and entrees are included in the buffet, which is available from 11:30 A.M. to 2:00 P.M. daily except Sunday. Or you might prefer to skip lunch and hold out for afternoon tea, a splendid affair served from 3:00 to 5:00 P.M. daily except Sunday in the Seasons Lounge. Choose between a fireside seat or one facing the lakefront near a tinkling waterfall as you sip and chat to the accompaniment of a live pianist who takes requests. Full tea, which includes finger sandwiches and pastries along with a pot of tea, is about $40 for two; add a few dollars more if you want a glass of champagne, too.

DAY TWO: evening

DINNER

Those who like to keep their meals on the three-squares program should be pleased that there is a place as casual as Seasons is formal in the 900 building at **Tucci Benucch** (312-266-2500). Thin-crust pizzas, delectable salads, and homemade pastas are served by pleasant, untuxed people in this agreeably "rustic" setting. The prices are a pleasant alternative to 900's rarefied atmosphere, too; dinner could come in at less than $40 for the two of you.

For a low-key evening, take in a movie at the **900 North Michigan Cinemas** (312-787-5279), where two screens give you a choice and crowds are rarely a problem. Perhaps you'd prefer to make it an even cozier evening by retiring to your Four Seasons room to watch a

Windy City Cinema

You say you'd like to see a Chicago movie that doesn't involve bloodshed? No problem! Here's a strictly subjective list of fun Chicago flicks with what the movie mavens call "a love interest."

Ferris Bueller's Day Off: *The very young Matthew Broderick plays a fatally charming high-schooler in this hilarious teen-fantasy romp throughout the city. Chicago never looked better than it does in director John Hughes's paean to friendship, young love, and a red Ferrari.*

My Best Friend's Wedding: *Even in the movies, how can a merely mortal male face a choice between Julia Roberts and Cameron Diaz? Here's the film that pops the question, as a radiant Roberts decides she, not Diaz, is the one her best buddy ought to wed. Don't miss the fabulously romantic declaration Rupert Everett delivers while dancing at the wedding.*

While You Were Sleeping: *In this lighter-than-air romance, Sandra Bullock poses as the fiancee of a comatose mugging victim, becoming entwined with his eccentric family—including an extremely attractive brother who isn't in a coma.*

Continental Divide: *A little-known 1981 romantic gem in which John Belushi plays a hard-boiled newspaper columnist for the* Chicago Sun-Times, *incongruously in love with ornithologist Blair Brown. Watch for Belushi's reaction when his wilderness guide mentions spotting a bear: "Am I pleased or frightened?"*

The Blues Brothers: *Released in 1980, this frenetically funny film features John Belushi, Dan Aykroyd, too many bluesmen to name, and the delicious sight of Jake and Elwood Blues terrorizing the elegant Chez Paul restaurant just by sitting down. Ya gotta love it!*

About Last Night: *The other Belushi, Jim, stars with a young Demi Moore, Elizabeth Perkins, and Rob Lowe in a funny, touching tale of yuppie love. The 1986 movie has been tamed considerably from its stage origins as David Mamet's* Sexual Perversity in Chicago, *although there's still a generous sprinkling of the f-word throughout.*

Chicago-made flick. The hotel will provide a VCR if you ask, and the concierge can find you a tape from our list of titles (see "Windy City Cinema" above) that'll keep you entertained while you try to spot local locations. Snuggle up in the plush terrycloth robes the hotel provides, and make this your most memorable movie-watching evening ever—especially if you've arranged for a surprise visit from the hotel's ice cream man. This room-service treat brings a fully equipped cart to your door, ready to adorn chocolate or vanilla scoops with pink sprinkles, gummy bears, and all the goodies guaranteed to bring out the kids in you.

DAY THREE: morning

BRUNCH

As you prepare to face the outside world again, fortify yourself with one more opulent meal at the Four Seasons. A lavish Sunday brunch is served in the restaurant from 10:30 A.M. to 1:30 P.M. with various "stations" serving Asian, Mediterranean, midwestern, breakfast, and dessert selections. The toughest decision of the weekend may be choosing whether to try the rosemary polenta or roast lamb—or maybe you should just go directly to the chocolate-dipped strawberries. It's all covered in the price of $51 per person, so don't be shy about lingering over cappuccino.

To end your 900 North idyll with a flourish, tell the hotel's concierge that you'd like to take a spin along Michigan Avenue as you depart. Your luggage can wait as you step into a horse-drawn carriage at the hotel's door. Expect this final touch of class to run about $30 for a half-hour ride, which is all you'll want if the day is cold. It's a chilly but charming way to say goodbye to your warm winter weekend.

A Romance with History

AFRICAN-AMERICAN CHICAGO

OVE WAS DESCRIBED BY SAMUEL JOHNSON as the triumph of hope over experience. Nowhere is this optimistic outlook more appropriate than in Chicago's African-American community, which got its start with the very first non–Native American to settle here. Jean-Baptiste Pointe du Sable, described in a post–Revolutionary War British report as a well-educated "handsome Negro," came around 1779, a successful trader who built his log cabin on the north bank of the Chicago River (demonstrating a good nose for prime real estate) before moving on to the wide-open spaces of Missouri in 1800.

Barely more than half a century later, the white Downstater who became known as the Great Emancipator was nominated here for the presidency. During the Civil War and after, Chicago proved a place of opportunity for freed slaves; and during the first half of the following century, Chicago became by far the most popular destination for southerners making the great migration north, where factory jobs and less blatant discrimination offered the promise of a better life.

Today, the triumph of hope over experience is driving redevelopment in areas such as Bronzeville, where many of the southerners settled. As you explore this and adjacent areas together (keep in mind that you needn't be African-American to do so), you'll be reminded over and over that here, as in your hearts and in the heart of every lover, hope springs eternal.

*R*om*ance*
AT A GLANCE

♦ Visit the Near South Side neighborhood of **Bronzeville,** where black Chicago flourished during the great migration from the South.

♦ Explore African tribal art, as well as works by modern masters, at the **DuSable Museum of African-American History** (740 East Fifty-sixth Place; 773–947–0600).

♦ Nourish yourselves with soul food at **Gladys' Luncheonette** (4527 South Indiana Avenue; 773–548–4566) or **Army & Lou's** (422 East Seventy-fifth Street; 773–483–3100).

♦ Glory in country-club opulence for everyone (and maybe swim or golf) at **South Shore Cultural Center** (7059 South Shore Drive; 312–747–2536).

♦ Applaud a show performed by one of the nation's most prominent African-American theater companies, **eta Creative Arts Foundation** (7558 South Chicago Avenue; 773–752–3955).

PRACTICAL NOTES: Public transportation is available throughout the South Side, where this itinerary is set. But you'll be able to move along faster—and, it must be said, perhaps more safely—if you're driving.

DAY ONE: morning

Start your day on the South Side in **Bronzeville,** the community that was a beacon for blacks heading north during the Great Migration of the early twentieth century. Bronzeville was known nationwide as a monument to the economic muscle that African-Americans could amass in unity. Today the neighborhood is no longer prosperous—and nearby public-housing projects should be avoided—but recent efforts to preserve its landmarks and salute its importance hold promise.

Begin at the **Monument to the Great Migration** statue (at Twenty-fifth Street near King Drive and the I–55 overpass), sculptor Alison Saar's larger-than-life bronze of a traveler whose bulging, cord-tied suitcase suggests more dreams than possessions. You can walk south along King Drive and examine, in the sidewalks on both sides of the street, the ninety-one bronze plaques in the **Walk of**

Fame, artist Geraldine McCullough's commemorations of notable Bronzeville events and people. On the same route, you'll see twenty-four benches at bus stops and median plazas, each designed by one of twenty-four artists to salute Bronzeville's past and present.

At the symbolic gateway to Bronzeville, Thirty-fifth Street and King Drive, stands a 14-by-7-foot bronze **street map** showing 120 historic sites in the area, including the homes of writer Lorraine Hansberry (*A Raisin in the Sun*) and the great gospel singer Mahalia Jackson, as well as the old Regal Theater and more. At this writing some Bronzeville sites had fallen into disrepair, but public and private efforts are now under way to preserve many.

These include the headquarters of what at the time were the nation's most prosperous black-owned businesses, including the **Supreme Life Insurance** company (3501 South King Drive). The **Eighth Regiment Armory** (at Thirty-fifth and Giles) was the home of an all-black military unit. And at the **Wabash YMCA** (3763 South Wabash Avenue), black historian Carter G. Woodson created what now is celebrated as Black History Month.

One building that has been recycled is the **Chicago Bee Building** (3647 South State Street; 312–747–6872). The *Bee* was a daily newspaper that boosted the Bronzeville promise to African-Americans nationwide. Appropriately, its old home now is the Chicago Bee neighborhood branch of the Chicago Public Library.

LUNCH

If walking has worked up your appetites, have lunch at a South Side institution that's a little south and west of Bronzeville. At **Gladys' Luncheonette** (4527 South Indiana Avenue; 773–548–4566), the soul food runs from hot links and eggs to salmon croquettes. "It's not fancy," says Gladys' fan Diane Hightower, "but when you sit down there, you really get the feeling that, wow, Louis Armstrong or Duke Ellington sat in this seat, too." The food is inexpensive, and the feeling is free.

DAY ONE: afternoon

Going east and south from Gladys', you'll come to Washington Park, which at the turn of the twentieth century

Classic Chicago Couples:
Grammie and Grandpa Sayre

Grammie and Grandpa Sayre starred in the most romantic travel story I know. One day in 1935 my mother's father, Louis T. Sayre, telephoned his wife, Mame, from the office. "Come right downtown and get a passport," he said. "We're going to Europe."

"Louis, you've lost your mind," replied Mame, who nonetheless went downtown and got the passport and some trunks and some lovely suitcases lined in blue velvet. Then she went home, made arrangements for the children, and sailed off with Grandpa for several weeks in the capitals of Europe. They mixed business with pleasure (even enjoying a private audience with the pope) in a love story we now tell to their great-grandchildren.

held a racetrack to which pleasure seekers flocked. Today, it's home to the **DuSable Museum of African-American History** (740 East Fifty-sixth Place; 773–947–0600), which got its start as a labor of love by Dr. Margaret Burroughs and her late husband, Charles, back in 1961. Burroughs, a painter and sculptor, wanted to showcase the history and art of her people; and though nowadays she's a civic pillar, it's a measure of how far her mission has come to note that she was the first woman many Chicagoans ever saw in colorful contemporary African dress.

At the museum (which called itself African-American long before the term entered the mainstream) you'll see works by many local artists who attained greater fame. One distinguished example is Archibald Motley, who painted Chicago's Negro life in vibrant compositions that are unmistakably 1930s American while recalling Henri de Toulouse-Lautrec in their clear-eyed, unapologetic focus on the artist's community. Motley was the subject of a major retrospective at the Chicago Historical Society a few years back, and his paintings also hang in the Art Institute as well as other major museums.

The DuSable Museum focuses as much on history as art, with many African artifacts and the stunning Robert Ames Freedom Mural, a 10-foot-tall mahogany carving that depicts highlights in African-American history. Special exhibits are also worth noting; at this writing these included a fascinating photography exhibit

Fight to Fly: Blacks in Aviation as well as a loving tribute to the late Chicago mayor Harold Washington. Admission to the museum is $3.00 for adults ($2.00 for seniors and students), except on Thursday, when everyone gets in free. Museum hours are 10:00 A.M. to 5:00 P.M. Monday through Saturday and noon to 5:00 P.M. on Sunday.

A couple of hours in the museum is enough to enjoy its collections and exhibits. Next take a leisurely drive south through Jackson Park toward the **South Shore Cultural Center** (7059 South Shore Drive; 312-747-2536). South Shore, once among the city's very best neighborhoods, remains a lovely area of fine old homes. Today's cultural center once was the very tony South Shore Country Club, to which I confess a sentimental attachment by way of my mother's treasured memories of swimming, riding, and playing there as a child.

A few years back my cousin was married at "the club" in one of the most glamorous weddings I've ever attended. The bride wore a vintage green satin short formal; the ceremony was held on the grassy area between the building and its beach, with the lake and city skyline as backdrop. The magic continued as we moved indoors to the ballroom and danced to the music of a local big band, complete with individual bandstands sporting the group's name. After dinner my mother guided us through the building, pointing out the room where movies were screened on Sunday nights, the children's play areas, and the grand staircase, beyond which lay the bedrooms for members who might not make it home.

A Break for Some Action

If you've had the foresight to come in summer and pack your swimsuits, you can take a dip in Lake Michigan at the South Shore beach. Or bring your clubs to the 2,900-yard, par-33 South Shore Golf Course at the Cultural Center. To reserve a tee time, call the twenty-four-hour answering system at (312) 245-0909. Either activity will give you a delicious feeling of playing hooky together as you savor some unexpected pastoral pleasures right in the big, bustling city.

Even without my mom's travelogue, you'll fall for the magic of South Shore, too. Now open to the public daily from 10:00 A.M. to 6:00 P.M. and operated by the Chicago Park District, the cultural center hosts many events that are open to the public, including dance and music performances that often are free. Call to have a schedule sent to you. When you visit, notice the stables, at one end of the gravel drive, where the Chicago Police Department's mounted patrol keeps its horses. Indoors, seek out the building's lovely old touches: a mosaic floor, grand windows, dreamy painted details. And savor the fact that what once was *veddy* private is now for everyone.

DAY ONE: evening

DINNER

Dinner is nearby at another South Side institution: **Army & Lou's** (422 East Seventy-fifth Street; 773–483–3100), where a beautifully refurbished building holds a restaurant that seems to have been here forever. A little more expensive and definitely more upscale than Gladys', Army & Lou's offers its own top-notch soul food, including excellent fried chicken and kosher short ribs. If you're here on Sunday, go for the roast turkey dinner that'll have you giving thanks, even in the heat of summer. And if you're really stuffed, agree on whether you'd rather split the sweet-potato pie or the peach cobbler.

Then take in a performance by the **eta Creative Arts Foundation** (7558 South South Chicago Avenue; 773–752–3955), a wonderful company that for more than thirty years has been producing shows that explore the African-American experience with heartfelt humor and serious emotion. Many eta shows spring from the music that was everywhere in the community's heyday; others focus on family. Shows address broader social issues, too, and all are guaranteed to give you plenty to talk about on the way home. Performances are at 8:00 P.M. Thursday, Friday, and Saturday, and 3:00 and 7:00 P.M. Sunday. Tickets are $25, and reservations are wise.

Chicago Christmas à Deux

ELEBRATING THE HOLIDAYS IN CHICAGO is enough to make you believe in Santa. There's magic in the miles of twinkling lights along Michigan Avenue, the towering tree right in the middle of the Loop, the glittering store windows decked out with intricate displays. The shopping is spectacular, even if you never leave North Michigan Avenue. And the festive, anticipatory atmosphere will have you wishing total strangers a happy holiday season. Lucky you, to have a sweetheart with whom to share the revelry!

PRACTICAL NOTES: Here's a weekend when you can leave the car at home. All this itinerary's highlights are within easy reach of each other.

DAY ONE: evening

Start your holiday weekend at the pinnacle of the Magnificent Mile by checking in at the **Drake Hotel** (140 East Walton Street; 312-787-2200). Although its address and entrance are on a side street, the Drake is something of a crown jewel on Michigan Avenue. It's the northernmost building on one of the city's very best streets, and one of the most venerable. All sorts of royalty have rested here, from the late Princess Diana to the very prominent society maven who resides in the penthouse. For the rest of us, there's a friendly and helpful staff, a posh afternoon tea, an excellent seafood restaurant that has earned the loyalty of generations of Chicagoans and out-of-towners, and a piano bar that's a legend in itself. And when

Romance AT A GLANCE

◆ Get set to twinkle at the **Drake Hotel** (140 East Walton Street; 312–787–2200); for dinner, savor the finny fare in the hotel's nautical **Cape Cod Room.**

◆ Ride down Michigan Avenue in a carriage drawn by a steed from **Noble Horse** (1410 North Orleans Street; 312–266-7878) to hear jazz at the **Hotel Inter-Continental** (505 North Michigan Avenue; 312–944–4100).

◆ Shop (or just window-shop) along **Oak Street, Michigan Avenue,** and the **Gold Coast**'s glittering side streets.

◆ Sip high tea to soothing harp music at the Drake's **Palm Court.**

◆ Join generations of Chicagoans for A Christmas Carol at the **Goodman Theatre** (170 North Dearborn Street; 312–443–3800) and festive trees in "Christmas Around the World" at the **Museum of Science and Industry** (Fifty-seventh Street and Lake Shore Drive; 773–684–1414).

◆ Purr with contentment in a bistro named for a tomcat: **Cafe Matou** (1846 North Milwaukee Avenue; 773–384–8911).

the Drake decorates for the holidays, it does so with enthusiasm plus panache. So give yourselves some time to linger in the lobby and enjoy the environment.

In its rooms as well as its public areas, you'll find the Drake is elegant but not stuffy, comfortable but never assuming. Maid service is provided not once, but twice daily, the better to replenish your supplies of fresh fruit and ice. No two rooms are exactly alike, but all offer a minibar, two telephones, and cozy terrycloth robes in the bathroom. Of course, just about every view is terrific; you can ask for a lake view or one that looks down on the festive twinkling of Michigan Avenue or Lake Shore Drive. The Drake's rates can top $300 a night for a deluxe room with double bed and lake view, but weekend packages can bring that figure down considerably. Ask about the shoppers' weekend, which is offered during the month of December; you'll do much better on rates this way.

DINNER

Once you've checked in and fully appreciated your accommodations, wander downstairs and take a look around the hotel's lovely public areas before heading for a splendid seafood dinner at the hotel's **Cape Cod Room**. The nautical theme here teeters between tasteful and retro, with lots of brass, dark wood, and red-and-white checked tablecloths. Get in the spirit with Bookbinder's red snapper soup, made famous in Philadelphia and made very well indeed here in the Cape Cod Room. Whatever seafood you favor is sure to be expertly prepared, but do ask your waiter for suggestions. Dinner will run about $50 per person, and you'll want reservations (make them when you book your room for the weekend).

After dinner, if you're feeling festive and the weather isn't forbidding, you might enjoy a carriage ride along the side streets of the two neighborhoods in this area, Streeterville and the Gold Coast. Historical sidelight: Streeterville is named for one of the city's genuine characters, a rogue named George "Cap" Streeter, who declared himself ruler of "the District of Lake Michigan" after running his steamboat onto a sandbar east of Michigan Avenue in 1886. Cap and his wife, Ma (I am not making this up), built up the sandbar with junk, remodeled the shipwreck into a shack, and refused to budge for more than twenty years, during which they sold beer on Sunday and performed their own sovereign "state's" marriages. As an irritant and a frustration to his neighbors, who even then included many of the city's very finest citizens (which, then as now, meant its very wealthiest), Cap remains legendary in local lore.

As for that carriage ride, you can make a reservation to be picked up at the hotel by calling **Noble Horse** (1410 North Orleans Street; 312–266–7878). Rush hour is off-limits, but evening rides are offered from 6:30 till midnight on weekdays and from 10:00 A.M. till after midnight weekends. A half-hour ride for two is $30, a full hour is $60.

For a swell after-dinner drink, park your carriage at the **Hotel Inter-Continental** (505 North Michigan Avenue; 312–944–4100), where the wonderful Erin McDougal performs most evenings in the lobby bar. The bar, says the *Chicago Tribune*'s man-about-town Rick Kogan, is "nicely furnished, with couches and soft chairs and a mon-eyed feel." Another plus: There's no cover, "though drinks ain't cheap."

Also cover-free is late-night entertainment in the Drake's own **Coq d'Or** room, a local landmark that opened the day after

Prohibition was repealed in 1933. Currently, on weekends Arlene Bardelle and Craig Lanigan sing and tickle the ivories till after you should be in bed.

DAY TWO: morning/afternoon

Dive into a day's worth of holiday shopping by crossing the street to **Arturo Express** (919 North Michigan Avenue; 312-751-2250), where a cappuccino and a bagel or muffin will get you going happily. Then head up the block to start at the top, in terms of browsing, on the fabulous **Oak Street** (1000 north). Oak Street's retailers are the crème de la crème of clothing and accessories, including star-power names from **Hermès of Paris** (110 East Oak Street; 312-787-8175) to **Barneys New York** (25 East Oak Street; 312-587-1700). Representing the cutting edge is **Betsey Johnson** (72 East Oak Street; 312-664-5901).

Tucked in among Oak Street's heavy hitters are local luminaries that you might actually prefer to scout more closely, since you can get those biggies elsewhere. Don't miss the spectacular **Ultimo** (114 East Oak Street; 312-787-1171), which is a name you can drop among the fashion cognoscenti anywhere. The shop carries high-style, highly sophisticated clothes for men and women, and the staff will help coordinate an outfit for you.

If these high-fashion shops are a bit much for your gift list, tone down the style statement with something a little less haute from **Sugar Magnolia** (34 East Oak Street; 312-944-0885). The overalls are long gone from this onetime Lincoln Park favorite, which has gone uptown gracefully with women's clothing and accessories that are good looking but less intimidating (and less expensive) than much of what the neighbors stock.

Beyond clothing, Oak Street and its neighbors offer both sexes the kind of personal grooming most of us only dream of—and you might just want to turn over your morning to it. At **Marilyn Miglin** (112 East Oak Street; 312-943-1120), you'll find skin-care consultation and products, makeup, and the exotic perfume Pheremone (Miglin's own concoction, and she swears it's every bit as effective as the hormones themselves). At the eponymous **Marianne Strokirk** (41 East Oak Street; 312-640-0101), stylists are renowned for their prowess in both cutting and coloring; Strokirk herself has worked on heads as famous as Hillary Rodham Clinton's. **Chatto** (102 East Oak Street; 312-640-0003) specializes in "multicultural hair," so dreadlocks will be handled with care. Facials and expert makeup applications can give you a new look for the holidays at **Anna Kay Skin Care Salon** (100 East Walton Street; 312-944-8500). You'll find pampering aplenty at **Kiva** (196 East Pearson Street; 312-840-8120), where you can get a conventional haircut as well as an array of New Age treatments, from a skin-soothing milk paraffin cocoon to a calming "shiro dhara" oil massage for your "third eye"(it's in the middle of your forehead). And remember—all these salons offer equal-opportunity luxury, so make plans for *two*.

There's lots more on Oak Street, but you don't want to short-change Michigan Avenue. This is where you'll find **Gucci** (900 North Michigan Avenue; 312-664-5504; www.gucci.com), **Chanel Boutique** (935 North Michigan Avenue; 312-787-5500), **Tiffany & Co.** (730 North Michigan Avenue; 312-944-7500), **Williams-Sonoma** (700 North Michigan Avenue; 312-787-8991), **Saks Fifth Avenue** (700 North Michigan Avenue; 312-944-6500), **Escada USA** (840 North Michigan Avenue; 312-915-0500), and many others from the shopping hit parade.

LUNCH

When your energy flags, get off the crowded shopping route with a detour to **Mrs. Park's Tavern** (198 East Delaware Place; 312-280-8882). Located in the Doubletree Hotel and Suites, Mrs. Park's atmosphere is pleasant and its menu is American—but everything is made with a bit of a twist. A chicken Caesar salad, for example, comes as a sandwich, and the accompanying chips are sweet potato. Lunch and dinner are served from 11:30 A.M. to 2:00 A.M. daily and won't cost more than about $35 total.

Revived, give over your afternoon to **Water Tower Place** (845 North Michigan Avenue), with its two anchor stores, **Lord & Taylor** (312-787-7400) and **Marshall Field's** (312-335-7700). Lord & Taylor carries classic clothing and accessories even Aunt Bertha will be happy to receive. And Field's offers a broader selection in the same territory, as well as such surefire gifts as crystal and jewelry. Be sure

Picture Perfect:

A twinkling, magical holiday weekend on Michigan Avenue is the perfect time to try one of my favorite romantic, playful things to do: Get a disposable camera as you start the weekend and start clicking—and don't be too shy to ask some nice bystander to get a shot of you together in a special place. When the roll's finished, have the film developed at a one-hour spot and take the results somewhere you can sit down and look over this instant journal of your time together. Then do it again!

to stock up on Frango mints, the Field's-made confections you can't get anywhere else. They're a perfect hostess gift and great to have on hand when you get an unexpected present from someone else.

More gifts? You're only steps from something for everyone in Water Tower Place's eight levels of shops; be sure to check out the small local ones, such as **Chiasso** (312-280-1249) and **Accent Chicago** (312-944-1354). You can wrap up treats for everyone from the sophisticated selection at **Godiva Chocolatier** (312-280-1133) or explore an all-candy version of Pinocchio's Pleasure Island at **F.A.O. Schweetz** (312-787-3773). (Toys are across the street at **F.A.O. Schwartz,** 840 North Michigan Avenue; 312-787-8894.)

The shopping is unsurpassed, but there's another reason to go to Water Tower: The people-watching is outstanding. The mall—let's face it, this is no more than that—attracts everyone. You'll see power shoppers, mall rats, ladies who lunch, and overstimulated families. I remember to this day a winter evening when I spotted, at a distance, a man I knew slightly, lingering near the sleek glass elevators with a beautiful, curly-haired blonde. Both were wearing head-to-toe black, berets included, and looked as glamorous and lucky in love as you could ever want to look.

Water Tower Place has a way of giving people a patina. Be happy, be in love, and it'll make you shiny, too.

DAY TWO: afternoon/evening

When you've finished your shopping (perhaps forever!), rest your plastic and your weary selves back at the Drake. Do it over afternoon tea, a sedate and highly civilized affair held daily in the **Palm Court.** Scones, finger sandwiches, and pastries will soothe you, as will the strains of harp music. You can choose a table with elegant upholstered chair or sink into a sofa for maximum comfort.

By the time you arise and stop in your room to change, you'll be ready to cab to the southern part of downtown for tonight's main event: a performance of Charles Dickens's *A Christmas Carol* at the **Goodman Theatre** (170 North Dearborn Street; 312–443–3800; www.goodman-theater.org). For almost twenty years, this show has delighted Chicagoans with its ever-changing production, including whiz-bang special effects that get better every year. It's truly a don't-miss holiday highlight, with shows at 7:30 P.M. (except Friday and Saturday shows at 8:00 P.M.) and tickets ranging from about $16 to about $35.

In your after-show glow, grab a cab to one of the city's hippest areas for a late dinner at **Cafe Matou** (1846 North Milwaukee Avenue; 773–384–8911), where the kitchen stays open for posttheater patrons. The name is French for alley cat, but there's a playful, feisty quality to the word—a sign of affection for the naughty cat who also serves as the restaurant's logo. You'll find moderately priced, characteristically French entrees here, as well as an oenophile's influence in the wine list and monthly dinner-tastings that spotlight a geographic area, grape type, or other aspect of wine appreciation. Put yourselves on the mailing list to receive notices of these events; it's a pleasant little jolt of memory every time you receive one.

If you're still feeling energetic, direct your cab to an upscale supper club where you can dine and dance the night away. At **Green Dolphin Street** (2001 North Ashland Avenue; 312–395–0066), *le jazz* is hot and so is the crowd, Wednesday through Saturday till 2:00 A.M. at least. The Green Dolphin's cover charge is about $10, but that's waived for those who have dinner here. If you do, you'll enjoy the fruits of one of the more innovative kitchens around town, with entrees like venison chops, smoked scallops, grilled quail, and tuna with wasabi and red curry. Don't miss a chance to linger on one of my favorite waterfront spots: The Green Dolphin has a "backyard" that ends right at the Chicago River, and it's land-scaped and lit for lovers. If the weather permits, see for yourselves by following the brick path to the water.

DAY THREE: morning

To get an early start on your Sunday, head for the breakfast buffet at **Beau's Bistro** (in the Ambassador West Hotel, 1300 North State Parkway; 312-787-3700). From 7:00 A.M. to 1:00 P.M., there's a big buffet of breakfast favorites, including eggs, bacon, hash browns, bakery treats, and more. And the price is right at just $13.95 per person. Beau's is a short cab ride (or walk, if the weather's friendly) west and north from the Drake.

BRUNCH

For a brunch that's more of an event, browse the American dim sum at **Park Avenue Cafe** (199 East Walton Street; 312-944-4414), where some thirty items give you a chance to sample much of what's coming out of this highly respected kitchen. Meats and fish, baked items, and more are offered in tempting little portions from 10:30 A.M. to 2:00 P.M. At $30 per person, it's definitely pricier than your average breakfast—but then, it *isn't* your average breakfast.

This being Sunday morning, even if you're not the churchgoing type, consider stopping in at services in the beautiful **Fourth Presbyterian Church** (126 East Chestnut Street, off Michigan Avenue; 312-787-4570). Its splendid stained-glass windows alone are worth the trip.

Then head south to enjoy the department store windows along State Street. Two big displays are at **Marshall Field's** State Street store (111 North State Street; 312-781-1000) and **Carson Pirie Scott & Co.** (1 South State Street; 312-641-7000). If you can stand a bit more time in retail establishments, don't miss Field's giant Christmas tree and Carson's glorious interior. Carson's is a Louis Sullivan building and one of the loveliest works by the city's pre-Prairie master, gracefully decorated and beautifully restored by caring owners.

If you happen to be in town on the right day, do try to take in a performance of Handel's *Messiah*. This magnificent piece has become a holiday tradition here as a do-it-yourself production that's a lot more polished than you might expect. The **Do-It-Yourself** *Messiah* generally has two performances on a weekend before Christmas, and although admission is free, you need tickets to get in. Write its sponsor, enclosing a self-addressed stamped envelope, at LaSalle Bank Do-It-Yourself *Messiah*, 135 South LaSalle Street, Suite 2905, Chicago, IL 60603. Check beforehand to learn when tickets become available and—very important—when the performances will be given.

To survey the many *Messiah* performances, as well as other special music programs around town, get a copy of *Chicago* magazine's December issue and consult its listing of holiday programs. They're too specific to discuss here, but it would be a shame to leave town without enjoying something from the rich array of holiday music that's available.

If you're ready for a taste of warmer climes, head over to **Caliterra** (633 North St. Clair Street; 312–274–4444), where chef John Coletta tosses a culinary salad of mixed influences—California, Tuscany, and seasonal freshness. Shrimp "cigars" are a signature appetizer, and the thin brick-oven pizzas are a big item. There's always a pizza or pasta for vegetarians, and carnivores go for the "surf and turf" combo of lobster risotto with a juicy filet of beef. The restaurant is open seven days, from 6:30 A.M. to 11:00 P.M., so you can come any time. Most evenings there's live music, too. Sipping a big red wine and scratching name after name off your gift-shopping list makes a perfect finale to your weekend of holiday magic in Chicago.

FOR MORE ROMANCE

Can you stand one more Chicago Christmas tradition? Make it a visit to the **Museum of Science and Industry's Christmas Around the World** (Fifty-seventh Street and Lake Shore Drive; 773–684–1414; www.msichicago.org), a collection of full-size Christmas trees decorated in the ethnic traditions of many nations. This loving display of pride and memory is sure to squelch any Scrooge tendencies (although I may be biased by the childhood wonder I still recall at seeing the Lithuanian tree, hung with intricate ornaments made entirely from white straws). There are performances of ethnic dance and music, plus all sorts of other special events for the season.

Finally, for a holiday experience that really tells you this is Chicago, take a holiday cruise on Lake Michigan with the *Odyssey* (630–990–0800; www.odysseycruises.com). Sunday jazz brunch cruises are offered year-round (assuming the lake isn't jammed with ice, and it almost never is). Just imagine telling everyone back home that you went on a pre-Christmas cruise for just 60 bucks each. (See "Swept Away: Romantic Lakefront Cruises" for more information on the *Odyssey*.)

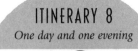

Amore!

CHICAGO ROMANCE ITALIAN-STYLE

ERE'S A QUESTION FOR YOU and your beloved to pon-
der: If we were planning a trip to the land of romance,
where would we be going? If you're from Chicago, the
answer is likely to be Italy. Leave snooty France, humid Florida, and
all those overcommercialized tropical islands to other, less discerning lovers. If you want great food, great culture, great people, and
great regard for *amore*, you've got to go for Italy.

Or the next best thing, which is immersion in Italia, Chicago-
style, and does *not* include anything that pertains to Al Capone,
thank you. Here's a lighthearted look at *la dolce vita*, according to
one of the city's proudest ethnic groups.

PRACTICAL NOTES: This itinerary calls for a car to permit travel from the western suburb of Stone Park to downtown locations.
The drive is about a half hour from downtown on I–290; exit north-
bound at Mannheim Road and look for signs.

DAY ONE: morning/afternoon

Get your cappuccinos *per andare* (to go) and head out to the **Italian
Cultural Center** (1621 North Thirty-ninth Avenue, Stone Park;
708–345–3842), where loving Italian-Americans have assembled
"Italians in Chicago," a photo exhibit displaying hundreds of
nineteenth- and twentieth-century pictures of their compatriots at
work, church, and home. An art gallery features paintings, sculp-
tures, and lithographs by Italian artists, as well as the little puppet
mouse Topo Gigio (think 1960s, *Ed Sullivan Show*). Other exhibits
include a stunning, built-to-scale wooden model of the Vatican's

◆ Get past Capone at the **Italian Cultural Center** (1621 North Thirty-ninth Avenue, Stone Park; 708-345-3842).

◆ Learn what becomes a legend most: sausage and cheese, when it's Chicago-style deep-dish pizza at **Pizzeria Uno** (29 East Ohio Street; 312-321-1000) or **Pizzeria Due** (619 North Wabash Avenue; 312-943-2400).

◆ Try playing a game of bocce at **McGuane Park** (2901 South Poplar Street; 312-747-6497).

◆ Cross over from audience to actors at **Tony 'n' Tina's Wedding** (Piper's Alley Theater, 230 West North Avenue; 312-664-8844).

◆ Sip a swanky Strega at **Spiaggia** (980 North Michigan Avenue; 312-280-2750).

Basilica of St. Peter and its columned courtyard, as well as miniatures of Pisa's cathedral, baptistry, and famous Leaning Tower. A library of some 3,000 volumes, about one-fourth of them in Italian, is open to the public but doesn't allow books to circulate, because too many have been lost.

The center's hours are 10:00 A.M. to 4:00 P.M. weekdays; usually the center's closed on weekends, except for the annual Italian Day picnic, which is held the first Sunday of August. An outdoor mass is celebrated in Italian before revelers settle down to catered food, tours of the center, and serious competition in bocce (an Italian version of bowling). If you want to make the picnic, call the center during its open hours for information.

LUNCH

Pretend you're in a little red Ferrari as you hit the Eisenhower Expressway (only out-of-towners and map readers call it I-290) and zoom downtown. You're headed for one of Chicago's premier destinations: **Pizzeria Uno** (29 East Ohio Street; 312-321-1000). At Uno's and its down-the-block sister spot, **Pizzeria Due** (619 North Wabash Avenue; 312-943-2400), what a grateful world knows as Chicago-style pizza was introduced by the late man-about-town Ike Sewell. This splendid slice of heaven starts with a crust thick enough to constitute a meal itself, topped abundantly with gooey mozzarella, a sauce that's more tomato than sauce, and, if you like, satisfying lumps of spicy sausage. Add a side salad (for health reasons) and a pitcher of soda or beer, and you'll know you're in Chicago.

Rolling out of these pizza palaces, you're likely to feel like bocce balls yourselves. And you might just like to try your hand at this little-known but pleasantly undemanding sport. Many Chicago Park District parks have bocce courts, and if they have time, the accommodating staffers will even teach you the basics—with the park's balls—at **McGuane Park** (2901 South Poplar Street; 312–747–6497). Be sure to call in advance and ask if someone is available when you plan to come.

If you want to explore a little-known corner of the city, take some time to look around about a mile west of the park's neighborhood, where Western Avenue holds some well-regarded Italian restaurants. This quiet old Italian area lies about a mile south of the Near West Side's better-known Little Italy, an immigrant haven where Jane Addams began modern social work with Hull House. As that neighborhood now is dominated by the University of Illinois–Chicago campus, so was this area once dominated by International Harvester's huge McCormick factory, whose jobs allowed many local residents to buy the tidy homes that still stand today. Some are owned by newer arrivals to the United States, while others remain in the families of those long-gone Italian factory workers.

DAY ONE: evening

Witness the most memorable nuptials ever. *Tony 'n' Tina's Wedding* (Piper's Alley Theater, 230 West North Avenue; 312–664–8844) is a participatory piece of comical theater that makes the audience the guests at a loony Italian-American wedding reception, complete with crackpot cousins, a champagne toast to the happy couple, a full buffet, dancing, and wedding cake for everybody. The cast makes it their business to draw audience members into the action, although you don't *have* to join the bunny hop to yuck it up at this goofy "occasion."

If it sounds totally *not* your cup of tea, consider going anyway. Reviewers have been surprised at how much they liked this wacky

Classic Chicago Couples:
Joe and Teresa

Joseph Sylvester Figliulo's family came from Naples, Italy, to Chicago's South Side neighborhood of Englewood. There he played as a child with Olivia Teresa Coleman, whose family had come from all over Ireland to the same neighborhood. Joe and Teresa grew up, fell in love, married, had two sons, worked, traveled, and doted on their seventeen grandchildren. They lived into their nineties and celebrated sixty-eight years of marriage.

Grandma and Grandpa Figliulo would have been a great couple anywhere. How lucky for me that they lived in Chicago.

evening—especially when they didn't expect to. To make your grab for the bouquet early, plan to catch the 5:00 P.M. show on Saturday. (Wednesday and Thursday, it's at 7:30 P.M.; Friday and Sunday shows are at 8:00 P.M.) Tickets range from $49 to $68 apiece.

DINNER

When you're ready to end your day of *la dolce vita* on a more sedate note, head back downtown toward the glittery stretch of North Michigan Avenue that holds **Spiaggia** (980 North Michigan Avenue; 312-280-2750) and **Cafe Spiaggia** (same address; 312-280-2755). Either of these extremely chic sibling restaurants can serve you the signature thin-crust pizza, with toppings as rich as the clientele. There are many variations, but the combo I like best is duck sausage and goat cheese. It's definitely different from pepperoni and anchovies, but trust me: You'll love it, too. Follow it by toasting each other with one of those bracing Italian liqueurs, such as Strega or grappa, and you'll feel like Mastroianni and Ekberg wading recklessly in the fountain of Trevi—except your fountain is more likely to be Buckingham. And, of course, you still believe in *amore*.

FOR MORE ROMANCE

Another Italian treat might be waiting for you at **Facets Cinematheque** (1517 West Fullerton Avenue; 773-281-4114), where art films have a happy home. Check the newspaper listings to see whether there's an Italian movie among them. If so, you can enjoy listening to the language (but reading the English subtitles) as you steep yourselves in the culture.

While you're in the neighborhood, consider exploring another culture while you're at it. Here are a few ideas to get you started.

The city has several restaurants whose menus draw from the British Isles, but the local Irish community meets, studies, and even eats at the **Irish American Heritage Center** (4626 North Knox Avenue; 773-282-7035; www.irishamhc.com). A small museum here holds Celtic treasures, and a regular class schedule offers Irish set dancing, music taught on traditional instruments, and Gaelic language instruction. On the premises, the **5th Province** pub (773-282-7035, ext.15) serves food on Friday and Saturday nights, with music from 9:00 P.M.

Get a glimpse of Jewish history at the downtown **Spertus Museum** (618 South Michigan Avenue; 312-322-1747; www.spertus.edu). Children's exhibits are highly regarded; the Asher Library is the area's largest Jewish public library, and the gift shop stocks all sorts of Judaica and books. To eat like in your own bubbe's kitchen , go to **Manny's** (1411 South Jefferson Street; 312-939-2855). This classic deli is open from 5:00 A.M. till 4:00 P.M. daily, and even if your heart's set on corned beef, get the chicken soup, too. If you'd rather try kosher fine dining, reserve at **Shallots** (2324 North Clark Street; 773-755-5205). Closed on Friday to observe the Sabbath, then open from sundown on Saturdayw, the moderately priced Shallots has made the kind of reputation any specialty restaurant wants: Rules and restrictions go unnoticed in the pleasure of good food.

Natural
Wonders

Adventures in Love

AN OUTDOOR AFFAIR

EING IN LOVE MAKES YOU FEEL as if you can do anything—so why not try it? Trust the one you love to be a
boon companion, in adventure as well as in love. Do
something neither of you has ever tried before, and give yourselves
a memory that will last forever.

Notice that this itinerary differs from others in that, although
two days are outlined, they're alternative rather than consecutive.
You could do one day after the other—but be sure to plan some
recovery time afterward.

PRACTICAL NOTES: Whether you're kayaking or canoeing,
dress for the outdoors and be prepared to get wet. Remember that
these activities are weather dependent. Rain, high winds, or other
inhospitable weather can delay your ballooning plans (although
you'll be rescheduled). Canoeing or kayaking can be done in bad
weather—but be realistic in deciding what constitutes bad.

DAY ONE: morning/afternoon

Taking to the water needn't mean a dip in Lake Michigan. The other
Chicago waterfront is a river, and there are several. You already
know the Chicago River and its branches, of course; out in the
'burbs, there are the Fox River, the Kankakee, and perhaps the most
user-friendly, especially for novice canoers, the **Des Plaines River,**
which reaches into the north and northwest suburbs.

Along these suburban stretches, "anything in the Vernon Hills
area is safe, because the river is only about 4 feet at its deepest

Romance AT A GLANCE

◆ Take to the wilds together by learning to kayak and going tandem on the placid **Des Plaines River** (north and northwest of the city).

◆ Balloon into the sunset over rural countryside with **Champagne Flights** (208 Harding Street, Libertyville; 847–604–1451).

◆ Stoke your stamina with a Polish feast at **Lutnia** (5532 West Belmont Avenue; 773–282–5335) or a cozy French dinner at **Cafe Pyrenees** (River Tree Court, Milwaukee Avenue at Route 60, Vernon Hills; 847–918–8850).

◆ Canoe the **Chicago River**—or go extreme by kayaking unpredictable **Lake Michigan.**

point," explains Fritz Hanselman, owner of the north suburban **Offshore Marine** (Milwaukee Avenue and Route 60, Vernon Hills; 847–362–4880). Located about an hour from downtown, Offshore is where you go to get outfitted for a canoeing expedition on the Des Plaines. The store provides everything you'll need, even if you don't know what to ask for. And if you're hesitant about your minimal skills, Hanselman is reassuring.

"Most canoe renters do fine, because there's not much to know," he says. "A canoe is a pretty stable craft, and if you're in calm waters, things should be OK." Just remember not to stand up and dance while afloat, and you should find yourselves enjoying a congenial paddle.

LUNCH

As for sustenance (food, not each other), pick up a *bellissima* picnic from **Convito Italiano** (Plaza del Lago, 1515 Sheridan Road, Wilmette; 847–251–3654). This Italian food-and-wine shop offers full take-out lunch menus, ranging in price from about $8.00 to $30.00 each, and not everything is pasta; plenty of salads and sandwiches are available, too. Be sure to call a couple of days in advance to order your picnic.

DAY ONE: evening

Want to celebrate your day together at the top of the world? Do it in a balloon! **Champagne Flights** (208 Harding Street, Libertyville; 847–604–1451) offers sunrise and sunset rides on its colorful hot-air balloons over its northern Illinois territory.

When you schedule your flight, you'll be told where to meet your pilot—maybe Champagne owner Ron Briley or maybe one of his employees, who average about seventeen years' experience aloft, Briley says. "Usually we meet at Hawthorne Mall," he notes, which lets you return your Offshore Marine gear conveniently. "From the time we start out till the time we bring you back where we met, it's about two, two and a half hours."

As you prepare to ascend, you're welcome to help your pilot make preparations as well, Briley says. Then, as you climb into the traditional wicker basket, drift skyward, and watch the earth recede, see if you don't feel like the Great and Powerful Oz floating above the Emerald City.

Returning to terra firma, you're again welcome to help your pilot deflate and pack up the balloon. Then you'll pop the cork on a celebratory bottle of champagne before returning to your point of origin. It's all pretty dreamlike, although there are a couple of practical points involved. One, of course, is price: about $150 per person for a weekend flight (weekdays are $130). Another is the rendezvous factor: Briley will notify you about your meeting place an hour or two before you fly, so you'll need a reliable cell phone, an answering machine you can call in to or a place where someone will take a message for you. (Maybe Offshore Marine will help.)

As you end your adventure, you'll probably be starving—so scout around for the mall's rest rooms, slip into the fresh clothes you presciently packed in the car, and you're off to a cozy dinner for two.

DINNER

At the charming **Cafe Pyrenees** (River Tree Court, Milwaukee Avenue at Route 60, Vernon Hills; 847–918–8850), the French food is lovingly prepared and beautifully presented in a setting that's *très romantique*. You'll find a terrific bargain in the $19.50 fixed-price dinner, which gives you three courses and takes nicely to an American or French wine from the list. If you go a la carte, consider the napoleon of grilled vegetables and goat cheese. Carnivores adore the grilled beef tournedos from the bistro-style menu. And chalk up the day's activity as justification for dessert if you're tempted by the luscious chocolate-caramel mousse cake.

ALTERNATIVE: morning/afternoon

What if you're up for a more challenging adventure? Make it kayaking in Lake Michigan! You can learn at the Thursday-evening classes offered by Offshore. "These classes are about three hours, and they're for the person who has never been in a kayak, or has minimal experience," Hanselman says. "We teach forward paddle strokes, turning techniques, and how to handle wet exits in an emergency" (in other words, what to do if you dump).

All lessons are offered in solo kayaks, "because it's always better to start in a solo," Hanselman explains. "You can control it better if you're alone. After a lesson, we'll rent you a tandem kayak, but you need to know what to expect. The tandems are short, wide, and not speedy." They're also much steadier than solo craft, a circumstance that offers an irresistible metaphor for you and your sweetheart.

To sign up for Offshore's lessons, call a week or two ahead. Lessons are $60 per person, starting at 5:30 P.M. from the Offshore store and conducted at nearby Big Bear Little Bear Lake. When you're ready for that tandem kayak, plan to paddle in the North Side shore area if you're headed for Lake Michigan. "Most people go roughly from Diversey to North Avenue, or between Fullerton and Belmont," Hanselman says. Everything you'll need for your day will cost about $125—except for lunch, which you could pick up on the way from Offshore to the lake at **Whole Foods Market** (1000 West North Avenue; 312–587–0648). There's a fabulous array of salads, sandwiches, and desserts at this big alternative supermarket, and you can assemble a dandy meal for two for about $15.

If you'd prefer to canoe the Chicago River or another nearby river, call **Chicagoland Canoe Base** (4019 North Narragansett Avenue; 773–777–1489), where the legendary Ralph Frese makes 'em himself. An expert on the seventeenth-century voyageurs who explored the Great Lakes and many area rivers, Frese might have time to chat with you about his work and passion for local waterways. Or he might just get you outfitted and heading for a good spot to put in along the river of your choice. Everything you'll need— canoe, paddles, life jackets, and rigging to carry the canoe on your car—costs $35 per person for the day, plus a $25 cash deposit.

LUNCH

Again you'll want to pack a lunch; Whole Foods is an option, as is **Chicago Diner** (3411 North Halsted Street; 773-935-6696; www.veggiediner.com), where the vegetarian menu can please vegans, too, at about $20 for two.

ALTERNATIVE: evening
DINNER

When you've returned your gear to Chicagoland Canoe Base, get cleaned up and do a little carbo-loading at **Lutnia** (5532 West Belmont Avenue; 773-282-5335). This is a slice of Chicago's Polonia, an old-fashioned restaurant where the service is proud and the pierogi even prouder. If you know Polish food, try the *bigos* (hunter's stew) or other familiar foods; if you don't, sip some borscht and ask for guidance. Prices are moderate; dinner for two shouldn't run more than $50, depending on your taste for vodka.

Love in the Great Outdoors

When is a poncho the most romantic gift imaginable? When it's from my next-door neighbor, Bill, to his wife, Lori. He adores the great outdoors; she likes all that, but she likes comfort, too. So the toasty-warm, water-resistant, top-of-the-line poncho Bill gave Lori for her birthday was more than a raincoat, it was a thoughtful gesture from a guy who understands what a woman needs to cope.

For More Romance

Here's a great way to impress an athletic sweetheart: Arrange sailboarding lessons for the two of you. Lessons are scheduled weekends from Memorial Day to Labor Day through **Windward Sports** (3317 North Clark Street; 773–472–6868). When you sign up for group instruction, you'll get directions to nearby Wolf Lake in Hammond, Indiana. There, lessons run about three and a half hours, and with a maximum of ten to a class with two teachers, you'll learn fast. Two lessons—which include guaranteed certification, a book, and five subsequent free rentals—run $140 per person and needn't be booked more than a week or two in advance. Windward caters to landlubbers with weekend Rollerblade rentals for $15 and winter snowboards for $35 a day, boots and all.

Love in Bloom
A GARDEN LOVERS' WEEKEND

HICAGO'S OFFICIAL MOTTO IS *URBS IN HORTO*, Latin for "city in a garden," and if you're here during the summer, you'll see just how appropriate that is. The city's "front yard" runs from the South Side's Jackson Park to Grant Park downtown to Lincoln Park on the North Side. At the city's outer edges and into the suburbs, the Cook County Forest Preserve maintains miles and miles of natural and recreational space. Beyond the city limits are gorgeous, growing monuments to nature, notably the Chicago Botanic Garden in north suburban Glencoe and the splendid Morton Arboretum in west suburban Lisle.

Chicago and its environs truly are in full bloom during late spring and well into fall. Sure, the weather can be wicked—too hot, too cold, too rainy, too dry—but when you're with the one you love, it all fades. And when the weather is good—as it often is—this glorious garden city is unbeatable. Here's a weekend and more of outdoor bliss.

PRACTICAL NOTES: This is a sunscreen–and–sensible shoes itinerary. Much of this itinerary requires that you visit during the summer, but not all of it; attractions that remain available during the winter are noted. You could spend a whole weekend outdoors reveling in Grant and Lincoln Parks, which would require only CTA public transportation. Going farther afield, the Metra-Union Pacific North Line (formerly the Chicago and North Western railway's North Line) serves Ravinia Park on the North Shore. The Chicago

Romance AT A GLANCE

◆ Savor music and a picnic under the stars at the **Grant Park Music Festival** *(Petrillo Music Shell, Columbus Drive and Jackson Boulevard; 312–742–7638)—and don't miss the lights playing over glorious* **Buckingham Fountain.**

◆ Spend the day hugging trees at the **Morton Arboretum** *(Illinois Route 53 at I–88, Lisle; 630–719–2400).*

◆ Contemplate the Japanese garden—even when winter reigns—at the **Chicago Botanic Garden** *(1000 Lake Cook Road, Glencoe; 847–835–5440).*

◆ Find your own "secret garden" in the lovely little **Shakespeare Garden** *(east end of Garrett Place at Sheridan Road, on the Northwestern University campus, Evanston).*

Botanic Garden and Morton Arboretum, however, can only be reached by car.

DAY ONE: evening

Enjoy a lovely on-site garden at the charming **Gold Coast Guest House,** a restored Victorian row house west of Michigan Avenue whose rooms are booked by owner Sally Baker at (312) 337–0361 (www.bbchicago.com). The comforts of a queen-size bed and private bath are considerable, and the house is full of delightful details, like the spiral staircases connecting its levels. The price is right, too, with rooms ranging from $129 to $189 per night.

You can explore the garden at your home base in the morning, when breakfast is served there (weather permitting, so pray for sun). Tonight, you're off to enjoy a picnic in the park—Grant Park, that is, where one of the city's great summer pleasures awaits. The **Grant Park Music Festival** (Petrillo Music Shell, Columbus Drive and Jackson Boulevard; 312–742–7638; www.grantparkmusicfestival.com) starts in spring and continues, several nights a week, through a season of top-quality music. Most evenings the Grant Park Orchestra performs classical programs, but you'll also find plenty of popular music. Show tunes are a frequent feature, as are jazz and even the occasional rock program. Dance, too, has a place in this eclectic lineup and the movies screened in the Outdoor Film Festival are hugely popular. Best of all, it's all free.

So pack your picnic basket—or let the park's own restaurant do it for you by calling (312) 377–0933 at least two business days in advance. Music starts at 7:00 P.M. Wednesday, Thursday, and Sunday evenings, and at 8:00 P.M. Friday and Saturday. If you can arrive early, by all means do so, and start your evening at the northern end of the park. That way you can appreciate another wonderful aspect of Grant Park, which is its **Wildflower Works garden** (Columbus Drive between Randolph and Monroe Streets). Some would call them weeds, but you know better. These indigenous beauties include pink evening primroses, purple coneflower, and the odoriferous wild onions from which Chicago takes its name. The park's **Rose Garden** is on your way south, so take the time to examine this gorgeous display.

A Hidden Garden

*If you don't mind a meandering drive to the Chicago Botanic Garden, go north on Lake Shore Drive to Sheridan Road, then continue north to Touhy Avenue. There, head west (away from the lake) and be patient for several miles, just until you cross the Chicago River. Turn to the north onto McCormick Boulevard, and, along the grassy area atop the riverbank, you'll see a garden that is little known beyond this neck of the woods: the **Skokie Park District's Northshore Sculpture Garden**. Park the car and stroll north through this pleasant expanse, with its large-scale modern works, and take a bit of time to enjoy this variation on cultivation, which remains available year-round, unaffected by the vicissitudes of weather that harm living things.*

DINNER

About that picnic basket: Think of it as just another name for take-out, and you're halfway there—on your way to the fabulously named **Zoom Kitchen** (923 North Rush Street; 312–440–3500). Calling itself "a cafeteria for the millennium," ZK serves up homey fare: meat loaf, real carved meats custom salads (no onions, please!), and the sides that say Mom, from mashed potatoes to melting-warm chocolate-chip cookies. Picnicking, of course, calls for food that travels well, but you may want to return to ZK one of these days to sit down and eat in while the food is still hot. Maybe you'll make a pilgrimage to the astonishing all-you-can-eat Sunday brunch at the bargain price of $8.00. In the here and how, however, just pick up a bottle of wine on the way down to the park (ask where to go before leaving Gold Coast Guest House), and you're set for a totally romantic evening.

Well, there *is* one more thing: Before heading back north, stroll over to **Buckingham Fountain** and enjoy the marvelous sight of its multicolored lights playing across spouts and streams of water. It's one of the city's favorite landmarks and not to be missed at night. The fountain operates from Memorial Day through Labor Day (often earlier and later, depending on the weather) and is a magical way to wrap up your evening on the city's spectacular lakefront.

DAY TWO: morning/afternoon

Enjoy your coffee in your B&B garden, then head up and out to the north. It's a short hop to the **Lincoln Park Conservatory** (Stockton Drive near Fullerton Avenue; 312–742–7736), where formal outdoor gardens complement the indoor cultivation. All is not hopeless if you happen to visit in the winter; you can refresh your spirits in the conservatory, which presents a special poinsettia display in December and a chrysanthemum show late in the winter. Like nearly all of its Chicago Park District siblings, the conservatory is free.

Another kind of complement to the formal gardens is just across the street and often overlooked when people visit Lincoln Park. Look for the **Grandmother Gardens** at the northwest corner of Webster Avenue and Stockton Drive, and enjoy its naturalistic stretch of ornamental grasses and flower beds. Most are perennials, and they're arranged as a freewheeling counterpoint to the orderly plantings across the street. Irregularly shaped beds give an unstructured feeling, and a long lawn "flows" down the garden's center, suggesting the curves of a river bordering the "banks" of flowers.

When you're ready to move on, drive a few miles west on Fullerton to the Kennedy Expressway, where you'll head about 30 miles north on I–94 to its Lake Cook Road exit. Go ½ mile or so east after exiting, and you're at the **Chicago Botanic Garden** (1000 Lake Cook Road, Glencoe; 847–835–5440).

The Chicago Botanical Garden, which is open year-round from 8:00 A.M. to sunset, charges no admission fee, but parking costs $4.00. The easiest way to get an overview of its 300 acres is to take a tram tour ($3.50) and note which areas you want to explore more fully. Some don't-miss parts include the splendid rose garden, the six-room English walled garden, the three areas of Sansho-En (a Japanese garden), and the six prairie types that reflect the state's natural beauty and heritage.

LUNCH

Plan to have lunch in the Botanic Garden's inexpensive cafeteria, which is open till 5:30 P.M. and serves soups, sandwiches, and salads. (If you're moving at breakneck speed, you might get here in time for breakfast, which is served till 11:00 A.M.) If you are interested in particular aspects of gardening, call the garden before you come to ask what programs are scheduled for the time you'll be there. Flower shows, sales, talks, classes, and demonstrations are offered year-round.

Which brings us to the fact that the garden is well worth a visit, even in the dead of winter. The garden's extensive greenhouses are filled with rare cacti, amusing topiary designs and figures, and lush, warming tropical plants. The Japanese garden, surprisingly, is also a joy during winter. Needless to say, you'll contend with drastically fewer fellow visitors during the winter, too.

DAY TWO: evening

As you leave the Botanic Garden, head east on Lake Cook Road until it bends into Green Bay Road. Look for signs directing you to parking for Ravinia, and watch out for the traffic jam you could find (especially on weekends).

While not itself a garden, **Ravinia Park** (Green Bay Road, Highland Park; 847–266–5100; www.ravinia.org) nestles in the tangled expanse of green that is the North Shore, providing a civilized, open-air haven for the entire Chicago area. Like the Grant Park music programs, the Ravinia Festival offers predominantly classical music, with enough jazz and other popular styles to attract the nonclassical crowd. Unlike Grant Park, Ravinia charges admission and, in addition to its expansive, well-groomed lawns, has a pavilion that you'll be glad you're sitting under if it rains.

Ravinia is the summertime home of the Chicago Symphony Orchestra, so you know you'll be hearing the best there is. The Ravinia Festival Orchestra also is featured, and both orchestras frequently welcome such guest artists as violinist Itzhak Perlman, pianist Andre Watts, cellist Yo-Yo Ma, and vocal luminaries from mezzo-soprano Frederica von Stade to bass Samuel Ramey. Programs come from the repertory, but you'll be enchanted at hearing them unfold under the stars.

Nonclassical programs include a long weekend of jazz, a week of dance toward the end of summer, and a season-long sprinkling of popular artists—for example, country stars Willie Nelson and Lee Ann Womack, popular acts from Jethro Tull to Michael Feinstein, Broadway chanteuse Bernadette Peters, Motown groups the Temptations and the Spinners, and festival favorite Tony Bennett typify the range of pop artists Ravinia presents annually.

DINNER

OK, there's the musical picture. Let's talk about food, which you'll want to have planned before you get here. My favorite dining option is **Instant Ravinia** (847–266–5100), which gives you a boxed supper, ticket for the evening's entertainment, and even a chair for comfort. It's all just $22, and your choices for dinner are universally yummy: Greek shrimp salad, chicken baguette, and Tuscan steak sandwich (grilled beef tenderloin, smoked Provolone, and sundried tomato pesto on focaccia), to name a few. All come with homemade potato salad. (Alcohol is allowed at Ravinia, so feel free to bring your own; it just isn't included in this dinner.) You must allow at least twenty-four hours' notice, so be sure to call ahead on this.

One more thing about Ravinia: I think it's one of the most romantic places in the entire Chicago area. I'd never want to have to choose between Ravinia and Grant Park, but there's an atmosphere of gentility here at Ravinia that makes you want to straighten your shoulders as you lean over to kiss.

DAY THREE: morning/afternoon

You've done the lakefront, the prairie, the wildflowers, and the cultivated gardens. Now, you're off to the woodlands at the west-suburban **Morton Arboretum** (Illinois Route 53 at I–88, Lisle; 630–719–2400; www.mortonarb.org). The arboretum's 1,500 acres hold more than 3,000 kinds of woody plants from around the world, with special strengths in such geographical groups as Appalachia, the Balkans, central and western Asia, China, Japan, Korea, and, of course, northern Illinois.

While there is some overlap with the area's other major gardens—a prairie/savanna reconstruction, a fragrance garden, landscaping galore—the arboretum is quite clear in its identity as a place of trees, shrubs, and vines. Come around Arbor Day (April 26), and you'll see that identity in full, uh, flower, with special programs and tree plantings.

First-timers usually start at the Visitors' Center, then strike out on the 13 miles of trails that are marked for easy self-education. You're even allowed to drive through on paved roads if you prefer (though bicycles and in-line skates are banned). Bird-watchers should be sure to bring their binoculars.

Morton Arboretum is open daily, year-round, from 7:00 A.M. till 5:00 P.M. or sunset, whichever comes earlier. Bring any questions about your woody plants back home, and you'll get polite, informed answers. You can even use the scholarly Sterling Morton Library from 9:00 A.M. to 5:00 P.M. Tuesday through Friday, and from 10:00 A.M. to 4:00 P.M. Saturday. Parking is $7.00. You'll probably want to stay for lunch at the restaurant, which is inexpensively priced and open from 11:00 A.M. to 3:00 P.M.

For More Romance

If you return to the city from the Botanic Gardens in daylight, detour east to the **Shakespeare Garden** (east end of Garrett Place at Sheridan Road, on the Northwestern University campus, Evanston). This exquisite nook, only 70 by 100 feet, is planted by local Garden Club volunteers with flowers, herbs, shrubs, and trees mentioned in the Bard's works. These include lavender, daisies, columbine, poppies, yarrow, hollyhocks, pansies, rosemary ("That's for remembrance—pray you, love, remember" said Ophelia), and more. The garden, designed by the landscape architect Jens Jensen, is ringed with a double row of hawthorn hedges original to the site. The flower beds are set off with a bronze relief of Shakespeare, a stone bench for sitting, a sundial—and the play of sunlight and shadow that was Jensen's trademark.

Nothing comforts the winter-weary Chicagoan like the **Chicago Flower & Garden Show,** held every year in March at downtown Navy Pier (East Grand Avenue at Lake Michigan; call either the Chicago Botanic Garden or the Morton Arboretum for specifics). You needn't be a gardener to enjoy this optimistic look at the green season, which includes exhibits from the area's garden centers and educational institutions, special programs for orchid enthusiasts, and sessions on many topics for everyone. Admission is $8.00—worth every penny during a midwestern winter—and there's a lot of walking involved.

Swept Away
ROMANTIC LAKEFRONT CRUISES

*A*HOY, YOUNG LOVERS! Get one look at the panoramic beauty of Lake Michigan, and you'll understand immediately why some Chicagoans leave home every summer. They don't go far, though—just to their boats, which they dock along the lakefront and live in until cold weather prevails. It's a totally romantic way to live—and you can get a taste of it by spending a weekend practically living in the lake.

PRACTICAL NOTES: Obviously, this weekend is intended for a summer visit to Chicago. It's quite a bit of cruising, but don't feel you must spend an entire weekend on the water. Any one of the options here will give you a terrific date without a weekend's commitment.

DAY ONE: afternoon

Even the street address will get you in the mood at the **Sheraton Chicago Hotel & Towers** (301 East North Water Street; 312–464–1000 or 800–325–3535). Located at the far east stretch of the Chicago River on its north bank, the hotel takes full advantage of its setting with gorgeous views and a charming, landscaped river walk at ground level. And, while it's fully fitted with exercise equipment, the swimming pool and sundeck are what you'll really enjoy in the hotel's health club.

Warm tones and lots of wood dominate the hotel's decor, the better to emphasize its magnificent views of lake and river. Nearly every room has a great view (ask for one when you reserve, just to

AT A GLANCE

♦ Practically sleep in the water at the riverside **Sheraton Chicago Hotel & Towers** *(301 East North Water Street; 312–464–1000 or 800–325–3535).*

♦ *Take a minicruise to dine and dance the night away on the sleek* **Spirit of Chicago** *(at Navy Pier; 312–836–7899).*

♦ *Learn about local history and ecology on a* **Chicago Historical Lake and River Cruise** *(Chicago from the Lake; 312–527–1977).*

♦ *Immerse yourselves in oenology at* **Bin 36** *(339 North Dearborn Street; 312–755–9463).*

♦ *Sail the lakefront on the* **Windy,** *a fabulous four-masted schooner (at Navy Pier; 312–595–5555).*

♦ *Drop a line from your own private cabin cruiser, chartered and captained through* **Chicago Sportfishing Charters** *(312–922–1100).*

make sure), and a really nice touch is in-room Starbucks coffee. The Towers rooms and suites offer extra luxury, and you can even book the presidential suite where Bill and Hillary stayed during the 1996 Democratic National Convention. (Of the hotel's three presidential suites, the Clintons favored the one with contemporary decor, says marketing manager Pam Vreeland.)

Room rates vary widely depending on when you're here and whether you want a suite. But you're likely to find a weekend package that will give you a rate as low as $149 per night or a $159 nightly rate that includes some nice perks, like breakfast for two.

Since you're heading for an aquatic weekend, you'll appreciate one more advantage the Sheraton provides: It's the only hotel in town with docking facilities. That means you can ask to be picked up right at the hotel when you take one of the cruises described in this chapter. (The *Odyssey* does this routinely, although usually for groups; others may need a bit of explaining.) Or ask the concierge to make your arrangements, and you'll *really* feel like royalty.

DINNER

Be sure to check out this possibility for your first evening's excursion: a dinner-dancing cruise aboard the sleek *Spirit of Chicago* (at Navy Pier; 312–836–7899). This black-and-white beauty is instantly recognizable when you see it from the lake, with its "striped" look and streamlined feeling. When you board for the evening's cruise (Navy Pier is a short cab ride from the Sheraton, if you can't get the *Spirit* to pick you up there), you can choose between taking in the fresh air on deck or heading to the air-conditioned comfort waiting below. To do both, check out the cash bar below, then take your purchases out to a table on deck.

When dinner is served, you'll find yourselves seated with several other passengers (as on a cruise ship) and perusing a menu that offers three entrees: salmon, chicken with a selection of sauces, or the day's pasta specialty. Dinner also includes salad, vegetables, and a luscious chocolate mousse for dessert.

After serving dinner, dessert, and coffee, the ship's waiters and waitresses sing and dance in a cabaret-style show. Then you and your fellow passengers can dance to a lively DJ—and all the while, the *Spirit* slices through the lake, going as far south as McCormick Place and as far north as Montrose Harbor. Altogether, it's a fun little getaway, a three-hour version of the kind of festive, "real" cruise you just might take together one day.

Dress code for the *Spirit* is casual but "nice"—no jeans or gym shoes, but jacket and tie aren't required. The cruise is a four-hour event, with boarding under way about an hour before departure and then a solid three hours on the water. A varied schedule generally sets departures at 7:00 or 8:00 P.M., depending on whether it's a weekday or weekend. The same variable affects the cost of the cruise; it ranges from $80.99 per person for a weekday evening to $102.99 for Saturday evenings. The *Spirit* offers special packages for passengers celebrating special occasions. Balloons, a keepsake photo, souvenirs, a cake, and more can all be yours if you want to surprise your sweetheart. Ask when you book.

If you've *really* enjoyed the trip, come back for more a few hours later. The *Spirit* runs moonlight cruises on most Friday and Saturday nights during the summer, leaving Navy Pier just after midnight and returning about 2:30 A.M. These cruises cost $32.21 per person; again, ask about special celebrations. Bring a sweater or jacket if you want to stroll on deck; the night air can get a tad nippy—or maybe you'll just have to hold each other a little closer . . .

DAY TWO: morning

Cruises can be more than just a good time, as you'll learn during the **Chicago Historical Lake and River Cruise** offered by **Chicago from the Lake** (435 East Illinois Street; 312-527-1977; www.chicago line.com). The history lesson starts as you board either the *Fort Dearborn* (named for the city's first military post, it was the first double-decker built to pass under all the city's many present-day bridges) or the *Marquette (*named for the seventeenth-century French priest who made his way through this wild territory, exploring and baptizing). Usually the history cruise travels aboard the *Marquette,* whose capacity of just fifty makes a mini-seminar of the cruise—though you won't have to worry about a pop quiz afterward.

Going all the way back to pre-European settlement by Native Americans, this short history course also addresses the river's ecology, which took a beating during industrialization but now has recovered somewhat. The tour also describes the many recreational uses of the river, including the fishing that seemed like a pipe dream back when Mayor Richard Daley (the powerful first one, who reigned from 1955 until his death in 1976) announced a plan to stock the river with sport fish. People were skeptical, but you'll see the late mayor's legacy in the quiet anglers along the riverbanks.

The ninety-minute history cruise is offered at 9:00 and 11:00 A.M. daily during the season, which runs from late May through late September. (Architectural cruises are offered more often, pretty much on the hour. Check with Chicago from the Lake, or see the chapter, "Love Built on Beauty: Architecture in Chicago," for information on architecture tours.) Tickets are $23, which includes Starbucks coffee and nibbles. Advance purchase of tickets is strongly recommended, so be sure to call before showing up—which, by the way, you do at North Pier, not to be confused (though it frequently is) with Navy Pier. North Pier is at the very east end of Illinois Street, but it's south of Navy Pier. Cabdrivers should know the difference, but if you're coming on your own, keep an eye out for street signs and other hints.

DAY TWO: afternoon

LUNCH

Break for lunch before boarding another craft. You'll debark from the *Marquette* hungry after all that fresh air. You needn't go far in search of a memorable lunch—one that involves flights rather than cruises—at **Bin 36** (339 North Dearborn Street; 312-755-9463). Located on the north side of the river and a few blocks west of Michigan Avenue, Bin 36 is a wine bar gone grand, with a retail area as well as a couple of dining rooms. Go for the romantic Cellar over the casual Tavern, and place your palates in the capable hands of the Bin 36 staff. The restaurant's real mission is helping patrons learn about wines by way of a "flight," which means tasting several wines from a single category, such as Italian reds or champagnes. Flights, which range from $13 to about $24, are separate from the menu, on which you'll find nibbles as well as meals to accompany your sipping spree.

Or you can stick around the North Pier vicinity by heading over to Navy Pier (the better to catch your next cruise on time), where you'll be happy with lunch from **Charlie's Ale House** (on Navy Pier; 312-595-1440). This sibling of an old-time pub on the North Side offers a super hamburger: half a pound of meat, plus a topping, potatoes, and coleslaw, all for $6.50. There's a solid chili, made with chunks of sirloin instead of ground beef, for $4.50. The ubiquitous Buffalo wings are here, too, and there's even a meat loaf dinner for $8.95.

Thus fortified, you might need a snooze out in the sun before picking up the pace again. Or you might even snooze during your next excursion, which offers a leisurely contrast to the morning's lessons. When you board the 148-foot schooner *Windy* (at Navy Pier; 312-595-5555), you're on a bit of nineteenth-century romance for folks who love the water. Holding some 150 passengers for three or more lake cruises daily, this tall ship will get the wind stirring your hair and your hearts—*and* it has modern conveniences (like plumbing). Cruises run about ninety minutes and generally depart every couple of hours, starting at 1:00 P.M. from Navy Pier. Boarding passes cost $25 per person ($15 for seniors or children) and are available at the dock, although you can't go wrong by reserving in advance.

To get the most water time from the remainder of the day and evening, figure on taking an early *Windy* cruise. You'll be on land by 4:00 P.M.—plenty of time to head back to the Sheraton, grab a nap or an early dinner, and walk over to the Michigan Avenue bridge.

DAY TWO: evening

Descend the staircase near the bridge, on the south side of the river, and you're ready to see the city's skyline fade into the sunset. The **Summer Sunset Cruise** (Mercury Cruiseline, on the south side of the river, Michigan Avenue and Wacker Drive; 312–332–1353) travels the lakefront Memorial Day to Labor Day for two twilight hours, starting at 7:30 P.M., when it's still light out. Much of the territory is what the *Spirit of Chicago* covers in its dinner cruise, but tonight, you're able to focus all your attention on the sights.

And they're grand! The skyline, backlit by the setting sun, is one of those star-struck, "how ya gonna keep 'em down on the farm" sights. Grant Park is visible, too, its swath of green and gardens spreading before the lake like a country estate's grounds. The highlight of the cruise is its lingering look at the light display at Buckingham Fountain, which assumes a magic all its own when viewed from the lake. See if you don't agree after visiting on land and then taking this cruise. Of course, you'll also enjoy the twinkling lights of downtown's buildings and the glittery Gold Coast. At $17 per person, the sunset cruise is one of the loveliest bargains in town. (Important note: Be at the dock an hour before departure to pick up your tickets.)

DINNER

If you're not completely starry-eyed when you dock, you will be after a late supper at **Redfish** (400 North State Street; 312–467–1600), where live music and a Louisiana menu keep the

Phantasm-y Cruise

*Hold each other tight as you check out the local version of a visit to Davy Jones's locker! The **Chicago Supernatural Cruise** is led by Richard Crowe, a lifelong Chicagoan who has made a vocation of ghost hunting. On Saturday nights in July and August (including Labor Day weekend), the cruises travel the river and lakefront while Crowe tells scary tales of their many spooks—including drowning victims, ghost ships, and even a "lake monster."*

Sound enticing? Go ahead, sign up. Tours cost $22 per person, and they run for two hours—11:00 P.M. to 1:00 A.M., since you wouldn't want to miss the witching hour. Cruise ships leave from the Mercury Cruiseline dock at Michigan Avenue and Lower Wacker Drive, on the south bank of the river. Book by contacting Crowe at P.O. Box 557554, Chicago, IL 60655-7544; his telephone number is (708) 499-0300, and he's on the web at www.ghosttours.com.

joint jumping till 2:00 A.M. Landlubbers can choose hickory-smoked barbecue, southern fried chicken, or Cajun-spiced meats and poultry, while fans of the fin will always find seafood and a blackened-fish daily special. Of course, everyone saves room for the pecan pie. Entrees average about $15, and the kitchen is open until 11:00 P.M. weekend evenings. The bar stays open later, if you want to linger and enjoy the live music weekends bring, usually from a rhythm-and-blues band. Redfish is just a couple of blocks west of Michigan Avenue and a little north of the river, across the street from Marina City—a short walk from where the sunset cruise docks, and not too far from the Sheraton, either.

DAY THREE: morning/afternoon

Here's a tough call: Should you spend Sunday fishing, or take one more fabulous cruise to round out a watery weekend?

If you want nothing so much as a quiet (albeit pricey) day of angling, call **Chicago Sportfishing Charters** (312-922-1100) and arrange your very own expedition on your very own cabin cruiser. Salmon and trout are the usual catch on these junkets. All the equipment you'll need is provided, and if you haven't gotten your annual Illinois fishing license and stamp, the charter company will help with that, too. All you bring is yourselves and your lunch.

Boats accommodate up to six people, but the price is the same whether it's just the two of you or a group. Five hours on the water runs $435, and a six-hour trip is $520. Early birds go out at 7:00 A.M. and return at noon, and late risers' fishing goes from 1:00 to 6:00 P.M.; six-hour trips are flexible.

LUNCH

And about that lunch: Ask your captain to put in at **Jackson Harbor Grill** (6401 South Coast Guard Drive; 773–288–4442), where lunch and dinner are served lakeside, daily during the April-to-September boating season, at a marina that's not widely known beyond its South Side neighborhood. Rest your sea legs at a terrace table or one indoors while you enjoy the kitchen's New Orleans–style fare (described in the chapter "Hyde Park Honeymoon"). If the fish just aren't biting, linger over dessert—a choice made simple because there are just two, rum raisin bread pudding with chocolate sauce and banana cheesecake with cranberries..

If fishing isn't your sport of choice, close out your weekend by sleeping in, then enjoying a final fling on the lake with the *Odyssey* **jazz brunch** (from 401 East Illinois Street; 630–990–0800). Cruise connoisseurs around town agree this is one of the very nicest. The ship is beautiful, a streamlined beauty in black and white, and the food and music are just as distinctive. "The food is wonderful, and I should know—I work in catering," says one anonymous informant.

The brunch buffet features lots of fresh fruit, pastries, hot and cold salads, and desserts. Entrees (one per person) span all three meals, ranging from poached eggs with smoked salmon or scrambled-egg quesadillas to chicken or pork chops. A cash bar is open during the cruise (although you can't buy liquor until noon on Sunday).

Music comes from three different jazz combos, one on each deck. On the outdoor observation deck, you'll hear music from one of these piped out. Boarding starts at 11:00 A.M., and the cruise runs from noon to 2:00 P.M. The whole thing, taxes and tips included, costs $60.72 per person, and reservations are a good idea. The jazz brunch cruises the lake from March through October, and since nearly all the ship is enclosed, cruises run even in the rain.

FOR MORE ROMANCE

Devote a fall day to learning more about the area's waterways on a **National Heritage Corridor Cruise** (through Mercury Cruiseline; 312-332-1353). This cruise, which leaves Michigan Avenue and Wacker Drive at 9:00 A.M. and returns at 4:00 P.M., constitutes a sort of minicourse in the natural history and development of Chicago's lake, rivers, and canals. It's offered on three weekend days every fall and is conducted by Dr. David Solzman, who is a professor of urban geography at the University of Illinois–Chicago. He's also a genial host and raconteur. (I knew him slightly as an undergraduate and remember how popular his classes were.) Reservations—the further in advance, the better—are essential for the cruise, which costs $69 per person.

You'll gather for complimentary coffee as you board, but you must bring your own lunch and beverage. To take the aggravation out of that, order a spiffy lunch in advance from the **Corner Bakery** (516 North Clark Street; 312-644-8100, catering department, 312-527-1956). This chic spot can feed you both for about $15 each, or ask for a basket of sandwiches, salads, and desserts for both of you. This package runs $50, but it includes a complete picnic setup, from tablecloth to cutlery. You'll want to scale down to a cruise-size basket, so let the kitchen know you don't need some of the accoutrements, and they'll oblige.

The Zoo for Two

WHAT IS IT ABOUT BEING IN LOVE that makes people want to go to the zoo? Maybe it's the animals' antics, which give you plenty to talk about when you're getting to know someone. Or maybe it's the free-spirited wandering that's so pleasant to do in a zoo. Or the cotton candy and popcorn to snack on, or the silly souvenirs you take home. Whatever the attraction, a zoo is a terrific place to while away a day with your sweetheart. And in Chicago, you can do it two days in a row, at two outstanding zoos.

PRACTICAL NOTES: This itinerary really calls for fair weather, although you don't need summery heat as long as you're not getting rained on. Both zoos are open year-round and are far less crowded in the cooler (spring, fall, and winter) months; weekdays, too, are less crowded than weekends.

DAY ONE: morning/afternoon

Visiting **Lincoln Park Zoo** (2200 North Cannon Drive; 312-742-2000; www.lpzoo.org) always reminds me of how I felt on discovering the Berlin Zoo—right in the middle of town, right across the *strasse* from the train station. How astonishing to find, at the heart of this bustling, aggressive city, a leafy, self-contained alternative world of animal life. Lincoln Park Zoo isn't quite in the middle of downtown, but it's about as close to that as you can get. It's a very doable, pleasant walk from the posh shopping strip of North Michigan Avenue. In fact, you could even walk to it without ever leaving the park and beach areas right along the lake shore.

*Romance
AT A GLANCE*

♦ *Escape the city at* **Lincoln Park Zoo** *(2200 North Cannon Drive; 312–742–2000), where you can rent a paddleboat, watch baby chicks hatch, mug with the great apes, and wander exquisite formal gardens.*

♦ *Get close to the butterflies in a living exhibit at the* **Chicago Academy of Sciences Peggy Notebaert Nature Museum** *(2430 North Cannon Drive; 773–549–0606).*

♦ *Go elegant with dinner at the spectacular* **Ambria** *(2300 North Lincoln Park West; 773–472–5959) or vegetarian at* **Red Light** *(820 West Randolph Stree; 312–733–8880).*

♦ *Visit half a dozen biospheres at* **Brookfield Zoo** *(First Avenue and Thirty-first Street, Brookfield; 708–485–0263).*

Even closer, however, is staying in a bed-and-breakfast on West Memomonee Street, just a little west of the zoo's south entrance, in the terrific Old Town neighborhood. Like several in the area, this apartment is booked through Bed & Breakfast Chicago (800–375–7084 or 773–248–0005), and it's a find. Appropriately for your animal-appreciating weekend, this B&B is dubbed **Fish out of Water** by its art-collecting owner. She's made the apartment home open not only to many guests but also to a large collection of folk, primitive, and out-sider art—enough to make you feel as if you're inhabiting your own private museum, maybe even enough to send you toward overstimulation as you try to take it all in. Just allow yourselves plenty of time during your stay to peruse and appreciate this amazing collection. You'll enjoy the owner's whimsical sensibility that is evident throughout, right down to the mirror-lined bathroom: All those mirrors are vintage handheld types, the kind a '40s siren might look into while brushing her silky bob—but here, they're mounted on the wall so you see their decorative backs, not their reflective fronts.

The comfort level at Fish out of Water is as pleasing as the abundant art, with a wood-burning fireplace on the first floor and a cozy upstairs bedroom furnished with a double bed. Smoking is allowed on the premises, a rarity among bed-and-breakfast accommodations. If you're lucky, the owner will be in town while you're here; she's glad to answer questions and talk about her collection.

Tearing yourself away from the art, head right back out to the park after settling into your weekend home. You're closest to the south end of the zoo, where generations of children have enjoyed the **Farm in the Zoo.** Cows, horses, pigs, and chickens are all here—but the most fun is in watching the hatching baby chicks. If you've never seen a tiny beak peck its way through a shell, take time to do it now. Visit the big barn, where several educational exhibits coexist with one of those two-dimensional cutout models that let you photograph your head on a farmer's body. Bring a camera and get a fellow zoo lover to shoot the two of you; you'll giggle over the picture forever.

The nicest way to do Lincoln Park Zoo's thirty-five or so acres is in a wandering mode. If you're knowledgeable about the animals, you'll appreciate one of the world's largest collections of gorillas here. The Primate House also holds an impressive colony of mandrills, colobus monkeys, and lemurs. The big cats are plentiful as well, and it's fun to watch the flamingos in their dome home.

One of the best entertainments at the zoo is renting a paddleboat on the pond where ducks vie for space with passing paddlers. It's easy to keep these big yellow boats moving, and you're considerably less likely to "dump" than in a canoe or kayak. Paddleboats rent for about $13.00 for a full hour, or $8.00 for half an hour. And even if you don't want to hop in and paddle, linger to watch the adventures of those who do.

LUNCH

If you're hungry by now, you're in the right place. The zoo's **Cafe Brauer** is right at the paddleboat pond. This nineteenth-century building fell into disrepair over the years but was restored to its original beauty during the 1980s. Today it is a focal point of special events at the zoo. If crews are setting up or clearing an event, you may be able to peek upstairs for a look at the building's elegant spaces and lovely mosaics.

Back downstairs, the lunch menu offers pizzas, salads, sandwiches, and a zoo specialty of animal-shaped french fries. Lunch won't run more than about $12 for both of you, although Cafe Brauer is likely to be crowded if the weather's good. You might prefer to leave the zoo proper and enjoy a lovely lunch at the charming **North Pond Restaurant** (2610 North Cannon Drive; 773–477–5845; www.northpondrestaurant.com), where modern American cuisine is served in an improbably beautiful pastoral setting and the accom-

modating kitchen can prepare a vegetarian or vegan repast with a
day or two's notice.

Another good spot to take a break is the central area around the sea
lions' pool (go down the ramp to watch them zipping by underwa-
ter). Popcorn, cotton candy, and similar snacks are available from
colorful vendors' carts here, and it's a good place to sit in the sun
and enjoy them. When it's too sunny, head for the reptiles' building,
which is cool and dim.

   As you head toward the zoo's northern end, stop at the gift shop
for a souvenir (rubber snakes, anyone?). Don't miss the wild, wooded
rookery, which counts several endangered species among its who-
knows-how-many birds. Two rookery inhabitants—the Guam rail and
the Micronesian kingfisher—are extinct in the wild. If you're lucky, your
visit may coincide with a spring or fall migratory period, which gives
you the opportunity to see even more aviary rarities.

   Just south of Fullerton Parkway, you'll come to the **Lincoln Park
Conservatory** (773–284–4770), where you may find a special event
highlighting some of its gorgeous flora. You don't need a special event
to fall for this intoxicating atmosphere of color and scent, though; just
linger and enjoy. Admission is free; hours are 9:00 A.M. to 5:00 P.M. daily.

   Be sure to stop across the way at the **Chicago Academy of
Sciences Peggy Notebaert Nature Museum** (2430 North
Cannon Drive; 773–549–0606; www.chias.org), with its Butterfly Haven
exhibit. This walk-through greenhouse lets visitors get delightfully close
to the gorgeous, elusive creatures it celebrates—and the intensely green,
humid setting is a little torrid, too. If you see only one exhibit here,
make it the butterflies. Or linger over others: an interactive exhibit that
lets you plan development, then explains the environmental impact of
your choices; one that showcases household pests; and one with dioramas depicting various ecosystems. The museum is open daily from
9:00 A.M. to 4:30 P.M., and admission is $7.00.

DAY ONE: evening

DINNER

When you're ready to head back to your bed-and-breakfast, be sure
you've brought something great looking to change into. You're

going to dine at one of the most romantic restaurants in town. I know of at least two couples who got engaged at **Ambria** (2300 North Lincoln Park West; 773-472-5959), and there's no doubt they aren't the only ones. You could find yourselves in the mood for just about anything as you luxuriate in this lovely room's cozy booths, wonderful service, and sublime food. Ambria is elegant yet friendly, posh yet comfortable, top-drawer yet accessible. It's expensive, too—expect to spend upwards of $150 total—but worth every penny to spend several hours with the one you love while savoring marvelous specialties from chef Gabino Sotelino. Let your waiter be your guide to the restaurant's many fine wines as well as its cuisine; or make it easy by choosing a degustation, which serves up multiple delights at a set price.

Maybe you're not up for such a splurge—or maybe the zoo has left you feeling acutely vegetarian. Not far to the north, the posthippie **Chicago Diner** (3411 North Halsted Street; 773-935-6696; www.veggiediner.com) proudly advertises itself as "meat-free since '83," and the years of refinements have yielded an inexpensive PC menu that's famous for yummy vegan desserts. South and west of Lincoln Park, in the hip Ukrainian Village area, **Bite Cafe** (1039 North Western Avenue; 773-395-2483) offers inexpensive vegetarian fare. If your taste in music runs toward loud and young, make a night of it next door at the **Empty Bottle** (1035 North Western Avenue; 773-276-3600). Or, to make a night of it all alone, plan ahead: Reserve the curtained private nook and ask for the vegan tasting menu ($65) at the hypertrendy home of the mango martini, **Red Light** (820 West Randolph Street; 312-773-8880; www.redlight-chicago.com).

After dinner, the best way to while away the evening is by strolling along Lincoln Avenue. Many bars and clubs lie within the immediate vicinity; and to the south, near the corner where Lincoln and Fullerton Avenues meet Halsted Street, is the notorious **Biograph Theater** (2433 North Lincoln Avenue). Here, on a sweltering July night in 1934, the FBI gunned down one of its most wanted criminals, John Dillinger, as the bank robber emerged after seeing a movie inside. He'd been turned in by his companion, the Woman in Red—perhaps an omen for the Biograph's romance potential, since the screen is dark nowadays. As you can see, though, there's more than enough to amuse yourselves along this lively strip.

DAY TWO: morning/afternoon

After breakfasting in your own B&B kitchen, hop into the car and head south on Lake Shore Drive to I-290 (known locally as the Eisenhower Expressway), and travel about an hour to the western suburb of Brookfield for something completely different: another day at another zoo. **Brookfield Zoo** (First Avenue and Thirty-first Street, Brookfield; 708-485-0263; www.brookfieldzoo.org) is one of the area's major cultural institutions, with just about everything on a scale far larger than what you saw at the comparatively snug Lincoln Park Zoo. Unlike Lincoln Park, Brookfield charges $7.00 per person for admission, plus $6.75 for parking; some exhibits carry an extra charge, too. (Zoo membership is $49 annually, so if you expect to come back, joining might be worthwhile.) Once you're in, however, the two of you will agree that it is money well spent. The zoo is nearly cageless, its many areas are beautifully kept, and its exhibits are fascinating.

Among Brookfield's attractions is "The Swamp: Wonders of Our Wetlands," which re-creates an Illinois wetland and a southern cypress swamp, complete with alligators. "Tropic World: A Primate's Journey" and "Habitat Africa!" explore animals' habitats in a larger context, reflecting the zoo's overall emphasis on environmental preservation and protection of fauna. The "Seven Seas Panorama" was the first local showcase for the dolphin presentations that are commonplace today; many Chicagoans treasure childhood memories of the mammals' splashing antics. Newer than these is "The Living Coast," which depicts the interrelationships linking plants, animals, people, and the environment along South America's western shores.

In other words, you'll probably learn a lot during your visit to Brookfield. But the nicest thing about Brookfield is its air of a day outing. You'll feel like kids again as you approach the big gates, anticipating the fun of observing our near and distant relatives in the animal kingdom. It's definitely a day's worth of attractions, and more. "Habitat Africa!" alone covers five acres, and "Tropic World" is one of the largest indoor exhibits in the world. The zoo's wide boulevards intersect at a lovely fountain ringed with bright flowers.

One good way to scope out the zoo is by boarding its Motor Safari train; stay on for the entire ride if you like, or exit at one of its four stops to take in an exhibit. (The ride costs $2.50 per person, and it can save some wear on your feet.)

Another Animal Attraction

Both Lincoln Park and Brookfield run animal "adoption" programs that give you the chance to show you care. Why not "adopt" an adorable baby bear or graceful swan in your sweetheart's name? Better yet—for those with a bit of a past and a good sense of humor—adopt a rhino, tarantula, or alligator and name it after the reviled ex you've heard so much about. Both zoos' adoption programs ask a minimum of $25, which entitles you to a certificate and other goodies. Call either zoo for more information.

LUNCH

Brookfield Zoo offers some welcome variations on the typical burgers-and-pizza lunch possibilities. Breakfast is available until 11:00 A.M., if you're hungry early. There's Mexican food at **Cafe Olé,** beer and wine coolers to wash down brats in a summertime beer garden, and gyros or Edy's ice cream for the indulgent. Lunches won't total more than $7.00 or so per person (although beer will add up). Or sample Peruvian specialties at **Bocaditos** where you can stay outdoors on the inviting veranda.

While you're here, be sure to find your way to **Indian Lake,** where you can sit on a shady bench and commune with each other in silence. A few ducks might come by, but you're likely to be the only humans at this quiet haven. Unleash a little animal passion on each other's lips!

For More Romance

Animal-loving Chicagoans eagerly anticipate annual events at each zoo. One that's especially popular takes place on a Sunday afternoon early in December, when animal lovers come to Lincoln Park Zoo for

"Caroling to the Animals." Singers of all ages and persuasions make a number of stops throughout the zoo, then repair to Cafe Brauer for cocoa and camaraderie. It's a wonderful way to enjoy the season and the zoo with someone you love. Watch the local newspapers for a date, or call the zoo at (312) 742–2000.

Another jolly celebration comes around every year on March 1, which the uninitiated may not recognize as National Pig Day. Brookfield Zoo celebrates what it dubs "the holler-day" with a pig-calling contest, pig polka music, and a program starring some of its most talented porcine population. Also popular (and very big with children) is the daylong Teddy Bear Fair, which takes place in mid-June each year. Call the zoo at (708) 485–0263 for more information on either event.

Arts and
Hearts

Love Built on Beauty

ARCHITECTURE IN CHICAGO

POETIC THOUGHTS on architecture and romance:

"Love built on beauty, soon as beauty, dies."
—John Donne, *Elegies*

"When we build, let us think that we build for ever."
—John Ruskin, *The Lamp of Memory*

You're building "for ever," and your solid-as-granite love will be richer for an immersion in Chicago's architectural riches. They're too great (and too scattered) to pack into one weekend—but that's no reason not to try. You'll find plenty of knowledgeable help in tours offered by the Chicago Architecture Foundation, whose volunteers are trained to explain how and why the work they show is important.

Take a full day to explore west suburban Oak Park, where architectural consciousness is incredibly high because the Prairie giant, Frank Lloyd Wright, lived and worked there. You can visit his home and studio, walk through a neighborhood where many other Wright works are located, and even stay in a bed-and-breakfast home designed by the master. Then come downtown to experience those who came before and after Wright. There's the great Louis

Romance AT A GLANCE

◆ Spend a day in Oak Park among Frank Lloyd Wright's residential masterpieces and **Unity Temple** (875 Lake Street, Oak Park; 708–383–8873).

◆ Stay in **Cheney House Bed and Breakfast** (520 North East Avenue, Oak Park; 708–524–2067).

◆ View downtown highlights from the comfort of the **Chicago Architecture Foundation River Cruise** (312–922–8687) on **Chicago's First Lady.**

◆ Stroll among the architectural masterpieces downtown; pause at the river, where nature counters architectural perfectionism.

Sullivan, Wright's mentor, perhaps the last architect to enjoy ornament unself-consciously. There's Sullivan's contemporary, Daniel Burnham, who is remembered not only for his buildings but also his statement about his bold, virtually citywide plan for Chicago: "Make no little plans; they have no magic to stir men's blood." And there are the later greats, most notably Mies van der Rohe, whose credo "Less is more" dictated the shape and feel of the later twentieth-century world. All of them lived and worked here in Chicago. Come and see what they did.

DAY ONE: morning/afternoon

Start a self-designed architecture-appreciation course in the first suburb to Chicago's west, **Oak Park,** which native son Ernest Hemingway scorned as a town of "broad lawns and narrow minds." Of course, Papa was a rolling stone who couldn't leave home fast enough, and he might just be surprised by the liberal bent of many Oak Parkers today.

But we're not talking politics here, we're talking architecture. And Wright is a good starting point not just because of Oak Park's concentration of his early work, but because Wright himself is a pivotal figure in the city's architecture. His mentor was Louis Sullivan, the hard-luck genius of the late nineteenth century, whose belief in functional yet beautiful buildings was carried out with an impeccable taste in decoration and absolute acceptance of the commercial nature of his work (which dictated a tall, proud appearance for the office buildings of the day). Like most artists, Sullivan relied on an underlying, romantic faith that his work would make the world a better place; he considered architecture essential to democracy, an art form that would reinforce the dignity of humanity and endow the commercial world with some of the same.

Wright and his like-minded contemporaries came to believe in buildings as horizontal as Sullivan's were vertical. Wright's principle of beauty in a building relied on taking the visual cues of its setting, and his setting was the prairie, a vast stretch of horizontal planes decorated by vegetation in muted shades (which Wright and other Prairie School architects represented with the stained glass that is one of their hallmarks). The geometric precision that assumes ever-greater importance in Wright's work comes into fullness in the work of a third, post-Wright giant of Chicago architecture, the Bauhaus master Ludwig Mies Van der Rohe. Here decoration comes to a halt; sleek, soaring lines are all, and the untrained eye is challenged to find the details in which Mies is said to have seen God.

OK, there's Chicago architecture in two paragraphs. You can plunge right into the subject by booking a room at **Cheney House Bed and Breakfast** (520 North East Avenue, Oak Park; 708–524–2067), a near-ly century-old home designed by Wright that is furnished with the master's furniture and fabrics. (Perfectionist that he was, Wright left nothing to the vicissitudes of others' taste.) "The happiest people who stay with me are those who are Wright fans," says owner Dale Smirl. "Everything is vintage Frank Lloyd Wright, nothing new or reproduced."

Cheney House has three B&B possibilities, two suites and one double bedroom. Both suites offer two bedrooms, a living room with a fireplace, dining room, kitchenette, and whirlpool-equipped bath. (You can see why Smirl says he sometimes has honeymooners who spend a week without his ever seeing them!) Then there's the double bedroom, which also has a nice big bed and private bath (sans whirlpool), and offers the greatest degree of privacy, including breakfast service in the dining room (suite guests make their own). Weigh your options and talk it over with Smirl before deciding which suits you best. Suites are $155 a night, and the double room is $100.

Smirl, who by day is a downtown attorney, likes to give guests tours of his home, which he has owned for almost twenty years. Like many local Wright owners, he has his share of difficulties in keeping up the structure, but he considers every bit of work, worry, and expense a good investment in history and beauty.

When you've seen Cheney House, head out to immerse yourselves in Wright's works. Discuss beforehand whether you prefer to go on your own or join a tour. If you don't know much about the subject, you're likely to learn more on a tour; but if you want an experience that's just for the two of you, you'll find plenty of printed material to help you along the way.

The excellent Chicago Architecture Foundation offers two Oak Park Wright tours: a walking tour and **Frank Lloyd Wright by Bus,** a three-and-a-half-hour junket that takes you into the neighboring suburb of River Forest to view Wright homes there. The bus tour, which is offered at 9:30 A.M. on the first Saturday of every month, departs from the downtown Chicago Architecture Foundation Tour Center, (875 North Michigan Avenue; 312–751–1380; www.architecture.org). It costs $25 per person, and reservations are required.

Once you're in Oak Park, though, the logical place to start is the master's own home, **Frank Lloyd Wright Home and Studio** (951 Chicago Avenue, Oak Park; 708–848–1976). Saturday and Sunday tours are ongoing, between 11:00 A.M. and 3:30 P.M. year-round. Admission is $9.00 per person. As you tour the house Wright designed for his own family, you'll see the development of his ideas about the organic arrangement of space—and you'll feel the rightness of how he did it. Enjoy, too, the gorgeous yet restrained beauty he created by using stained glass to suggest prairie flowers. Imagine yourselves taking root—together—in this warm, enchanting space.

The house's **Ginkgo Tree Bookshop** is the starting point for various, more wide-ranging tours of the **Frank Lloyd Wright Prairie School of Architecture National Historic District,** which includes thirteen Wright-designed homes. You can do your own self-guided map tour from 10:00 A.M. to 5:00 P.M. daily; choose an audiocassette-guided tour from 10:00 A.M. to 3:30 P.M. daily; or sign up for a guided Chicago Architecture Foundation walking tour, starting on the hour from 11:00 A.M. to 4:00 P.M. Saturday and Sunday from March through October. This tour costs $8.00 per person and often sells out fast, so heed the first-come, first-served ticket policy.

On your own or with a group, what you'll see here in Oak Park is a remarkable, living museum of architecture. The area's thirty-plus Wright buildings constitute a treasure trove of the master's work, and more: a real-world context in which to view the works. These are the streets for which the houses were designed, the sites on which they were built, the neighbors with which they lived—and except for Wright's own house, every one of these remains a privately owned home. Seeing so many, one after another, is a sort of intellectual voyage during which you can watch the development of ideas and the flowering of brilliance. Architecture can be appreciated adequately only in situ; here is Wright's.

The two most important Wright buildings in Oak Park are Wright's home and studio, and one of his greatest works, **Unity Temple** (875 Lake Street, Oak Park; 708-383-8873). Wright himself called the structure his "little jewel," and its smooth, straight, graceful lines belie the complex assemblage of spaces that together create a massive yet intimate whole. This is still a functioning church, so tours are sometimes modified to meet the congregation's needs. The basic schedule, however, includes guided tours at 1:00, 2:00, and 3:00 P.M. Saturday and Sunday, plus summertime open hours of 10:00 A.M. to 5:00 P.M. weekdays. Guided tours are $6.00 per person.

Between the Wright home and Unity Temple are many Wright designs; sorting them out is best done on a tour, which helps assure you won't miss anything. If you're going solo, be sure to note the **Arthur Heurtley House** (318 Forest Avenue), which is near the Wright home and, having been built in 1902, is one of the very

Flawed Genius

When you visit Frank Lloyd Wright's home, you'll surely be touched by the majestic quality of the house and especially by the beauty of the playroom he built for his six children there. What you may not know is the scandal surrounding Wright's departure from the house. Domestic life apparently did not suit the architect, who left his wife and children when he ran off to Europe with the wife of a client. The Wrights continued to live in the house minus Dad, and the house you see today has been restored to its state in 1909—the last year he lived there.

earliest and finest examples of Prairie design. At the corner of Forest
and Superior Street is the **Nathan Moore House** (333 Forest
Avenue), Wright's 1895 blend of Prairie and Tudor. Forest Avenue
also holds the 1906 **Hills-DeCaro House** (313 Forest Avenue), the
Peter A. Beachy House (238 Forest Avenue), and the 1901 **Frank W.
Thomas House** (210 Forest Avenue). As you travel Forest Avenue,
keep an eye out for Elizabeth Court, where at the bend you'll find
the lovely **Mrs. Thomas Gale House,** a 1909 design that shows the
way to what many consider Wright's greatest house, Fallingwater
(which unfortunately is not in Oak Park, but in Bear Run,
Pennsylvania).

LUNCH

When the two of you are ready to sit down and break from
this architectural overload, do it with lunch at **Petersen's
Restaurant & Ice Cream Parlor** (1100 Chicago Avenue, Oak Park;
708-386-6130). Sandwiches, soups, and other lunch fare here are
good, but greatness is in the ice cream. Petersen's creamy, butter-
fat-laden treat has kept Oak Parkers and others coming here for
better than seventy-five years, currently from 11:00 A.M. to 10:00 P.M.
every day.

Back on the architecture beat, make time for a stop at the **Pleasant
Home Mansion** (217 Home Avenue, Oak Park; 708-383-2654). It's
a good reminder that Wright wasn't the only practitioner of Prairie;
this thirty-room mansion, done in 1897 by Prairie School member
George W. Maher, now belongs to the Historical Society of Oak Park
and River Forest, which opens it to the public. Admission is $5.00
per person, and tours are offered at 12:30, 1:30, and 2:30 P.M.
Thursday through Sunday. (On Friday, admission is free.)

If you're Hemingway fans—and what lovers aren't, once
they've read *For Whom the Bell Tolls?*—be sure to visit his
birthplace in the family's Victorian home (339 North Oak Park
Avenue, Oak Park) and the **Ernest Hemingway Museum** (200
North Oak Park Avenue, Oak Park; call 708-848-2222 or visit
www.hemingway.org for both sites). The home focuses on his family, while the museum holds his childhood diary, early writings,

letters, photos, and more. Admission is $6.00 per person for both sites, and home tours are offered from 1:00 to 5:00 P.M. Thursday, Friday, and Sunday, and from 10:00 A.M. to 5:00 P.M. on Saturday.

DAY ONE: evening

DINNER

After your wanderings, go to dinner at one of the town's favorite spots, **Philander's Oak Park** (in the Carleton Hotel, 1120 Pleasant Street, Oak Park; 708–848–4250). This elegant restaurant was among the first to take advantage of the repeal of Oak Park's dry laws, not so very long ago, and has since prospered sufficiently to add **Poor Phil's Shell Bar** (round the corner, 139 Marion Street, Oak Park; 708–848–0871). Either can give you top-notch seafood, and Philander's often adds live music, from cabaret to Caribbean to the splendid jazz pianist Judy Roberts. Dinner will run about $60 for the two of you any evening but Sunday, when it's closed.

Nightlife tends to be quiet in Oak Park, but summer brings the treasured institution of **Festival Theater Shakespeare in the Park** (Austin Gardens Park, Lake Street and Forest Avenue, Oak Park; 708–524–2050). The mosquitoes can be vicious, but the shows are a pleasure, especially with ticket prices comfortably less than $20 apiece.

DAY TWO: morning/afternoon

Depart Oak Park for downtown Chicago and a whole different perspective on the Windy City's architectural life. When you arrive downtown, check in at the **Inter-Continental Hotel** (505 North Michigan Avenue; 312–944–4100), where the art deco atmosphere will lure you right out of the Wright world and back into a richly decorated look of luxury, 1930s-style. Beautifully restored in recent years, the Inter-Continental is right in the middle of the famous Michigan Avenue shopping zone, the Magnificent Mile, and thus a good location from which to survey this high end of downtown.

The hotel also offers a fully equipped fitness center, but its real attraction—in looks as well as the pursuit of fitness—is a stunning, junior Olympic-size swimming pool whose cool green tempts the tired traveler. Be sure to get a look, at the very least, at this beautifully embellished pool area. And note that the lobby bar here (where pianist Erin McDougal holds forth many evenings) serves a martini that ranks among the very best in town—down to the extra that comes to you in a very 1930s flask chilled to frosty perfection in an ice bucket.

Whether or not you dive into the pool (or into one of those martinis), you'll want to get started on sampling the riches of downtown. Again, the easiest way to be sure you won't miss anything major is to sign up for a **Chicago Architecture Foundation (CAF)** tour. Consider a Loop double header, "Historic Skyscrapers" and "Modern Skyscrapers." Each is offered on a schedule that allows people to do both with a lunch break in between, although schedules vary enough that you'd best call for the times. Each tour is $10 per person, but buying both at one time is a bargain $15. For recorded information on tour schedules, call (312) 922–8687.

If you want a more in-depth look at some of the city's highlights, choose the appropriate CAF tour. Two Daniel Burnham buildings have tours of their own: the **Marshall Field and Co.** store (111 North State Street), which Burnham did from 1902 to 1907, and the 1888 **Rookery Building** (209 South La Salle Street), where the exterior was the work of Burnham's partner, John Root, and the stunning, light-filled interior—with a staircase that's pure poetry— was Burnham's plan (remodeled years later by none other than Frank Lloyd Wright). Another Root building that's well worth a look is the 1891 **Monadnock** (53 West Jackson Boulevard), one of the last skyscrapers built without a steel frame; one thing you may not learn from a tour is that the Monadnock is the professional home of V. I. Warshawski, the fictional detective heroine created by Sara Paretsky.

More greatness? Certainly. Learn about the work of Wright's mentor, Louis Sullivan, at his magnificent **Auditorium Building** (70 East Congress Boulevard). Historical sidelight: Here the city's first air-conditioning system blew air over blocks of ice to cool summertime theatergoers. Or explore Sullivan's **Carson Pirie Scott** (1 South State Street) store, where the master's more subtle ornament took a backseat to focusing shoppers' eyes on big windows showcasing merchandise. Each building is the subject of a CAF tour.

Or leap in the opposite direction, to the latter half of the twentieth century, with a look at the local masterpieces of Mies van der Rohe. Driven from Germany by the rise of the Nazis, Mies settled in Chicago and created the buildings of the South Side's Illinois Institute of Technology. His austere geometry can be seen in the **860–880 North Lake Shore Drive** apartment building, though it's not easy to get a good perspective on how the buildings' mass balances. Another downtown Mies building, done near the end of his career, is the grand **IBM Building** (North Wabash Avenue at the Chicago River). This imposing tower offers a good lesson in form not following function. Its large, featureless plaza leaves pedestrians prey to Chicago's often savage weather, especially the sweeping winds that necessitate emergency ropes for passersby to cling to as they struggle through this impressively austere but impractical expanse.

And let's not forget some of the city's best-known landmarks. Architect Bruce Graham's 1969 **John Hancock Building** (875 North Michigan Avenue) was the city's first 1,000-foot-plus skyscraper and remains one of its most instantly recognizable buildings. Just as distinctive, and built just a few years earlier, is Bertrand Goldberg's **Marina City** (300 North State Street), the two cylindrical towers some call corncobs and others call great. And, of course, there's the **Sears Tower** (a full city block, bounded by Adams Street, Franklin Street, Jackson Boulevard, and Wacker Drive), the 1974 behemoth that is still arguably the world's tallest (Chicagoans are tenacious; that building in Malaysia counts antennae, which we believe is cheating).

LUNCH

The downtown area offers lots of good places for lunch, depending on where you find yourself. If you're in Sullivan's Carson Pirie Scott building or Burnham's Marshall Field and Co. building, eat at Field's seventh-floor restaurants. Farther south in the Loop, head for the **Berghoff** (17 West Adams Street; 312–427–3170), an institution since 1898 and one of the places where, not so long ago, women weren't allowed at the bar. In those days, the Berghoff's menu was strictly German; nowadays, there's pasta next to schnitzel, plus lighter fare for those who prefer it. Whatever you eat, though, don't skip the chance to try the restaurant's own beer. Figure about $20 to $30 total for lunch, and don't feel rushed if it's busy; the Berghoff is *always* busy.

DAY TWO: evening

DINNER

As you return to the Inter-Continental, think of that gorgeous pool to revive your weary feet. Then think about dinner—but, surprisingly, it's not so easy to get a nice dinner in an architecturally significant building. A happy exception is the John Hancock Building's **Signature Room on the Ninety-fifth Floor** (875 North Michigan Avenue; 312–787–9596). The view, of course, is unbeatable; ask for a window table on arrival, if you're willing to wait.

The room has had its ups and downs over the years, but the current management is doing well with a health-conscious menu that offers fish, chicken, and vegetarian selections alongside the power-lunch steaks and thick lamb chops you might expect. (A weekday lunch buffet is a fabulous bargain at $13.95 per person.) There's live music on Friday and Saturday evenings, and the lounge (one floor up) has jazz on other nights. Dinner entrees range from about $21 to about $37. You'll definitely need a reservation, and several weeks in advance is none too soon for a weekend evening. Sunday brunch is available here, too ($35.95), and it's a wonderful treat to come here in daylight when the weather is good. (On the other hand, I've been here during a thunderstorm and actually felt the building sway.)

To continue your appreciation of the city's architecture by using its beautiful spaces, take a cab south on Michigan Avenue to catch a play at Louis Sullivan's glorious **Auditorium Theatre** (50 East Congress Parkway; 312–902–1500). It's truly a beautiful place to see a show; the building's grandeur serves well whatever takes the stage. For up-to-date information, check the Friday or Sunday entertainment listings in the *Chicago Sun-Times* or *Tribune*.

DAY THREE: morning/afternoon

BREAKFAST

Two full-tilt days, and you've barely scratched the surface of Chicago's architectural glories! Talk it all over at breakfast—maybe near your next destination, which is the Chicago River. You'll be right there, and right in the middle of Marina City, if you go to the gospel brunch at **House of Blues Hotel** (333 North Dearborn Street; 312-923-2000; www.hob.com). The buffet is loaded with home cooking, and the music lets you know it's Sunday morning, without a doubt. Each week brings a different local choir, which performs at each of three seatings: 9:30 A.M., noon, and 2:30 P.M. All three generally sell out, so you'll want to order at least a couple of weeks in advance by calling (312) 923-2000. Tickets bought in person are $38.00; for telephone orders, add a $2.50 surcharge.

After breakfast, stroll downtown and pick out the buildings you've been studying, as well as some riverside notables—**333 West Wacker Drive,** for example, a glass-sheathed 1980s beauty whose curve seems to echo the river's own. Then put it all in perspective with one last tour, the **Chicago Architecture Foundation River Cruise** (312-922-8687), a ninety-minute trip that spotlights fifty-three historic and/or architecturally important sights as you ply the Chicago River. The cruise takes place aboard *Chicago's First Lady,* and commentary comes from (who else?) CAF guides. From May through October, several daily cruises are offered, throughout the day, at varying times depending on the season. Tickets are $21 per person; a cash bar is open on board. Again, it's wise to buy in advance.

Now's the time to take your drink to a comfortable seat and relax while someone else does the talking. Hold hands as you let yourselves go with the flow, musing over what you've seen in the past few days—and how much more there is to do, another time, together.

Words of Love

A Literary Getaway for Lovers

CHICAGO HAS ALWAYS LOVED WRITERS, and the affection is mutual. It was our own Charles MacArthur, playwright and man-about-town, who, when he met the great actress Helen Hayes, offered her a handful of peanuts, saying he wished they were emeralds. We like to think of our town as Carl Sandburg's brawny "City of the Big Shoulders," but in fact Chicago is a very accommodating place for any wordsmith. Early in the twentieth century, *Poetry* magazine was born in a Michigan Avenue building, where its home remained for many years. More in the local image is another Chicago product, the poetry slam, in which poets read for tough, often raucous audiences.

The city's daily newspapers have nurtured countless writers, from Sandburg and Theodore Dreiser to early slammer Patricia Smith. Two daily papers remain. The *Chicago Tribune* is home paper to curmudgeonly columnist John Kass, while at the rival *Chicago Sun-Times,* film critic Roger Ebert turns his famous thumb to typing beautifully crafted essays disguised as routine movie reviews. Even Bill Zehme, who wrote exquisite celebrity profiles for *Esquire* magazine before taking to television, got his start at Loyola University's school paper.

We Chicago-philes have other favorites, too: Sara Paretsky of Hyde Park, whose detective heroine V. I. Warshawski is every inch a Chicagoan, and North Sider Nicole Hollander, whose opinionated comic strip, "Sylvia," appears daily in the *Tribune* and other newspapers all over the country.

If your romance rests on a passion for words, if you thrill together in a love of language, this is your city. Explore the down-

*R*omance
AT A GLANCE

♦ Snuggle up with a good book—and a very good friend—at the cozy **Claridge Hotel** (1244 North Dearborn Parkway; 312–787–4980).

♦ Savor conversation over a world-beat dinner at **Savoy Truffle** (2728 West Armitage Avenue; 773–772–7530), or go French in Little Italy at **Chez Joel** (1119 West Taylor Street; 312–226–6479).

♦ Lose track of time in specialty bookstores and bibliophilic coffeehouses.

♦ Take yourselves on a tour of the treasure trove at the **Newberry Library** (60 West Walton Street; 312–255–3510); linger long at the stunning **Harold Washington Library Center** (400 South State Street; 312–747–4300).

♦ Salute your sweetheart in a poetry slam at the **Green Mill Jazz Club** (4802 North Broadway Avenue; 773–878–5552).

town library, snuggle in wonderful bookstores, read (or gasp) at a poetry slam. In a word, wow!

PRACTICAL NOTES: This itinerary works at any time of year. You don't really need a car to reach these locations; impoverished writers travel by CTA bus or train. Also, if you want to seek out one of the city's many chain bookstores, such as Borders or Crown, just check the yellow pages.

DAY ONE: evening

Begin your rendezvous by checking into the **Claridge Hotel** (1244 North Dearborn Parkway; 312–787–4980), a small, 1920s-vintage Near North Side hideaway where you can snuggle by a fireplace while reading.

The Claridge's suites—there are two—command its highest prices, which are upwards of $375. But the rooms with a fireplace—there are three—are considerably less expensive at about $260 a night. Suites and rooms with a fireplace all feature king-size beds, or choose a room with a queen-size bed and a terrific city view for just $155 a night. All the suites and rooms come with some dandy freebies: continental breakfast daily and hot coffee served gratis in the lobby around the clock, with cookies every afternoon baked on-site at the Claridge's restaurant, **Foreign Affairs** (reason enough to stay, if you ask me).

D I N N E R

Naturally, you've brought a book (maybe a few?), and you could get so comfortable, you don't even want to go out for dinner. No problem. The Claridge's concierge can provide you with menus from several nearby restaurants that deliver to the hotel. Just ask, and you'll be able to choose from at least two spots offering Chicago-style pizza and other Italian fare. Or maybe you'd prefer a top-notch steak from **Gibsons Steak House** (1028 North Rush Street; 312-266-8999).

If you prefer to go out for a dinner that takes a whole evening, head to the fashionable yet anti-chic Wicker Park/Bucktown neighborhood, which is loaded with artists who aren't all starving. Some are auteur chefs in small restaurants who serve up vision along with dinner. One of this breed is chef-owner Wendy Gilbert, whose **Savoy Truffle** (2728 West Armitage Avenue; 773-772-7530) is all for romance. "I've seen many a good date here," Gilbert declares. "It's intimate; I have little candles and great lighting, so everybody looks good here. Plus, I do all the cooking, and I don't have a liquor license, so what you do here is bring a bottle of wine and sit and talk."

Now there's an evening for lovers—and so much the better if you have Gilbert's cooking to keep you company. A world traveler who lived in India for several years, she brings an Eastern influence to her classical French training. Place your palates in her hands by asking what's great today, and she'll take great care of you. Prices are moderate, and Gilbert herself is a pleasure.

DAY TWO: morning/afternoon

Just outside the Claridge is one of the city's most bustling neighborhoods, which makes its quiet oases all the sweeter. One such retreat is the **Newberry Library** (60 West Walton Street; 312-255-3510), an independent research institution whose strengths include cartography, Native American, and family and community history. The library supports a center for scholarly study in each of those specialties. It's also a second home for bookbinders, calligraphers, and genealogists from all over the world. But you don't have to have a Ph.D. to appreciate this stately, beautifully kept old building and the library's holdings of rare books, maps, and manuscripts.

To get an overview, join the tour that's offered at 10:30 A.M. on Saturday.

You'll get even more from the Newberry by perusing a schedule of its programs before you visit. Call well in advance and ask to have one sent to you. Events at the library include stimulating exhibits, lectures, readings, and performances by the resident Newberry Consort, which draws most of its thirteenth- to seventeenth-century music from the library's collections. And if you happen to have a research interest that fits into the Newberry's collections—genealogy is the most common for nonscholars—you can gain a remarkable access to the collections by becoming a Newberry reader. All you have to do is bring a photo ID and register, although it's important to have your topic clearly defined for maximum help from the staff.

When you're ready for a breath of fresh air and respite from the Newberry's rarefied atmosphere, pause in the small park across the street to contemplate how the other half thinks. This is **Bughouse Square**, the time-honored free-speech space where, during the late nineteenth and early twentieth centuries, anyone could find an audience by mounting a soapbox (literally—they were bigger and sturdier then!) and offering opinions. Today it's almost as quiet as the Newberry itself.

LUNCH

The area around the Newberry is loaded with restaurants, though not all are open for weekend lunches. You could walk a couple of blocks south and a couple of blocks west to **Cafe Iberico** (739

Double Word Score

Enjoy an indoor evening with the bibliophile's favorite game, which also makes a great gift for the two of you. Look wherever games are sold for a compact travel Scrabble set with titles as magnetic as the game's appeal. Pack it for your weekend, and you'll be able to enjoy an evening of killer Scrabble. You might even want to award yourselves bonus points for words of love.

North La Salle Drive; 312–573–1510), a tapas bar that's as lively as the Newberry is staid, for a late lunch that can be as light or substantial as you wish. Excite your taste buds with the grilled wild mushrooms, tortilla espanola (an omelette with potatoes), and tender octopus. Nibbles do add up, but $40 will cover lunch for the two of you.

When you're ready to move on, walk or hop the El to one or more of the specialty bookstores that are all over town. Here are a few favorites:

◆ **Prairie Avenue Bookshop** (418 South Wabash Avenue; 312–922–8311; www.pabook.com), just a block east of the Harold Washington Library, is the nation's largest bookstore specializing in architecture.

◆ **Brent Books & Cards** (309 West Washington Street; 312–364–0126), north and west of the Washington library, is owned by the son of renowned bookseller Stuart Brent, whose Michigan Avenue shop now is closed and frequently lamented. Look here for fine fiction and nonfiction, and bring on the special orders.

◆ **Myopic Books** (1468 North Milwaukee Avenue; 773–862–4882), in the hip Wicker Park neighborhood, offers used books and tons of atmosphere.

◆ **The Stars Our Destination** (705 Main Street, Evanston; 847–570–5925; www.sfbooks.com) is a haven for fans of science fiction, horror, and fantasy.

◆ **Women & Children First** (5233 North Clark Street; 773–769–9299; www.womenandchildrenfirst.com) is a friendly North Side hang-out in which to browse for kids' and feminist books.

◆ **Centuries & Sleuths** (7419 West Madison Street, Forest Park; 708–771–7243; www.centuriesandsleuths.com) is a happy home for mystery lovers like owner Augie Aleksy and his wife, Tracy.

◆ **Transitions Bookplace/Cafe** (1000 West North Avenue; 312–951–7323; www.transitionsbookplace.com). Personal growth is a full-time job at this serene, New Age-y store.

◆ **The Savvy Traveller** (310 South Michigan Avenue; 312–913–9800; www.thesavvytraveller.com). Guides to everywhere are here, as are maps, language aids, and accessories to smooth your way.

◆ **Barbara's Bookstore** (five locations; call 312–624–5044 for information). The city's top indie, Barbara's offers a thoughtful stock and wonderful service.

◆ **Sandemeyer's Bookstore in Printers Row** (714 South Dearborn Street; 312-922-2104). In the historic Printers Row area, this quiet spot specializes in children's and grown-up literature as well as travel books.

◆ **Unabridged Books** (3251 North Broadway Avenue; 773-883-9119). Look for the staff's recommendations throughout this extensive store's shelves.

DAY TWO: evening

Where, oh where, have your bibliophilic wanderings led the two of you by nightfall?

DINNER

No matter where you've landed by now, no matter how hungry you are, the sure thing is that you're up for more romance. Find it at **Chez Joel** (1119 West Taylor Street; 312-226-6479), an *île de la belle France* in what once was the city's Little Italy. Today it's trendy, thanks to the growth of the nearby University of Illinois–Chicago campus—though construction began only after a bitter fight that pitted local residents against City Hall. The locals lost, but the resultant prosperity seems to have soothed everyone's feelings—and lately, everyone's talking about this authentically charming bistro.

And everyone *is* talking! I don't think I've ever heard so many romance-minded recommendations in such a short time than in the months just after Chez Joel opened. People love Chez Joel's soft, flattering lighting; its mood-making French music; and its classic menu—coq au vin for the Francophile carnivore, fish and vegetable specials for *les nouvelles*. The service is wonderful, even when there's a crowd, and prices are a lot lower than you could pay for a lot less: $70 or so should cover dinner, and the atmosphere's free.

After dinner, if the weather's good, stroll east to the university campus (not west; that can be dicey) and contemplate its ultra-modern architecture. Its flaws have become evident over time, but like a dysfunctional family, UIC works anyway. Or, for sheer entertainment, hop the Halsted Street bus up to the North Side and catch a double feature at **Brew & View at the Vic** (3145 North Sheffield Avenue; 312-618-8439; www.brewview.com). This lovable old theater programs a pair of movies every night, plus a midnight feature on Thursday, Friday, and Saturday. Movies may be bumped by popular demand for communal TV viewing of such specials as the Grammys, Academy Awards, or series finales. Seating is chairs at tables, stadium-style in the balcony; admission is a dirt-cheap $5.00, and three full-service bars keep things loose.

DAY THREE: morning/afternoon
BREAKFAST

Roll out of bed for a way-cool breakfast at **Wishbone** (1001 West Washington Street, 312-829-3597). The menu at Wishbone is pure Southern comfort, from crab cakes to corn muffins to pecan pie. And the prices are comforting, too—breakfast isn't likely to set you back more than $18 or so for the two of you. There's a second Wishbone location farther north, but this Washington Street location is a quick cab ride from the Claridge. And it places you another quick cab ride from your downtown destination, which is the pride of Chicago's populist-bibliophiles.

The **Harold Washington Library Center** (400 South State Street; 312-747-4300) is named for the city's first African-American mayor, elected in 1983, who succeeded the first woman mayor, Jane Byrne. This one-two punch of affirmative action greatly riled the City Council's powerful old-timers, who made Washington's initial four years in office a spectacle of continuous wrangling. The big, genial man known universally as Harold was hugely popular among the voters, however, and his second term followed a landslide electoral victory in 1987 that brought the City Council to its senses. Too late, however: Washington died after a heart attack within the year, leaving the city bereaved and the aldermen in a state of bafflement that lasted pretty much until the present mayor, Richard M. Daley, took over in 1989.

Meanwhile, a suitable monument to Harold took shape. The new library opened in 1991, housing 1.6 million volumes. Get an eyeful of the gargoyle-like owls on the outer corners of the building, then head inside. As you enter the library itself, pause to look at the wall exhibit of Chicago-related memorabilia. Inside, ascend to the second-level balcony for a good view of the grand lobby's lovely mosaic floor, with its touching words from Washington about the city's many faces. Also off the first few floors' open stairways is a lovely tinkling fountain into which many visitors toss coins.

Guided tours of the building are given at 2:00 P.M. daily, starting at the third-floor information theater. Meanwhile you can entertain yourselves by consulting wall directories for your own special interests. If you know anything about children's literature—even a rusty recall of nursery rhymes from your youth—be sure to stop in the kids' area and examine the librarians' dollhouse, which holds more than seventy references to fairy tales, Mother Goose classics, and modern works. Maybe you'll be inspired to share some pleasant childhood memories with your partner.

Also note that a good half-dozen exhibits are up at any given time of year, most highlighting aspects of the library's own special collections. These include a wide variety of Civil War artifacts and extensive holdings on Chicago's life and times. Photography, fine art, and other work by local talents usually are on display, too, and Washington himself is the topic of a permanent exhibit. "Called to the Challenge" examines Harold's most important contributions to his beloved city.

If you want to catch an arts program here—they're free, of course—write for a monthly calendar before you visit. Dance, theater, readings, music, and lectures are all represented in a brimming schedule that's available a couple of weeks before the start of each month. Or just call (312) 747–4649 when you're in town.

To relax with a pair of books, head upstairs to the glorious **Wintergarden,** a sunny, skylit atrium where chairs and tables offer comfortable reading areas. Note, however, that you're not supposed to eat in the Wintergarden. For that you'll have to leave the building. A good destination, just a little to the south, is **Prairie** (500 South Dearborn Street; 312–663–1143). Located in the Hyatt on Printers Row, Prairie serves lunch from 11:30 A.M. to 2:00 P.M. daily except Sunday, when the same hours bring brunch instead. At either meal, you'll find yourselves lulled into serenity by the Prairie School decor and inspired cuisine. Using local ingredients wherever possible, the kitchen places its own spin on all sorts of classics: pot pie made with buffalo, roasted sturgeon from Minnesota, pasta pillows filled with ostrich, and lots more. (Vegetarians, don't despair: There's always at least one entree for you.) Prices are on the high end of moderate, and be sure to take a look at the wine list.

If Prairie is a little rich for your blood, all you have to do is look around and choose from one of the many coffeeshops and small restaurants in the area. If the weather is good, you might want to take lunch out to the little park immediately north of the library, where you can sit (and read while eating) near a fountain that helps muffle the downtown noise.

If the two of you get tired of wallowing in words (impossible!), take a walk. Write notes to the folks back home (who never have time to devote a day to books), or get one of those magnetic-poetry kits and amuse yourselves by assembling words at random.

Too Risky?

Remember the movie that made Tom Cruise a star? The Brown Line is the El route that Cruise and Rebecca de Mornay rode in Risky Business. If you haven't seen the movie, you'll have to guess at how they passed the night in their deserted El car.

DAY THREE: evening

DINNER

Dinnertime already? You bet, and here's where you get your noses out of a book long enough to hop the El route that gave the Loop its name. The Brown Line (formerly known as the Ravenswood Line) traces a rectangle bounded on the north by Lake Street, on the east by Wabash Avenue, on the south by Van Buren Street, and on the west by Wells Street. Leaving the library, get on the El a block north, along Van Buren, and enjoy the clackety din.

You're heading north, of course, for the trendy River North area, where dozens of restaurants, clubs, and other festive possibilities await. For a dinner you're not likely to have back home, get off at the Merchandise Mart stop and head for **Tizi Melloul** (531 North Wells Street; 312–670–4338), where the cuisine cuts a swath as wide as Moorish forces did in the Middle Ages. You'll taste Spain in almond sauces, Morocco in the couscous, and practically every nation in between in just about everything. Come ready to participate, ideally by relaxing on low-to-the-floor seats while making your way through five courses at the remarkable price of just $30 each. (Note, though, that if you want to follow dinner with a poetry slam at the Green Mill, as outlined below, it might be best to remain upright and make dinner a little less lengthy.)

After dinner, head north to the **Green Mill Jazz Club** (4802 North Broadway Avenue; 773-878-5552), a Prohibition-era spot that now is the home of the poetry slam. Slams and other competitive poetry events are held all over town, but this regular Sunday-evening slam is reliably interesting and varied. Poet-ringmaster Marc Smith hosts an evening that combines performance art with pro wrestling as poets read their work in competition for audience approval. It's sport, but not blood sport; often exhilarating, never boring; a fascinating glimpse into a creators' culture of men and women, younger and older, office types and ex-hippies, WASPS and people of color, all propelled by an inner voice that makes them write and read out loud.

Come early—by 6:30 P.M. is smart—and if you *really* want to impress your sweetheart, slip a word to Smith that you'd like to read during the early open-mike part of the slam. Then get up there and address something to your beloved. You don't have to read your own work, although most do; if you choose someone else's piece, just acknowledge the poet and get on with the reading. They're kind to newcomers, but the audience *will* let you know if they don't like you. So be brief and be fearless. "Macho poet" is no oxymoron at a slam.

When you're finished, sit down, breathe deeply, and enjoy the rest of the slam, as well as the jazz that, if you're lucky, just might be scheduled for after. You can stay put for that after-dinner drink you've earned. Maybe your honey will buy it for you.

FOR MORE ROMANCE

Check out the terrific regional library on the city's North Side. **Sulzer Regional Library** (4455 North Lincoln Avenue; 312-744-7616) was built to replace the old Hild Library down the

Book That Fair!

*Every year, Chicagoans who love books flock to the **Printers Row Book Fair**, a celebration of the printed and spoken word that's mostly outdoors, mostly free, and totally fun for two. It's held on a June weekend, in a south-of-the-Loop neighborhood whose century-old printing houses now are fashionable lofts with charming shops and restaurants galore. Prominent local authors appear at the fair to read from and/or sign their work. There are also performances by theater groups for kids and adults, plus music, refreshments, and general festivity. For more information, call (312) 987–9896.*

street (itself now home to the performance space of the **Old Town School of Folk Music**).

Sulzer is a shiny new haven for book lovers, with row after row of English- and foreign-language newspapers, audio and video rentals, computer terminals, and a great children's area—and that's just the first floor. Upstairs are the quiet stacks bibliophiles dream of, with plenty of seating and good librarians. It's open seven days a week, the better to offer movies, speakers, and other programs in its auditorium.

Sulzer's neighborhood, Lincoln Square, is a charming one to visit, too, an eclectic mix of ethnic influences that accommodates Greeks and Hispanics and Eastern Europeans along with the old German places. Right across the street from the Sulzer library is **Welles Park** (2333 West Sunnyside Avenue; 312–742–7511), where you might catch a baseball or soccer game or, during the season, a kids' basketball game indoors. Or you can just stroll this spacious, well-kept park's inviting grounds. Going north on Lincoln Avenue brings you to the **Davis Theater** (4614 North Lincoln Avenue; 773–784–0893), a great spot to catch current movies for just $5.00 at an early show. There's also a time-suspended German institution, **Merz Apothecary** (4716 North Lincoln Avenue; 773–989–0900), an old-fashioned pharmacy where rows of herbs and curatives gleam on wooden shelves, right next to the toothpaste (also herbal).

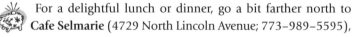 For a delightful lunch or dinner, go a bit farther north to **Cafe Selmarie** (4729 North Lincoln Avenue; 773–989–5595),

a sweet little bakery-plus-restaurant that serves salads, sandwiches, and more substantial fare, all made from scratch on the premises. Prices are very moderate, although this is one spot where you can't help budgeting calories for dessert, since you have to pass the bakery cases on the way to your table. Many patrons plan dinner around what they've just perused.

Another local favorite is **La Bocca della Verita** (4618 North Lincoln Avenue; 773–784–6222), a snug trattoria that has become a word-of-mouth success among North Siders. You can cozy up at a little table while you enjoy well-prepared pastas—go for the salmon fettuccine with portobello mushrooms, if at all possible— or free-range chicken, or perhaps a whole fish, at prices as low as $12 for an entree. Feel free to dress casually. La Bocca is open Tuesday through Sunday from 5:00 to 11:00 P.M.

Art and Soul

THE ART INSTITUTE AND MORE

RUTH, BEAUTY, YOU, AND YOUR SWEETHEART—what could be more romantic? It's all within easy reach when you devote a day to nourishing your souls as well as your relationship. The space of a few downtown-Chicago blocks holds a world-class art museum, some of the city's top-notch theater venues, sultry spots for late-night music—plus charming places for lunch, elegant dinner options, and just the right nightcap.

PRACTICAL NOTES: This day works at any time of year. Be sure to check on what's playing at the theaters mentioned; they are popular, and you may need to order tickets well in advance.

DAY ONE: morning/afternoon

Get in the mood for art over café au lait and a croissant right across the street at **Artists' Restaurant** (412 South Michigan Avenue; 312–939–7855). As you cross Michigan Avenue and ascend the grand stone steps to the **Art Institute of Chicago** (Michigan Avenue at East Adams Street; 312–443–3600), you'll pass between the famous lion statues that "guard" the entrance. They're one of the city's favorite landmarks—part meeting place, part civic treasure, adorned with evergreen wreaths at Christmas, and, when a local team wins big, with the appropriate colors or logo. (Chicagoans still fondly remember the huge Bears helmets the lions wore for 1985's Super Bowl victors.)

Whether it's your first or your five-hundredth visit here, keep the map you'll receive as you enter; it offers a floor plan with photos of well-known works from each area. There's more information in the guides to the collections that you'll find at the entrance to

♦ Spend an art-drenched day at the **Art Institute of Chicago** *(Michigan Avenue at East Adams Street; 312–443–3600), with lunch in its* **Garden Restaurant** *or elegant* **Restaurant on the Park.** *Browse in the museum's well-stocked gift shop.*

♦ *Dine on sophisticated American fare (in guy-size portions) at* **Printers Row** *(550 South Dearborn Street; 312–461–0780).*

♦ *Take in a show at the* **Goodman Theatre** *(120 North Dearborn Street; 312–443–3800).*

♦ *Stay up late listening to the blues at* **Buddy Guy's Legends** *(754 South Wabash Avenue; 312–427–0333).*

each major area. For 25 cents, you get an illustrated discussion of major pieces and a preface explaining their context and importance.

The Art Institute is best known for its magnificent collection of French Impressionist works. These include Georges Seurat's pointillist panorama, *Sunday Afternoon on the Island of La Grande Jatte,* and Pierre Auguste Renoir's *On the Terrace,* a glowing portrait of a beautiful woman and her daughter on a sunny afternoon. Renoir's *The Rowers' Lunch* is a don't-miss for lovers, as is Henri de Toulouse-Lautrec's famous *At the Moulin Rouge.* Claude Monet's *Irises* is glorious, but get a look at his luminous *Haystacks,* too. You'll want to jump right in—together.

There's also a glow to *The Place de l'Europe on a Rainy Day,* Gustave Caillebotte's precise and subtle marriage of geometry and mood, known to many simply as "the umbrella painting." And luminosity reaches new heights in Marc Chagall's stunning, exuberant stained-glass windows. They're guaranteed to fill your hearts with love and joy, and if you remember a certain heartfelt moment in the movie *Ferris Bueller's Day Off,* you'll realize Ferris was kissing his girlfriend before these irresistible windows.

Two of the Art Institute's most famous works are American, and you'll recognize them the moment you see them. Edward Hopper's *Nighthawks,* the shadowy late-night diner that is perhaps the quintessential picture of loneliness in America, will definitely make you appreciate your sweetheart. And the poker-faced farmers in Grant Wood's *American Gothic,* another instantly familiar work, just beg

Timeless Treasures:
Eight Romantic Masterpieces

When you're looking through the eyes of love, just about everything is gorgeous. So you may need to pare down the possibilities of a day at the Art Institute. Here's a strictly subjective list of lesser-known works that speak of romance. Be on the lookout for others to call your own!

Are They Thinking of the Grape?, Francois Boucher. *Probably not! A shepherd lolls at the knee of a shepherdess about to feed him a grape in this ripe, racy eighteenth-century painting.*

The Buddha God Ilevajra Embracing His Consort, Nairatmya. *The fierce yet joyful god wraps all sixteen arms around his love in this Nepalese gilt bronze statue from the sixteenth or seventeenth century.*

Venus and Cupid, Luca Cambiaso. *Love's favorite deities, in a sweet mother-and-child representation.*

Lovers, Sugimura Jihei. *A man, a woman, a couple of cats—all lying down, or about to, in this Japanese woodblock print.*

Solitaire, Balthus. *If you've ever agonized over a love letter, you know this painting's feeling.*

Veranda Post Representing an Enthroned King and His Senior Wife, Olowe of Ise. *Here's a power marriage. He's the king, but she brings the woman's* ashe*—"power and force in all things"—to their union in this Yoruba wood carving.*

Sky Above Clouds, Georgia O'Keeffe. *Hanging over a huge, circular double staircase, this massive canvas looks like a lovely brick walk straight to heaven.*

Uma Maheshvara. *Casual gods, indeed. Shiva caresses Uma's breast as the couple rides a bull, surrounded by their sons and other acolytes, in a ninth-century sandstone sculpture.*

for mischief. If only you could put your own faces on their bodies to create one of those goofy fake photos.

LUNCH

When it's time for lunch, you can stay right here and do very well. The **Garden Restaurant,** which is open during the summer, lets you relax over an inexpensive light lunch in a beautiful, relatively quiet outdoor courtyard. (You'll appreciate the quiet if you check out the overpriced, mediocre Court Cafeteria, which is likely to be crowded with school groups.) For a real treat, though, go upstairs to what a tuxedoed waiter calls "the best-kept secret in Chicago." The **Restaurant on the Park** is open to the public for lunch only, so don't make the mistake of expecting to return later for dinner. This white-tablecloth oasis of civility looks out over Grant Park toward the lake. (Although reservations are accepted, they won't promise a window table—but you can try!) The menu, whose elegant appetizers and entrees run from $4.50 to $30.00, features several dishes inspired by artist Claude Monet's cooking journals. Wine, beer, and luscious desserts are available, too.

You can also **picnic in the park** without having to pay a second museum admission, since your ticket is good for the day. All of Grant Park awaits you at the Art Institute's east end, although you'll have to leave your picnic backpack at the front entry and walk around the block after retrieving it. You might want to picnic near the Isamo Noguchi sculpture that many call "the fountain"; it's a horizontal, loglike piece with flowing water that calms the sound of traffic.

Later, when you've had your fill of gallery wandering, stop at the museum shop to browse through art books, souvenirs, jewelry, and gifts. Don't forget to choose a beautiful postcard and write a note of thanks to the person who introduced you to each other. As you leave at the main entrance, stop for a peek behind the northernmost lion. You'll find a staircase that's perfect for a secluded snuggle and a secret smooch.

DAY ONE: evening

DINNER

A curtain-conscious early dinner is easy to find at restaurants near the Art Institute. One good choice is **Printers Row** (550 South Dearborn Street; 312–461–0780), a dignified place where the fare is sophisticated and satisfying; foodies enjoy nouvelle-ish entrees, and guys rejoice in man-size portions of venison. Dinner ranges from about $75 to about $95 for two; it's served from 5:00 P.M., so you'll have plenty of time to make your show. Another good bet is **Russian Tea Time** (77 East Adams Street; 312–360–0000), a very popular spot where dinner is available early (from 4:00 P.M.) and runs to about $60 per couple. Closing as late as midnight on weekends, the restaurant also is a good place for a drink after the show.

And which show will it be? An outstanding possibility is close by the Art Institute. The **Goodman Theatre** (170 North Dearborn Street; 312–443–3800) is in the city's new Theater District, several blocks west and north of the Art Institute. Goodman is known for its lavish annual staging of *A Christmas Carol* and has an admirable record ranging from Shakespeare to Tom Stoppard. One felicitous pairing is the Goodman's productions of plays by Eugene O'Neill featuring the actor Brian Dennehy. Dennehy, the well-known television and movie actor with the canny Irish face, solidified his local reputation in *The Iceman Cometh* a few years back at Goodman; more recently he starred in *Death of a Salesman* there. If you have the chance to see him, do. But anything on the Goodman's stage is worth taking a chance; I've seen a few clunkers, but many a mesmerizing show there. If you're seeing a Goodman show, you can dine next door at **Petterino's** (150 North Dearborn Street; 312–443–0150), where the menu of "lite" dinners stays well below $15—and you can go from Petterino's to Goodman without going outdoors.

Two other great prospects downtown are the **Chicago Shakespeare Theater** (Navy Pier, 800 East Grand Avenue; 312–595–5600), whose new home at one of the city's major tourist attractions has boosted the Bard's popularity remarkably among local audiences; and **Lookingglass Theatre Company** (312–337–0665; www.lookingglasstheatre.org), which at this writing was about to move into its new home at the old Water Works pumping station on Michigan Avenue at Water Tower. Lookingglass has pioneered a gracefully physical theater by partnering with the Actors' Gymnasium, and I recommend taking a chance on anything they do. The company's members include the actor David Schwimmer and the acclaimed director Mary Zimmerman, whose *Metamorphoses* took home the Tony and whose bewitching The *Odyssey* lured me back for a second viewing.

After the show, finish your evening with a dose of the famous Chicago blues at **Buddy Guy's Legends** (754 South Wabash Avenue; 312–427–0333), where the longtime bluesman books buddies and talented lesser-knowns. You might happen upon a recording session, like the live-album set that captured Son Seals. And if you're cosmically fortunate, you'll catch the likes of Eric Clapton, who played a three-night stand here not long ago. The location is perfect if you're downtown, and cover charges aren't more than $10 or so. There's even a kitchen that serves up tasty Louisiana specialties, including red beans and rice, at inexpensive prices till midnight.

Opera Lovers' Tryst

EVEN PEOPLE WHO DON'T KNOW an aria from an airplane fall in love with the Lyric Opera, Chicago's world-class entry in this most rarefied stratum of show biz. Everything at Lyric is top-notch, from musicianship to set design to gracious ushers, so newcomers and old-timers alike are assured an evening that's the best of its kind.

Many novices fear they'll spend an evening at the opera wondering what the heck everyone's singing about. That's not a problem at Lyric, where supertitles projected above the stage translate lyrics to help you track the onstage action. It's easy to see why this addition has contributed to opera's surging popularity in recent years; knowing what's going on *does* enhance your enjoyment of the music.

Realize, too, that at Lyric, what's onstage is definitely not the whole show. The company owns its home, the grand old **Civic Opera House** (20 North Wacker Drive; 312–332–2244), an opulent fantasyland of marble and velvet and gilt, gilt, gilt. Better yet, your fellow operagoers make a fascinating pageant that you'll enjoy watching (and eavesdropping on!) before curtain, during intermissions, and as you depart.

PRACTICAL NOTES: Where to begin? You'll need two things to begin planning your night at the opera: a schedule and a head start. A season consists of eight different operas, with performances starting in September and finishing in March. Schedules are available early in the year for the shows starting in September, with season subscribers getting first pick of seats. A mailing that lists available single tickets goes out in July, and orders begin in August. Don't expect the selection to be plentiful.

◆ Enter the world of opera from behind the scenes with a backstage tour of the **Civic Opera House** (20 North Wacker Drive; 312–332–2244), home to Lyric Opera of Chicago, one of the world's great opera companies.

◆ Make your pretheater dinner world-class, too, at one of the city's finest restaurants, **Everest** (440 South La Salle Street; 312–663–8920).

◆ Discuss opera over a nightcap at the opera lovers' hangout, the **Italian Village** (71 West Monroe Street; 312–332–7005).

Your first task, then, is to get a schedule from the Civic Opera House box office, which is open year-round (312–332–2244; www.lyricopera.org). When you've received it, you can begin deliberating on which production you'd like to see. Although some people consider Mozart synonymous with exquisitely beautiful music, opera has other heart-tuggers, too, and they're never absent from a Lyric schedule, says general director William Mason, a Lyric lifer who joined the children's chorus at the age of ten. Mason recommends "anything by Richard Strauss, who is the height of romantic. The prelude to *Tristan und Isolde* is extraordinarily sensual—really sexual, almost pornographic. Verdi is the one for spectacle; there's no one more honest and direct. All the Puccini can't help but touch us. *Madame Butterfly, Tosca, La Bohème*—I always remember the writer Harry Golden saying, 'Never take a girl to *La Bohème* or you'll wind up marrying her!'"

Opera is replete with fates worse than that, but yours is bound to be happier if you do a little preshow self-education with readings and recordings from the public library. You might even rent a video of a title you're considering. *Tosca*, for example, was filmed not long ago in Rome, in a real-time production that critics and fans loved. There are films of *Carmen, Madame Butterfly*, and many others. (*La Bohème* is the opera that moved Cher and Nicolas Cage to tears in *Moonstruck*.) All of these, by the way, are among the great romances of opera.

When you've chosen your title, be flexible on which performance you want. Getting tickets to a Lyric production is by no means a cinch, as its sellout rate of more than 100 percent attests. (Baffled about the math? They do it by getting season subscribers, as well as individual ticketholders, to notify the box office when they won't be using seats already bought. These turned-back seats give the ticketholder a tax break and Lyric a chance to sell the same ticket twice.)

As you might expect, opera tickets aren't cheap, but you won't go bankrupt, either. Tickets for a single performance can be bought for as little as $30 apiece, although main-floor seats on a weekend evening can ascend well into three figures. Ask about sightlines when you buy; the box office personnel are patient and knowledgeable.

Be careful, though, to get seats together. (And if your definition of *together* is "side by side," specify that, or you'll end up seated one in front of the other in consecutive rows or in the same row but separated by an aisle.) This is trickier than getting single tickets, but your first opera is no time to go it alone. Unlike airline passengers, operagoers are not likely to trade seats so you can sit with your sweetheart.

DAY ONE: afternoon

If you really want to learn more about what goes into making an opera, plan to take in one of the afternoon tours of the Opera House that are offered from time to time during the season. Rehearsal rooms, dressing rooms, workshops, and the stage itself are included in the two-hour tours, which cost $17.50 per person. Ideally, you can choose a backstage tour that coincides with the performance you want to see; check with the box office when you buy tickets to arrange this.

This is one evening that demands attention to correct attire—but, happily, it's pretty simple to be correct at Lyric. Dressing up is always acceptable for the opera, although black tie and formal gowns are mostly seen at opening night and, sometimes, at Saturday-evening performances. Weekends are dressier than weeknights, when many patrons come directly from work. Since you'll be appropriate in just about anything snazzier than blue jeans, feel free to get as gussied up as you wish.

Plan an early dinner before the opera, because the curtain goes up at 7:30 P.M. sharp and nobody is seated afterward. (Late arrivals are stuck watching the show on a television monitor in the lobby.) It's wise to arrive by 7:00 P.M., so you can check coats, find seats, locate rest rooms, and get in a little people-watching in the lobby before the performance begins.

☆Operatic Alternatives

*If you don't think you can muster the stamina for a full night at the opera, get a pleasant, undemanding taste—free!—by attending a show featuring Lyric singers as part of summer's **Grant Park Music Festival.** Early in the season, you'll find an evening starring some of the best young stars-in-training from Lyric's own Center for American Artists. Then, just after Labor Day—when Grant Park's season is winding down while Lyric's is getting started—Grant Park hosts the annual **Stars of Lyric Opera** show, featuring lead singers in town to rehearse for their roles in the early shows of the fall schedule. This offers an incomparable chance to hear some of the finest voices in the world— and did I mention it's free? For more on the Grant Park concerts, including suggestions about a picnic dinner, see the chapter "Love in Bloom: A Garden Lovers' Weekend."*

DINNER

Several fine restaurants offer pretheater dinners that will send you on your way in good time. One of the city's very finest restaurants, **Everest** (440 South La Salle Street; 312–663–8920), serves an early menu that consists of four courses of spectacular French food from 5:30 to 6:30 P.M., at the equally spectacular price of $44. You even get valet parking, although it's a bit of a hike over to the Civic Opera House and back. A pleasant one, though, if the evening is mild and your shoes are comfortable; or tell your valet when you'll be back and take a cab both ways.

Even closer to the Opera House (and considerably less steep in price) is **Rivers** (30 South Wacker Drive; 312–559–1515; www.riversrestaurant.com), where office folk from the financial district mingle with opera-going diners. Tables next to the windows offer the best view of twinkling lights and leisurely strollers along the Chicago River—that is, when the weather cooperates; but even in winter, the water is a pleasure to watch. Rivers's menu is modern American, with signature dishes such as rack of lamb, Florida grouper, and seafood stew. Entrees begin at a surprisingly affordable $16, and the kitchen is very accommodating about getting you out fast.

Classic Chicago Couples:
Hizzoner and Sis

Chicago's Irish community has produced many local luminaries, none brighter than Hizzoner—the late mayor, Richard J. Daley, father of the current mayor, Richard M. Daley. Far less well known is Richard J.'s wife, Eleanor, known as Sis. Never one for the spotlight, Sis kept house and tended to the kids in the quiet, old-fashioned neighborhood of Bridgeport, where Hizzoner was born. Many's the night that her husband came home for dinner and went right back out again, to a wake or a meeting, while Sis stayed put, taking care of the family.

After Hizzoner's death, Sis remained in Bridgeport. The story is told of a day when her son Rich called his wife, Maggie, to tell her he felt ill and was leaving work to go home. He sounded awful, so she, too, went home. He was nowhere to be found—until Maggie thought to check at her mother-in-law's. There lay Rich, in bed, recuperating with Vicks. At home.

The love story of Hizzoner and Sis is really a family story. And who wouldn't want their own love story to be just that?

DAY ONE: evening

When you arrive at the Opera House, ushers will guide you in the right direction and, as you locate the right aisle, help you find your seats. If you aren't familiar with the opera, read the plot synopsis in your playbill. Note, on the title page, how many intermissions you'll have. Usually there's one, but often there are two.

Once the music starts, strict silence is the norm; if you have a bit of a cold, bring cough drops, and if you have a beeper or cell phone, turn it off. Don't fret about whether or when to applaud; take your cue from the people around you. And relax. Let the music embrace you.

At intermission you'll find refreshments ranging from champagne to coffee to chocolate chip cookies at counters in the lobbies on almost every level. Lines are long, but you can pass the time by observing your fellow culture vultures' appearance, conversation, and pick-me-up practices. Intermissions often are lengthy—fifteen to twenty minutes, but sometimes as long as half an hour—so you should have time for a snack and a visit to the washroom.

As the performance ends, stay in your seat long enough to applaud the conductor as well as the performers; he or she will come onstage after the first round or two of bows. Then head out into the night for a snack, a nightcap, and/or a postshow wrap-up. According to Lyric's old-timers, the **Italian Village** (71 West Monroe Street; 312-332-7005) has been the unofficial restaurant of fans and musicians alike ever since Lyric began, more than forty years ago. The reason is simple: The kitchen serves up good, moderately priced Italian food and stays open late enough for operagoers.

You can walk there if the weather's reasonable (and since cabs are nearly impossible to get after the show, you may have to!). The building actually holds three Italian restaurants, each with its own identity and menu. At the main level, **Vivere** (312-332-7005) is a postmodern vision of swirling flourishes and startling colors, with a sophisticated Italian menu of pastas, fish, and some meat. It's a good place to wrap up your equally sophisticated night at the opera. Romantic in a very different way is the upstairs **Italian Village,** a Chicago favorite of such long standing that some of your fellow diners may be high schoolers on the same postprom trip downtown that their parents made. Get one of the room's little tucked-away nooks for two, and settle in to decide for yourselves whether those twinkling lights are charming or hokey. The menu is as reliable as the clientele, with filling pastas and traditional entrees. Downstairs, the pleasant **La Cantina** (312-332-7005) is decked out as a fishing village, suggesting its specialty of fine seafood.

FOR MORE ROMANCE

A night at the opera is a late night; why not extend its pleasures by reserving a room at a downtown hotel? Lyric sometimes puts up its out-of-town singers at the Drake or the Four Seasons, and both are ideal for continuing the evening's feeling of grandeur. If you'd like to rub some famous elbows in these elevators, call the Drake at (312) 787-2200 or the Four Seasons at (312) 280-8800 for reservations. (For a detailed description of the Four Seasons, see the chapter "Let it Snow: A Cozy Winter Weekend for Two"). Or consider the felicitously named **Allegro Hotel** (171 West Randolf Street; 312-672-6143), whose West Loop location is fairly convenient and whose light touch is all about comfort.

Another possibility is the hotel many people think of immediately when they think of Chicago. Even after the feverish hotel-building boom of the 1980s, the **Hilton Chicago** (720 South Michigan

Avenue; 312-922-4400), formerly the namesake Conrad Hilton, remains one of the city's premier hotels. Rooms—there are 1,543 of them—are decorated in pale peachy shades and warm cherrywood furnishings, and baths feature Italian marble and brass fixtures. In the Executive Class upgrade, guests enjoy their own concierge, a separate registration area, and lots of deluxe perks. A fully equipped fitness club offers plenty of machines, a spacious pool, and a sauna and whirlpool for working out and relaxing afterward. Rates for a double room start at $165 per night, but look for a weekend package to bring that down to around $140 and include a continental breakfast, too. (Suites are pricey—$440 and up.)

One of the Hilton's biggest attractions is its pub, **Kitty O'Sheas,** which is among the most authentically Irish spots in this Eire-loving town. It's especially packed around St. Patrick's Day, but the Irish staff are here year-round, and there's often Irish music performed by bands from the Auld Sod. The kitchen serves up corned beef and cabbage, fish and chips, shepherd's pie, and more from 11:00 A.M. to 9:00 P.M., so if you knock off that continental breakfast early, you're positioned for a hearty lunch. Best of all, nothing at Kitty's runs more than $12.

Also at the Hilton is **Buckingham's,** its top-of-the-line steak house, where entrees include plenty of fish and seafood, running from about $17 to about $35.

You'll be in town when Lyric's season is over? No problem: There are at least two other opera possibilities in Chicago during Lyric's downtime. **Chicago Opera Theater** (70 East Lake Street; 312-704-8414; www.chicagooperatheater.org) offers three productions every season, all sung in English, at the North Side Athenaeum Theater (2936 North Southport; 773-935-6860). This is the company whose *Orfeo* wowed New York not long ago. So you'll want to plan ahead to get tickets to one of their shows.

Another way to see opera here is in the first suburb north of Chicago at **Light Opera Works** (927 Noyes Street, Evanston; 847-869-6300), which specializes in high-quality music that isn't heavy-duty—Gilbert and Sullivan rather than Richard Strauss, Leonard Bernstein rather than Philip Glass. Light Opera Works produces three shows each summer and a holiday show as well; call for seasonal information.

The Food of Love
MUSIC IN CHICAGO

I F SHAKESPEARE WAS RIGHT in calling music "the food of love," then Chicago is an all-you-can-eat buffet. Feast on three courses—jazz, folk, and blues—on Friday. Make a double entree of rock and pop on Saturday. And on Sunday, brunch with gospel and go till teatime with the Chicago Symphony Orchestra. Here's a weekend that invites you to bop till you drop with three gluttonously, gloriously tuneful days—and nights.

DAY ONE: evening

Make a base for your musical explorations at **Windy City Inn,** a cozy, centrally located bed-and-breakfast guest house in New Town. Your hostess owns **Bed & Breakfast Chicago** (800–375–7084), so you can count on being well cared for during your stay. A self-contained former coach house offers three roomy, beautifully renovated apartments, and more guest rooms are available in the equally beautiful main house. Rates range from $124 to $325. (*Hint:* Those apartments can sleep at least four and are often booked for business meetings or even entire families attending a wedding.) All Windy City guests are welcome to enjoy an exquisite landscaped courtyard, too.

If you prefer to stay downtown, the obvious choice is **Loews House of Blues Hotel** (330 North Dearborn Street; 312–245–0333; www.loewshotels.com), for its central location in Marina City and, better yet, for its proximity to the top-notch entertainment next door at the **House of Blues** (329 North Dearborn Street; 312–923–2000; www.hob.com). Room rates at the Loews House of

Romance AT A GLANCE

◆ Mastermind your music-packed getaway from the gorgeous courtyard garden at the **Windy City Inn** (booked through Bed & Breakfast Chicago; 800–375–7084).

◆ Kick off the weekend the way Chicago's own jazz fans do: with lunch at **Andy's** (11 East Hubbard Street; 312–642–6805).

◆ Go globe-trotting in the universal language of music at the **Old Town School of Folk Music** (4544 North Lincoln Avenue; 773–728–6000).

◆ Get funky at **B.L.U.E.S.** (2519 North Halsted Street; 773–528–1012); don black leather for a show of cutting-edge rock at **Metro** (3730 North Clark Street; 773–549–0203).

◆ Uplift yourselves with the gospel brunch at **Dick's Last Resort** (435 East Illinois Street; 312–836–7870) and a matinee performance by the **Chicago Symphony Orchestra** (Symphony Center, 220 South Michigan Avenue; 312–294–3000).

Blues Hotel start at $149 a night; for $1,500, you can get close to some of Dan Aykroyd's gear from *The Blues Brothers* film by staying in the Blues Brothers suite, where the memorabilia is on permanent display.

LUNCH

Arriving on Friday means you can start taking in tunes as soon as you've unpacked. If you're really early, you can catch the lunchtime set at **Andy's** (11 East Hubbard Street; 312–642–6805), a friendly bar-restaurant where downtown workers recover from the morning with a burger and quality jazz from noon to 2:30 P.M. weekdays. Some even come back after work for more, though you'll find yourself sitting near jazz-loving out-of-towners as well as ad execs. In Chicago everyone who knows jazz comes to Andy's. There's no cover for the noon shows, and covers vary in the evening.

DINNER

Make your way north to the lively Lincoln Square neighborhood, where you'll find a world of possibilities for dinner and an evening's musical entertainment. Plan to eat at the exotic **Simplon Orient Express** (4520 North Lincoln Avenue; 773-275-0033), a restaurant named for the train whose route provides its menu theme. Entree choices reflect its eastern European starting point (Wiener schnitzel from Austria) and other specialties from points beyond (notably Turkish stuffed grape leaves and various grilled sausages from different areas of the former Yugoslavia). The accordion music is suitably foreign, and the meal won't set you back more than $40 or so for two—far less expensive than actually booking a sleeper.

Or squeeze into the fashionable **She She** (4539 North Lincoln Avenue; 773-293-3690), where the BYOB policy keeps costs down and the menu is as eclectic as the clientele. Don't be startled when you see spots: The staff wear the same leopard print that's on the chairs.

Just a few doors to the north is your after-dinner destination, another spot that brings together influences from the four corners of the world. The **Old Town School of Folk Music** (4544 North Lincoln Avenue; 773-728-6000; www.oldtownschool.org) has overhauled a former Chicago Public Library site to become a shiny new performance-and-classroom space.

An institution nationwide as well as in its hometown, the Old Town School has nurtured and hosted absolutely everyone in the folk world. That's partly because its definition of folk music embraces every sort of folk: African as well as Celtic, eastern European as well as all-American, joyful noise as well as angry protest, challenging rhythms as well as pretty voices.

And there's history as well as musical anthropology. Consider the talent lineup that was scheduled for the concert celebrating the new site's opening. Topping the bill were Joni Mitchell and Richard Thompson—two of the biggest, two of the best. At the same time, the Old Town School is vital to keeping alive Chicago's own folk scene; here you'll find both shows and classes featuring the likes of the Holstein brothers, Ed and Fred, who have been indispensable fixtures of the city's musical life since the days when Steve Goodman and John Prine were frequent performers at legendary Lincoln Avenue spots like Somebody Else's Troubles or the brothers' own Holsteins.

Now as then, when you call the Old Town School to ask who's playing during your weekend, it's wise to be open-minded to anything they care to program here. You won't be sorry. Depending on the show, tickets usually run about $20, and the music usually starts around 7:30 P.M.

That leaves you plenty of evening left to explore another Chicago specialty, the blues. If you want an authentic neighborhood to go with the music, catch a cab down to the **Checkerboard Lounge** (423 East Forty-third Street; 773-624-3240). This legendary name still attracts well-known players and fans from all over town and all over the world. Cover charges vary, but the music always starts after 9:30 P.M. If you come, realize that the neighborhood can be rough, and don't go wandering. Close to the Old Town School is a pair of reliable blues bars: **B.L.U.E.S.** (2519 North Halsted Street; 773-528-1012) and **Kingston Mines** (2548 North Halsted Street; 773-477-4646; www.kingstonmines.com). Both offer high-quality local talent from about 9:00 or 9:30 P.M. at variable cover charges.

DAY TWO: morning/afternoon

Sleep late, breakfast in your kitchen, then take the El downtown for a free-form day. Don't neglect to tip the street-corner musicians you're sure to encounter as you make your way to the **Harold Washington Library Center** (400 South State Street; 312-747-4300). You may not think that this would be the natural place to look for music, but this is no ordinary library. (The library itself is described in more detail in the chapter "Words of Love: A Literary Getaway for Lovers.") Be sure to call before coming and ask about the music programs scheduled during your stay. There are sure to be some. Among the library's most popular events are the sessions in which blues performers play and talk about their work and lives. Or you might catch a performance by an up-and-coming local classical artist. It's always worth a look.

Also worth checking out is the **Chicago Cultural Center** (78 East Washington Street; 312-346-3278), which used to be the city's main library. Outgrown but not outdated, the lovely building now serves as an exhibit and performance space for a wonderfully eclectic schedule of programs. You might catch a show by a resident company, such as the Chicago Children's Choir or City Lit Theater. On Wednesday at 12:15 P.M., the Dame Myra Hess Memorial Concerts offer classical artists whose performances are broadcast live on WFMT radio, a station that calls itself "Chicago's fine-arts station."

DAY TWO: evening

DINNER

Before heading into more music back north, stop for sustenance at the **Outpost** (3438 North Clark Street; 773–244–1166). Much as the selections at Simplon Orient Express are inspired by its name-sake's train route, the Outpost takes its culinary influences from the worldwide wanderings of the old China clippers. An ever-changing menu gives new meaning to the term *free-range*, with wontons next to risottos and ceviche alongside New Zealand venison. The wine list is equally peripatetic, drawing from Europe, the Americas, and Australia. And dining to this world beat is cheaper than traveling—unlikely to total more than $60 or so for two.

Next up is a 7:00 P.M. all-ages show at **Metro** (3730 North Clark Street, 773–549–0203). Call it Metro or call it Cab Met (from its for-mer name, Caberet Metro), but don't ever call it boring. This long-time fixture on the city's rock/alternative scene is where you might have caught Smashing Pumpkins, Nirvana, or other big names before they were big, and the club's frequent all-ages shows let a younger crowd enjoy the music at a reasonable hour. The attraction for grown-ups is that there's no alcohol, so things are likely to be less rowdy than they will be later. The place is funky—and the wash-rooms are downright scary—but Metro has a vibe that can't be denied. Ticket prices vary, so be sure to call. And stop in at another fixture, the downstairs Smart Bar, before you leave.

The early hour leaves time for the two of you to see another set at another location. Good bets are at the **Double Door** (1572 North Milwaukee Avenue; 773–489–3160), which books both local and national rock acts and keeps cover charges reasonable at $10 per per-son, tops. Also check out the very-off-the-beaten-path **Empty Bottle**

(1035 North Western Avenue; 773-276-3600) or, closer to Metro, **Martyrs** (3855 North Lincoln Avenue; 773-404-9494). Both present solid rock as well as more fringe-y music that could turn out to be a highlight of your weekend. Or see what's happening downtown at **Hot House** (31 East Balbo Avenue; 312-362-9707), where local impresario Marguerite Horberg considers the world her talent pool and books accordingly. Most performers can fit under the umbrella of jazz, but not a week passes without some category-defying, mind-expanding set from Africa, Central or South America, or Europe. Go and find out for yourselves.

If you aren't drawn to one of these, put part of your leisurely day to use in choosing the evening's entertainment. The best source for complete music listings is the weekly Chicago *Reader*, a free paper that's available in stores, libraries, and other public places all over town. No matter what you choose, keep in mind that a great place to talk it over afterward is **The 3rd Coast** (1260 North Dearborn Street; 312-649-0730), a cross between cafe and coffeehouse that's open to 2:00 A.M. daily and to 4:00 A.M. on Friday and Saturday nights. It's a quiet alternative (complete with wine list and full bar) to the more raucous nightlife in this Division Street area. Also open late—though the neighborhood can be dicey—is the authentically art deco **Green Mill Jazz Club** (4802 North Broadway Avenue; 773-878-5552), where the crowds thin after a poetry slam or jazz show, and you can drink in a quieter atmosphere.

DAY THREE: morning

BRUNCH

It's worth getting out of bed to take in the unlikely but wonderful Sunday gospel brunch at **Dick's Last Resort** (435 East Illinois Street; 312-836-7870). Like some reprobate hustled off to church every Sunday by a God-fearing wife, Dick's transforms itself weekly from a raucous good-time bar into a respectful home for soul-stirring gospel singers from all around the area. The food is almost as heavenly as the music, with dozens of entrees, any breakfast item you can conjure, and a sinful dessert table to tempt even the straight-and-narrow dieter. It's all here from 11:00 A.M. to 3:00 P.M. every Sunday, at moderate prices.

DAY THREE: afternoon

When you're thoroughly redeemed, head west to Symphony Center (220 South Michigan Avenue; 312-294-3000) for a splendid finale to your musical weekend: a matinee by the **Chicago Symphony Orchestra.** One of the very top orchestras anywhere, the CSO has traveled the world to universal acclaim and given the city something to brag about besides Al Capone and Michael Jordan. Any program you happen to catch, it goes without saying, will be first-rate. Perhaps you'll even hear a performance of works by Romantic composers. Even if you're not a fan of classical music, taking your seat in this venerable house and listening to some of the world's best musicians warm up gives you the thrill that comes with knowing you're in the presence of greatness. Tickets are not as hard to get as you might expect, but it's always wise to plan ahead; and because prices vary widely, you'll need to pin down a date before ordering.

FOR MORE ROMANCE

There's yet another way to enjoy music on a late Saturday night: Join **Rosa's Blues Cruise.** Tony Mangiullo, the Italian-born owner of this friendly Northwest Side bar (it's named for his mom), organizes a cruise or two every summer for regulars and people who've never set foot in the bar. He books top performers—Otis Clay, Syl Johnson, Melvin Taylor, and Sugar Blue are past cruise stars—and the fun runs into the night. "It's a nice combination of people," Mangiullo says. "We get lots of couples, and we get groups of five or eight or ten. Rarely does anyone buy only one ticket. We get tourists, too—I just got a fax from some Germans who are planning their trip to make it."

Rosa's Blues Cruise sails on the *Spirit of Chicago,* so the ride is smooth and the engines don't drown out the tunes. Tickets, which include Italian submarine sandwiches and two free passes to visit Rosa's, are $35 per person (a cash bar is open throughout). The three-hour cruise boards at midnight, departs at 12:30, and returns at 3:30 A.M. To find out future dates and order tickets, call Mangiullo at Rosa's (3420 West Armitage Avenue; 773-342-0452).

If classical music isn't what you want on Sunday afternoon, hang loose to 4:00 P.M., when the **Jazz Showcase** (59 West

Grand Avenue; 312–670–2473) presents its matinee show of the weekend's attraction. Don't even fret about who's appearing—it's certain to be a high-quality talent because it's booked by Joe Segal, a godfather of Chicago jazz, without whose tasteful tenacity we would all be culturally poorer. Sunday afternoons are a relative bargain at $15 per person (other weekend shows are $20), and the bands are cooking.

Shall We Dance?

HERE'S AN AD FOR A FLAMENCO SHOW that played here not long ago, with a sentiment that speaks directly to lovers. "The vertical expression of horizontal desire," says the headline. Indeed, isn't that what much of dance—from ballet to salsa—really is about? And doesn't it make terrific sense to devote yourselves to pursuing it? The vertical, of course. The horizontal—well, there you're on your own.

As for watching dance, you'll find the best variety in town during the springtime Festival of Dance, usually held in May and offering everything from classical ballet to avant-garde dance. To find out what's shaking at any time of the year, call the Chicago Dance and Music Alliance hot line at (312) 987–1123 (www.chicagodance.org) for information on scheduled performances. If the groups mentioned below aren't on the performance list, don't despair. Take a chance on a different company—Ballet Chicago, Muntu Dance Theater, anything at Columbia College or from the spectacular step dancers of the Trinity Irish Dance Company—all are good bets and could be a dance experience you'll remember always.

PRACTICAL NOTES: Most of this weekend is within easy reach of the Omni Ambassador East, but you'll need a car to get to Willowbrook Ballbrook.

DAY ONE: evening

Make your headquarters for a romantic weekend in motion at a spot that just might make you feel like dancing right away. The **Omni Ambassador East Hotel** (1301 North State Parkway; 312-787-7200; www.omnihotels.com) offers sumptuous surroundings, deluxe suites, and rooms for which "comfort" is an absurd understatement.

Romance AT A GLANCE

♦ Take a whirl on the dance floor at one of Chicago's most glamorous spots—the **Pump Room** (1301 North State Parkway; 312-266-0360)—right in your hotel, the **Omni Ambassador East** (1301 North State Parkway; 312-787-7200; www.omnihotels.com).

♦ Delight in the city's most popular movers and shakers, the **Hubbard Street Dance Theater** (312-850-9744).

♦ Browse through the fascinating **Ann Barzel Dance Collection** at the **Newberry Library** (60 West Walton Street; 312-943-9090).

♦ See a breathtaking performance by the **Joffrey Ballet** (312-739-0120 or 312-987-9298 for the Chicago Dance Coalition hot line).

♦ Swing your sweetheart at **Kustom** (1997 North Clybourn Avenue; 773-528-3400); step out in style at the **Cotton Club** (1710 South Michigan Avenue; 312-341-9787); or lose yourself in a dance trance at **Square One** (1561 North Milwaukee Avenue; 773-227-7111).

♦ Dance ballroom by daylight at **Willowbrook Ballroom** (8900 South Archer Avenue; 630-839-1000).

Ask about special packages when you call to book; at this writing, the L'affaire d'amour package offers a continental breakfast in the hotel's Pump Room (on which more below), along with champagne and a blooming rose when you arrive, all for $191 per night. Or spring for the Hollywood Night splurge at $588.50. That buys you a sumptuous suite complete with champagne and flowers, dinner in the Pump Room, a carriage ride, and breakfast the next morning, again in the Pump Room.

Lest you think the Ambassador East has nowhere to sit but the Pump Room, just look across the hall into Byfield's. Here's a little lesson on how to make a hotel ballroom comfy and welcoming: Open it to all your guests, unless it's booked for a private party. Add a fireplace and keep it crackling all winter long—summer too, if the weather warrants. Put in a television and a piano that's anyone's to play; open a full bar and, during the convivial cocktail hour, add a pianist. There you have Byfield's, and wouldn't you like to spend a little time here while you're staying at the hotel?

DINNER

In any case, bring something glamorous to wear to dinner. You're going to a Chicago icon, the **Pump Room** (in the Omni Ambassador East, 1301 North State Parkway; 312–266–0360; www.omnihotels.com), where generations of stars and stargazers have dined and danced. Rescued some years back from a drift into downslide, the pricey Pump Room has returned to its former glory as a chic spot to meet and eat. The kitchen's mostly French food ranges from salmon to duck to filet mignon, all served with delightful flourish; but it's the atmosphere that really draws people to this high-style room, with its hall-lining photos of glitzy Big Names, all shot on the premises. Past the pix there's the room's polished service and its posh booths— where *you* just might receive a phone call. I've interviewed several show-biz personalities here, and I can tell you that they love it every bit as much as the regular folks.

Everybody also loves the intimate dance floor, where you can get your evening off to the right start with a whirl or two—or maybe even a dip. Before you know it, though, you'll be off to a performance by the city's foremost nonclassical dance group. The **Hubbard Street Dance Theater** (www.hubbardstreetdance.com) led for years by their beloved teacher and choreographer Lou

Dancing to Different Drummers

When you've gotta dance, you want variety—and you'll find it all over town. Several fabulous places to dance are described in this book's other chapters, so check out your options before putting on your dancing shoes. If you like to polka, go to the **Baby Doll Polka Club** (see "Hyde Park Honeymoon"). For country-western line dancing, point your boots to **Willowbrook Ballroom** on a Friday evening (see "City Slickers' Western Weekend"). And for super-sizzling salsa, you'll love **Nacional 27** (see "Love in the Hot Zone").

Conte, has developed into a versatile group of performers whose work is very accessible and wonderfully energetic. Beyond their hugely popular standards by Conte and others, Hubbard Street recently has broadened its horizons by creating a working relationship with the choreographer Twyla Tharp.

To find out when Hubbard Street is performing around town, call the company at (312) 850-9744. If possible, catch them at the Cadillac Palace Theater (151 West Randolph Street)), a great old venue for a show. Tickets range from $18 to $65.

Leaving a Hubbard Street show, you'll probably have energy to burn. Luckily, the Cadillac Palace is a short cab ride away from a chic club where you, too, can dance the night away. The **Cotton Club** (1710 South Michigan Avenue; 312-341-9787) attracts a youngish professional crowd that divides its allegiance between the tasty jazz in one room and an insistent beat in another. Take your pick and boogie. Cover charges range from $4.00 to $20.00, and the club is open to 3:00 A.M. on Friday and Saturday.

DAY TWO: morning/afternoon

A night at the Cotton Club means a late morning after. When you've bestirred yourselves and breakfasted down in the Pump Room, take a leisurely walk over to the **Newberry Library** (60 West Walton Street; 312-943-9090; www.newberry.org), where the history of dance in Chicago lies in some 400 boxes. The **Ann Barzel Dance Collection** is the life's work of a passionate lover of dance— a tiny, omnipresent former schoolteacher known to all as Miss Barzel. She works on the collection once or twice a week at the Newberry and is attending shows to this day—and you can bet that when you see her, she'll be clutching the evening's program to add to her collection. Her posters, books, programs, photos, films, and other items go all the way back to the Century of Progress Exposition of 1933.

Admission to this marvelous collection is free, but bring a solid idea of what you'd like to see, plus a photo ID, when you come to the library's front desk. You'll receive a Newberry card and be guided to the Special Collections department, where librarians can help locate your chosen topics. Subjects are classified mostly by company or regional area, so think in those terms. The Newberry is open on Tuesday, Wednesday, and Thursday from 10:00 A.M. to 6:00 P.M., Friday and Saturday from 9:00 A.M. to 5:00 P.M. If you're inspired by Miss Barzel's collection, know that a band of volunteers who help with cataloging might very well have room for two more.

DINNER

When you've feasted on Miss Barzel's collection, head back to the hotel to change for the evening. Then hop the bus or flag a taxi back to the South Loop area of the Cotton Club for an early dinner at an Italian spot where drollery is in the air—and in the name. **Gioco** (1312 South Wabash Avenue; 312-939-3870) means "game" or "joke," and playfulness is evident even in the jester who dots the i in Gioco's logo. When you call for reservations, ask about the nook in back, where overstuffed chairs offer comfy seclusion while you peruse a solidly Italian, stylishly *nuovo* menu. My favorite is the Chicago classic, chicken Vesuvio, here a luscious leg tricked out to look like a pear standing proud on the plate. It's funny *and* delicious. Gioco's prices are toward the high end of moderate (entrees run about $16 to about $30), but it's not just dinner, it's an experience.

Then—it's off to the **Joffrey Ballet** (312-739-0120; www.joffrey.com). The former New York stalwarts have relocated to the Midwest, which is mighty glad to see them. Chicago's own ballet history has been difficult, with several companies starting in great promise and going through quantities of money before collapsing. The Joffrey came to us established, and many local dance lovers are hoping the company's presence will help to build a stronger scene here.

Meanwhile you can enjoy the Joffrey in its new environment. If you visit during the spring season, you should be able to see them at the Auditorium Theatre, where they're likely to present a mix of old favorites from choreographer Gerald Arpino and others, plus newer pieces by up-and-coming choreographers. The company also devotes attention to rarely seen works, such as a recent presentation of early contemporary pieces by Branislava Nijinska. Tickets generally run from $34 to $74. For information, call the Chicago Dance and Music Alliance at (312) 987-9296.

After the Joffrey, step up to salsa, swing, or stomp at a local institution for dancers of every persuasion. Shifting identities daily with the versatility its name suggests, **Kustom** (1997 North Clybourn Avenue; 773–528–3400) devotes itself to swing on Thursday and a supercharged dance mix on Friday and Saturday. No matter when you come, Kustom is lively and the crowds are friendly, and cover is never more than $12.

On the funk scale, you're about as far as you can get from ballet—and from Kustom, for that matter—when you get in the healthy groove at **Square One** (1561 North Milwaukee Avenue; 773–227–7111). This hot Wicker Park juice bar, which also functions as a haven for magazine maniacs and a sometime screening room, vibrates to a DJ-driven dance imperative on weekend nights. (The weekend, incidentally, starts on Thursday.) There's no alcohol, but Square One's exotic juices and scrupulously healthy eats are a buzz in themselves.

DAY THREE: morning

BREAKFAST

Have a super morning—not too early, of course—at the **Breakfast Club** (1381 West Hubbard Street; 312–666–3166), where owner Elaine Joyce serves up breakfast and lunch seven days a week from 6:00 A.M. to 3:00 P.M. This off-the-beaten-path spot offers everything you've ever wanted to start the day, from squeezed-to-order OJ to the city's richest French toast to a chaste egg-white omlette. Pancakes and waffles are popular, too, as are a huge variety of omelettes and frittatas. Breakfast for two will run you about $12 to $14, and the coffee's plentiful.

DAY THREE: afternoon

By about 1:00 P.M., you'll want to head for the suburbs, where a very special afternoon awaits. Out in west suburban Willowbrook, you'll find a haven for ballroom dancers in the **Willowbrook Ballroom**

(8900 South Archer Avenue; 708-839-1000; www.willowbrook.com). The ballroom brings in a ten-piece orchestra on Sunday, from 2:00 to 5:30 P.M., for the kind of dancing everyone did before the twist— the kind in which you actually touched your partner. Take Lake Shore Drive to I-55, exiting I-55 at La Grange Road. Continue south on La Grange Road until you see a turnoff for Archer Avenue. Take this, and after about 2 miles, you'll see Willowbrook on the right side of the road.

Some of the Willowbrook crowd is older than forty, but younger dancers increasingly make the scene, too, often outfitted in vintage finery that fits the music to a T. And speaking of Ts, don't even think of wearing your jeans to Willowbrook. Women wear anything from 1930s frocks to nice pantsuits to after-five dresses; for men, a tie is optional but a jacket isn't. The cover charge for dancing is $10 per person, and if you work up an appetite, an a la carte buffet is open from 3:00 to 5:00 P.M., offering entrees, soups, salads, desserts, and coffee, all at modest prices.

For more romance

If you're in town during the summer, cut a rug outdoors at **Chicago Summer Dance** (Spirit of Music Garden in Grant Park, 601 South Michigan Avenue; 312-742-4007). On Thursday, Friday, and Saturday evenings as well as Sunday afternoons, free lessons are offered, and there's live music afterward. The festivities start with hourlong lessons at 6:00 P.M. (2:00 P.M. on Sunday) and continue to 9:30 P.M.

Are you one of those couples who dread weddings? For whom dancing is a divisive force, rather than a uniting one? Is your two-left-feet sweetheart slowing you down? Help him or her take the cure with private instruction from teachers you'll find through the Chicago chapter of the **U.S. Amateur Ballroom Dancers Association**. Write for the organization's newsletter at Dance Connection, 3317 North Clybourn Avenue, Chicago, IL 60657, or call (773) 404-0006.

Stages of Romance
A THEATER LOVERS' WEEKEND

AH, THE STAGES OF ROMANCE! Introduction, flirting, first kiss, commitment . . . Whoa—not *those* stages! We're speaking here of the other stages. The ones on which our dreams, hopes, fears, and joys come to life. The ones where, whether you're on a first date or celebrating an umpteenth wedding anniversary, the show always gives you something to talk about. The ones that, to Shakespeare, were all the world—and the men and women on it all players.

In Chicago, one of the world's best cities for theater, there's always plenty to see onstage. To sort out the most romantic possibilities, I called on a good friend and foremost expert, Hedy Weiss. Hedy is theater critic for the *Chicago Sun-Times*, a woman who combines an optimistic outlook with a critic's omniscience. Most important, Hedy knows romantic when she sees it.

Here are her picks for the most romantic prospects on the stages around town, arranged into a fabulous, theater-hopping weekend for those who love "the theatah" *and* each other.

PRACTICAL NOTES: If you stick with in-town shows, you really won't need a car. The best way to sort out theater options is to consult the *Reader*, a free weekly newspaper that offers extensive listings and reviews. Both the *Chicago Tribune* and the *Chicago Sun-Times* also carry theater listings in Friday's editions. And don't neglect Hot Tix.

DAY ONE: evening

When you're devoting yourselves to the theater, you won't want to spend a bundle on your hotel room. So consider a bed-and-breakfast location that lets you save the big bucks for the-

Romance AT A GLANCE

◆ *Stage your theater-going fling from a cozy bed-and-breakfast in the hot Wicker Park neighborhood—**Maud Travels** (book through Bed & Breakfast Chicago, 800–375–7084).*

◆ *Tap your toes to a musical—after a long, chatty drive—at **Marriott Theater in Lincolnshire** (south of Route 22 at Milwaukee Avenue, Lincolnshire; 847–634–0200).*

◆ *Thrill to a show at one Chicago critic's choice of the most beautiful place in town: The **Auditorium Theatre** (50 East Congress Parkway; 312–902–1500).*

◆ *Find bargains at **Hot Tix** (two locations: 78 West Randolph Street and 163 East Pearson Street) with half-price tickets for the day of a show.*

◆ *Break for visual art—but check for performance art—at the **Museum of Contemporary Art** (22 East Chicago Avenue; 312–280–2660).*

◆ *Discuss your opinions over steak frites at **Le Bouchon** (1958 North Damen Avenue; 773–862–6600), varnishkas at **Russian Tea Time** (77 East Adams Street; 312–360–0000), or gelato at **Vinci** (1732 North Halsted Street; 312–266–1199).*

ater tickets. One good choice, represented by Bed & Breakfast Chicago (800–375–7084), is **Maud Travels,** a snug B&B in the hot Wicker Park/Bucktown neighborhood. Located on a quiet side street—so parking isn't a nightmare—this cozy home offers good access to expressways, yet it's close enough to Lakeview and downtown theaters that cab fares wouldn't be prohibitive. Your host, Bob, is a theatrical, genial guy who knows absolutely everything about the area and almost everything about this house, built just after the Great Chicago Fire. Maud Travels' accommodations run from $75 to $95 per night; make sure to get a queen-size bed, and try for the room with its own Jacuzzi.

Once you're settled in, start your theater getaway by getting away from the city. You'll need to drive to the **Marriott Theater in Lincolnshire** (south of Route 22 at Milwaukee Avenue, Lincolnshire; 847–634–0200). To get there, travel north on I–94 till you reach Half Day Road, also known as Route 22. Exit and turn left to head west for a couple of miles to Milwaukee Avenue. Turn left to go south; the first light you reach will be Marriott Drive, and that's where you turn left into the theater's hotel home. (Depending on traffic, this could take anywhere from about forty-five minutes to quite a bit longer.)

When you arrive, don't be deceived by the far-far-suburban location or the hotel ambience. The Marriott is a respected, long-time fixture on the Chicago theater scene, and a musical here is the real thing: smart staging, good acting, and fine singing in top-notch material.

"Musicals are great to do on a romantic date," notes Hedy, and a Marriott musical is likely to contain some familiar tunes you already can hum in harmony. *Damn Yankees, Carousel, Finian's Rainbow,* and the musical version of *Elmer Gantry* are among its recent offerings. If you're here during the holiday season, be sure to check out the Marriott special production. The theater's Equity casts include many of the area's top names, most of whom are good enough to take on the coasts but prefer the steady work and relatively sane atmosphere Chicago offers its actors.

DINNER

It's fine (and usual) to buy show-only tickets to a Marriott production, but come on a Thursday and you're in luck: Dinner at the hotel's restaurant is included in the price of a show ticket, which is about $40. If you'd like to do dinner on any other evening, a fixed-price option gives you a choice of entrees at a very reasonable $23.50. You'll want to allow at least an hour for dinner before show time, so plan your driving time and dinner time accordingly. Shows are at 8:00 P.M. Wednesday, Thursday, and Friday; at 5:30 and 8:30 P.M. Saturday; at 7:30 P.M. Sunday; and matinees (think lunch) are at 2:00 P.M. Wednesday and 2:30 P.M. Sunday.

As you applaud the cast's final bows and head out to the car, you'll have lots to talk about during your ride back to the city. It's bound to be quicker than the drive out, and when you get back to Bucktown, you'll find a bit of France at a little bistro that cooks till midnight. And a good thing it's late, because if you came at dinnertime you'd have quite a wait at **Le Bouchon** (1958 North Damen Avenue; 773–862–6600). At this hour, you might still be tempted by such classics as snails in garlic butter or steak frites, but dessert could be enough. In any case, you wouldn't spend more than $70 or so even for a full dinner for two. Dessert and coffee, of course, will run much less.

DAY TWO: morning

Rise and shine—you're off to glory in a doubleheader day of Chicago theater! Breakfast is whenever you want it in your little B&B kitchen. Your host makes morning coffee and supplies everything from cereal to yogurt and muffins for guests; if you're in a cooking mood, check the refrigerator for eggs, too. (The kitchen is available to all three guest rooms, so dress before coming down!)

Head downtown to the **Hot Tix** booth at 78 West Randolph Street or, near Water Tower Place, at 163 East Pearson Street. Both are open from 10:00 A.M. to 6:00 P.M. Monday through Saturday and noon to 5:00 P.M. Sunday.

And what is Hot Tix? It's a service that offers half-price, day-of-show tickets to just about everything in town that isn't sold out. It's a perfect way to cut your ticket costs, if you're willing to make the trip and to be flexible in what you'll see. I recommend it strongly.

Unless you linger very late in your B&B, you'll have some time before your matinee curtain (generally between 2:00 and 3:00 P.M.). Why not spend it at the **Museum of Contemporary Art** (22 East Chicago Avenue; 312–280–2660; www.mcachicago.com)? After a couple of years in its current, custom building, the MCA is bursting with activity: traveling shows of such modern masters as Sol LeWitt, Chuck Close, and Cindy Sherman, as well as frequently changing samples from the permanent collection. The museum often programs performance art, too, if you want to stick with your weekend theme. Be adventurous; whatever's up is worth a look, and the museum's manageable size is a plus. When you've finished perusing the galleries, hit the street again. The neighborhood is prime for another secret pleasure of theater fans: people-watching.

LUNCH

If you've become hungry again, the neighborhood is loaded with good places for lunch. Or you can lunch right in the museum's

Hot Time with Hot Tix

As you choose the shows you'll see during a theater weekend, remember that many terrific ones aren't the product of an established theater company. Venues to check: Briar Street Theatre (3133 North Halsted Street; 773–348–4000), the multiple stages at the Theatre Building (1225 West Belmont Avenue; 773–327–5252), the Royal George Theatre (1641 North Halsted Street; 312–988–9000), and the Mercury Theater (3745 North Southport Avenue; 773–325–1700).

Chicago's theater scene is just too much for the normal matinee-and-evening hours. Late-night and midnight shows are interesting at the very least and could be the best surprise of your weekend. A couple of examples: Too Much Light Makes the Baby Go Blind *is a long-running, always changing set of quickie bits that's described more fully in "Sweet Home Chicago: A Weekend in Andersonville." On the whacked-out side, there's such homegrown hilarity as* Life Is a Cabaret with the Weird Sisters *(Noble Fool Theater Company, 16 West Randolph Street; 312–726–1156).*

restaurant; with its Wolfgang Puck imprimatur, you know lunch will be as modern as the art, though thankfully at inexpensive prices.

DAY TWO: afternoon

Consider making your matinee a show at **Court Theater** (5535 South Ellis Avenue; 773–753–4472; www.courttheater.org). A 3:00 P.M. matinee here will let you get back downtown for an evening show, and coming during the day gives you the chance to stroll around the theater's beautiful Hyde Park location. You can simply drive south on Lake Shore Drive—a pleasure in itself—and exit at Fifty-fifth Street, then continue west and look for street signs. The trip is an easy twenty minutes or so from downtown.

Court does the classics with style and verve in a lovely theater that attracts lots of University of Chicago types as well as art-minded folks from all over the area. You'll find a more detailed description of Court in the "Hyde Park Honeymoon" chapter of this book. Whatever the show is, it's bound to be good—and the neighborhood is charming.

DAY TWO: evening

DINNER

As you return downtown from your matinee, you might want to park in the city lot across from your evening destination, the Auditorium Theatre at 50 East Congress Parkway—on which more will come later. Before the show, however, walk a few blocks north on Michigan Avenue to Adams Street, then turn left and indulge yourselves at the chic, bustling **Russian Tea Time** (77 East Adams Street; 312-360-0000). Open from 11:00 A.M. daily, Russian Tea Time serves up a luscious lunch or dinner of borscht, varnishkas, latkes, beef Stroganoff, and other Russian/Ukrainian specialties. Depending on the time you're here, lunch or dinner can cost as little as $40 for two, and the atmosphere, with just a hint of intrigue, is appropriately dramatic.

Now, the centerpiece of your theater weekend: the **Auditorium Theatre** (312-922-2110; www.auditoriumtheatre.org). This 1889 gem, designed by the great local architect Louis Sullivan, is "probably *the* most beautiful space in the city," according to critic Hedy Weiss, and there's no argument from me. The Auditorium is a classic lost-and-found story of urban architecture, a gorgeous building that fell on hard times and, at its nadir, saw its stage used as a bowling alley. Today, its upper floors are occupied mostly by Roosevelt University; the theater area, happily restored to its former glory, is the venue of choice for the biggest shows, from *Les Miserables* to *Riverdance*.

At this writing, the next big show scheduled at the Auditorium is the spring season of the Joffrey Ballet, whose home floor is here. But no matter what's onstage, go. Just being in the Auditorium is an intoxication. I often remember seeing a show here not long after the theater's restoration and being far more entranced with the building than the program. I had never seen such splendor and sheen, such plush seats and lavish ornament. Even the lightbulbs, their tiny filaments glowing golden, were fascinating. Years later, at a high-society open-

ing night of *Phantom of the Opera*, I looked around the lobby and con-
cluded that the house itself was every bit as glamorous as this glittering A-list throng.

Especially if you and your sweetheart have never experienced
this sort of splendid, old-fashioned theater, do your best to see a
show here. Afterward, stay in the show's spell by wandering north
on Michigan to the **Artists' Restaurant** (412 South Michigan
Avenue; 312–939–7855). It's just a cut above a short-order spot, but
there's a nice sidewalk cafe in good weather—and besides, the
Artists is always full of, well, artists. Especially after a show, your fellow diners are sure to be interesting in this inexpensive place for a
drink and/or dessert.

Or head back to Bucktown and talk over the evening in one
of that neighborhood's many late-night spots—perhaps the
tongue-in-cheek **Lava Lounge** (859 North Damen Avenue;
773–772–3355). The "lava" comes, of course, from the lava lamps
lined up behind the bar in this retro-'70s spot. The rambling room
feels like one big, funky living room, with old sofas, recliners, and
easy chairs for its groovy Gen-X clientele. Drinks are reasonably
priced, and the place is open to 2:00 A.M. nightly.

DAY THREE: morning

BRUNCH

Are we awake yet? If so, head for brunch at the friendly, trendy
Jane's (1655 West Cortland Avenue; 773–862–5263), where the
kitchen's astir from 11:00 A.M. till 2:00 P.M. on Saturday and Sunday.
(Dinner is served from 5:00 to 10:00 P.M. Sunday through Thursday,
to 11:00 P.M. Friday and Saturday, with the Sunday menu changing
from brunch to dinner at 2:00 P.M.) Brunch dishes range in price
from about $7.00 to a salmon favorite that's just under $13.00, and
there are salads and pastas galore—even plain cheese quesadillas or
mashed potatoes, for comfort-food seekers.

DAY THREE: afternoon

For a convenient (2:30 P.M.) matinee, challenge yourselves at
Steppenwolf Studio (1650 North Halsted Street; 312–335–1650;

www.steppenwolf.org). The space itself is an offshoot of the famous Steppenwolf, built by the now-prosperous company where stars including John Malkovich, Joan Allen, Terry Kinney, Laurie Metcalf, and Gary Sinise got their start as writers and directors. Unlike the high-profile Steppenwolf, however, the Studio stages "more experimental works," critic Hedy Weiss says. Give whatever's here a try, especially if you came to see theater beyond the mainstream.

DAY THREE: evening

DINNER

Stay in the neighborhood for dinner at **Vinci** (1732 North Halsted Street; 312-266-1199), a casual but spiffy Italian spot. The delicious *nuovo* menu offers a wonderful polenta, as well as lots of grilled selections and, for dessert, homemade gelato. Sunday also brings a brunch, so think of that, too. Dinner will run about $60 for two.

An even better bargain lies a couple of miles north, at **Yoshi's Cafe** (3257 North Halsted Street; 773-248-6160). Until a few years ago, chef Yoshi Katsumura cooked strictly at the high end, but this charming spot keeps prices low without compromising quality. Fish is a good bet, as is a reward for the open-minded diner: well-seasoned, nicely chewy tofu "steak." Or you could just go for desserts; a platter holding samples of half a dozen temptations is less than $10.

Still up for something offbeat? Check out anything offered by the incredibly imaginative **Redmoon Theater** (2936 North Southport Avenue; 773-338-9031; www.redmoon.org). I'll never forget the first Redmoon show I saw, a magical outdoor spectacle in which silent silhouettes told a love story against a dusky sky as the sun set. The Redmoon spell is cast partly by the group's astonishing use of puppets—life-size or bigger—in addition to human actors, and partly by its pleasantly pagan fondness for elements like light, water, and the air itself—not to mention its annual Halloween and Christmas festivals. Go to the Web site, then go to whatever show is up.

If you're interested in Hispanic-American cultures, check out a show by the Bucktown-based **Teatro Vista** (312-494-5767). Billing itself as "theater with a view," this is the city's premier Equity Latino company, with twenty members hailing from across the northern stretch of Latin America, from Cuba and Puerto Rico to Mexico and Colombia. Like many other local companies, Teatro Vista lacks a permanent home, so call for information or the season's schedule, which is sure to contain works by new Latino playwrights.

Among established companies, consider anything from **Chicago Shakespeare Theater** (Navy Pier, 800 East Grand Avenue; 312-595-5600); for new Irish works, **Victory Gardens** (2257 North Lincoln Avenue; 773-871-3000); Sondheim specialists **Pegasus Players** (1145 West Wilson Avenue; 773-878-9761); or the tiny but dynamic **Lifeline Theatre** (6912 North Glenwood Avenue; 773-761-4477). In Evanston, check out **Next Theater Company** (927 Noyes Street, Evanston; 847-475-1875) and its neighbor, **Piven Theater** (927 Noyes Street; 847-866-8049); or **Organic Theater Company** (1420 Maple Avenue, Evanston; 847-475-2800); in Skokie, **Northlight Theater** (North Shore Center for the Performing Arts, 9505 Skokie Boulevard, Skokie; 847-673-6300); and in Highland Park, **Apple Tree Theater** (595 Elm Place, Highland Park; 847-432-4335).

Above all, don't get hung up on what to see. Just go together and share an experience. I've seen some unforgettable shows—and some terrible ones—at the city's best theaters and at its small, struggling ones. I always remember who was with me. Good or bad, going live creates a bond that lasts.

Small Pleasures

W HEN YOU'RE IN LOVE, there's nothing nicer than taking a day off together. A day without responsibilities, chores, or entanglements; a day whose only goal is to revel in each other, enjoying whatever comes your way. It's the sort of break that makes people fall in love all over again.

These things don't just happen, of course; it's smart to lay some plans, and that's just what this itinerary does for you. Starting from the assumption that your love is bigger than life, why not devote your lazy day to the appreciation of the *little* things? From train sets to tapas, dollhouses to dim sum, here's a collection of good things painstakingly placed in small packages, the better for you to enjoy them together. And if it all sounds a tiny bit precious, set your sights on ending the day sipping cocktails in a smart bistro called—what else?—La Sardine.

All you need is each other and a car (hey, make it a compact!) to make your way through this collection of small pleasures. They'll add up to a big day to remember.

PRACTICAL NOTES: This itinerary goes from the South Side to downtown to the North Side, so driving is the most practical way to go.

DAY ONE: morning

BREAKFAST

A romance without a sense of humor is no romance at all. So start your day at any Dunkin' Donuts, where a breakfast of Munchkins donut holes will get you feeling small.

♦ Bring a magnifying glass to the **Museum of Science and Industry** (Fifty-seventh Street and South Lake Shore Drive; 773–684–1414) to enjoy the **Great Train Story** and **Colleen Moore's Fairy Castle.**

♦ Get small for lunch with dim sum at **Phoenix** (2131 South Archer Avenue; 312–328–0848).

♦ Survey centuries of style in the miniature Thorne Rooms at the **Art Institute of Chicago** (South Michigan Avenue at Adams Street; 312–443–3600).

♦ See what generations of Chicagoans love in the dioramas at the **Chicago Historical Society** (North Clark Street and North Avenue; 312–642–4600).

♦ Nibble tapas at **Cafe Ba-Ba-Ree-Ba!** (2024 North Halsted Street; 773–935–5000), then examine tiny treasures at **Think Small by Rosebud** (3209 North Clark Street; 773–477–1920).

♦ Cozy up in a classic French bistro, **La Sardine** (111 North Carpenter Street; 312–421–2800).

Then proceed to the **Museum of Science and Industry** (Fifty-seventh Street and South Lake Shore Drive; 773–684–1414; www.msichicago.org), where people who love tiny things could spend hours enthralled at two spectacular permanent exhibits. Choosing which one to begin with is up to you.

For the train enthusiast, there's the ultimate basement layout. The **Great Train Story** is a sprawling, bustling maze totaling 1,200 feet of track on which dozens—no, surely hundreds—of Santa Fe locomotives, boxcars, flatcars, sleepers, and cabooses travel endlessly along a realistically reconstructed route. A few years back, the museum got a fast reminder of how much the trains are loved when it closed the previous railway exhibit. The immediate outcry brought hasty assurance that the closing was merely a break for renovation, and the spiffed-up spread now appears to be safe in its popularity.

You can watch the trains as long as you like, and that's likely to be a long time. Be prepared to discuss them with fellow buffs who gather and linger around the exhibit. Then, when you're ready to move on, you can head for the museum's other monument to smallness: **Colleen Moore's Fairy Castle.** Moore was something of a fairy tale herself: a movie star in the silent era who left Hollywood to become the socialite wife of a wealthy Chicagoan. Over the years, she indulged her love for miniatures with the construction and fitting of this dreamlike palace. The Fairy Castle now lives in a velvety darkened room, the better to heighten its dramatic splendor. Lit so that it seems to sparkle, the castle is surrounded by a ramp along which visitors move—never very fast—to view its many rooms, its grounds, even its exquisite little lightbulbs, while listening on earphones to the lilting voice of Miss Moore herself. A guidebook to the castle is imperative and may be bought in the museum shop—perhaps on the way in, rather than as you leave, so you can use it as you look at the castle.

LUNCH

Leaving the museum, take Lake Shore Drive north to Thirty-first Street, then go west to State Street. Heading north on State, you'll soon reach Chinatown and a lunch of yummy little dim sum—bite-size portions of egg roll, dumplings, and more—at **Phoenix** (2131 South Archer Avenue; 312–328–0848). This upstairs room's large windows are as tempting as the extensive dim sum menu, so corral a waitress right away and decide which tidbits to order, then enjoy the view as one dish after another arrives at your table. A bountiful lunch won't set you back more than $25.

DAY ONE: afternoon

From Chinatown, you can drive right up Michigan Avenue to downtown when you reach the entrance to the Grant Park underground parking lot, drive right in. Then head for the **Art Institute of Chicago** (South Michigan Avenue at Adams Street; 312–443–3600; www.artic.edu), where the legacy of Narcissa (Mrs. James W.) Thorne is a breathtaking collection of sixty-eight miniature rooms, each decorated with scrupulous accuracy in a period style, like tiny models for stage sets. Like her friend Colleen Moore, Mrs. Thorne was a wealthy, socially prominent Chicagoan whose fondness for miniatures developed into a full-scale passion. The ambitious goal Mrs. Thorne set was creating and furnishing rooms that would constitute a history of European and American interior design from the sixteenth to the early twentieth century. To carry out her mission, she employed old-world artisans and top-notch architects (many of them available only because of the Great Depression); one of these likened her to Walt Disney in her vision and personal presence in every detail. The Thorne Rooms are known all over the world—one depicting a library at Windsor Castle is in London's Victoria & Albert Museum—and it's easy to see why when you look at them for the merest fraction of time it took to create them.

The museum shop has a good guide to the **Thorne Rooms,** and again, it's smart to buy it on the way in. It's impossible to take in all the pleasures and subtleties of the rooms in one visit, so you can enjoy the guide as a souvenir and in future visits.

If you're in the mood for an antidote to the painstaking prettiness of Mrs. Thorne's tasteful rooms, search out the museum's collection of works by another sort of miniaturist. Joseph Cornell is as modern as Mrs. Thorne was classical; his boxes and small houselike structures carry an air of mystery, sometimes menace, that's fascinating. Cornell's pieces are in the twentieth-century area, upstairs from the Thorne Rooms; museum guides can show you the way.

Now head north on Lake Shore Drive, exiting at North Avenue, for the **Chicago Historical Society** (North Clark Street and North Avenue; 312–642–4600; www.chicagohistory.org). Here you'll find another small-scale exhibit that has entranced generations of Chicagoans, young and old. In their own darkened room, eight dioramas re-create moments from the city's history in a collection of miniatures more in sync with model trains than French salons or fairy castles. The leaping flames of the Great Chicago Fire are the favorite of many children, but others love the soldiers meeting Native Americans in the very first installment. There are also a sweet, snowy scene depicting the city's earliest hotel and another showing the leisure class out for a day at the races in a century-old glimpse at Washington Race Track.

DAY ONE: evening

DINNER

The Historical Society closes at 4:30 P.M.—time to choose between driving or leaving the car and hopping the westbound North Avenue bus to Halsted Street. There, a few blocks north of North Avenue, you'll find the lively **Cafe Ba-Ba-Ree-Ba!**

(2024 North Halsted Street; 773–935–5000), a shrine to the appealing Spanish custom of whiling away the hours over drinks and tapas—sample-size servings of appetizers in wondrous variety. Tangy Spanish ham is always on the menu, but consider the daily specials and remember that even little bites add up; decide at the outset to save room for dessert. Depending on how much you drink, dinner can be as inexpensive as $30 for the two of you. And remember to make reservations; Ba-Ba-Ree-Ba! is a *very* popular place.

If you're game for a stop at one more small world, make it **Think Small by Rosebud** (3209 North Clark Street; 773–477–1920). This shop, which is open late (until around 9:00 P.M.) many evenings, carries supplies for enthusiasts who build their own dollhouses. The folks at the store may let you take a look at the houses in progress in their downstairs workroom, and they'll get you started if the day has inspired you to tackle a tiny project together.

End your small-scale day in an upscale way at **La Sardine** (111 North Carpenter Street; 312–421–2800). From its gleaming dark-wood bar to the tiny shades on its wall lamps, La Sardine evokes the French bistro so successfully that you're likely to forget you're in Chicago—till you glance out the window and behold, right across the street, the Harpo Inc. complex that houses Oprah Winfrey's media empire. Still, the small screen surely will be the last thing on your minds as you sip a glass of wine, perhaps order a classic bouillabaisse and individual souffles, and make small talk about the big things in life. Starting, of course, with each other.

Or feed your inner jokester with a visit to everyone's favorite relative, **Uncle Fun** (1338 West Belmont Avenue; 773–477–8223), a teensy treasure trove of kitschy toys, books, postcards, and other stuff your mom threw out years ago—in other words, the perfect place to shop for that brother-in-law who loves gag gifts and really needs a new cap gun. Uncle Fun is closed on Monday and Tuesday but is open from 11:00 A.M. to 7:00 P.M. other days.

The Sporting Life

Football Fantasies

"FOOTBALL" AND "ROMANCE" may not seem like a perfect fit, but many couples eagerly anticipate the season, both for the sport itself and for the companionship afforded on a crisp, fall day, walking into the stadium arm in arm, carrying a warm woolen blanket. Even when you're half of a couple in which your other half lives and dies by the sport, love will find a way for both of you to revel in the glory of the gridiron. Beyond the NFL razzmatazz of the downtown Soldier Field crowds supporting the Chicago Bears, you can enjoy a rousing college game in Evanston, the first lakeside suburb north of the city limits. The most famous local heroes here are the Northwestern University Wildcats, who climbed from the bottom of the Big Ten barrel all the way to the Rose Bowl itself in 1996. Even though they lost that last big one, the winning season left a warm glow around the entire campus.

Northwestern's campus is pretty much aglow year-round anyway. It's a woodsy sprawl of lovely old buildings and spiffy new ones that occupies a good stretch of Evanston's northern lakeshore area. The town of Evanston is a leafy, liberal enclave of gracious old homes and even older trees. Altogether, it's a charming setting in which to enjoy a slice of collegiate life during an autumn weekend.

PRACTICAL NOTES: Of course, you'll have to plan ahead for tickets to a Northwestern game—although it wasn't long ago that you could have wandered in and bought tickets an hour before kickoff. Those days may be gone, but non-Northwestern folks can still come by tickets. Start in the spring by calling the university's athletic department at (847) 491–2287. Ask to have a schedule for

◆ *Whisk yourselves off to the weekend you didn't have in college—complete with vastly improved creature comforts—from home base at the **Omni Orrington** (1710 Orrington Avenue, Evanston; 847–866–8700).*

◆ *Ramble along the twists and turns of Sheridan Road to reach the North Shore's most romantic landmark, the **Baha'i House of Worship** (100 Linden Avenue, Wilmette; 847–853–2300).*

◆ *Snuggle under a cozy blanket as you join a stadium full of fans in cheering the **Northwestern Wildcats** football team.*

◆ *Linger over a heavenly dinner at **Va Pensiero** (1566 Oak Avenue, in the Margarita Inn, Evanston; 847–475–7779).*

the upcoming season sent to you. Then, when you've chosen the game you want, wait for individual tickets to go on sale (after the season ticket holders order theirs). This happens early in August for the following fall, and tickets cost about $24 each.

DAY ONE: evening

When your weekend arrives, get comfortable in style at the **Omni Orrington** (1710 Orrington Avenue, Evanston; 847–866–8700). Here, right at the outset, is where you'll see the advantage of enjoying a football weekend *after* you've departed your own halls of academe. The Orrington is miles nicer than any dorm. Located just steps from the Northwestern campus (whose buildings, while marked, blend seamlessly into those of the town), the Orrington welcomes visitors with a doorman and, thankfully, on-site parking to shield you from the trials of trying to park in downtown Evanston—a charming but traffic-jammed shopping area that faintly resembles a modern English town.

The Orrington has something of an English look, with a chandelier-and-staircase lobby to greet you and rooms decorated in soothing pastels. Georgian-style furniture, built-in bookshelves, and pretty fireplaces add to the cozy but elegant ambience. If you need more space, minisuites and one-bedroom suites are available, too, with rates ranging from $149 to $209 per night for a double room to upwards of $205 for a suite.

DINNER

Once you're on the North Shore—which is what the well-to-do sub-urbs hugging the lakefront are collectively called—you have an amusing dinner choice between two classic French bistros. Both are utterly romantic and evocative of *la belle France*; what's amusing is that one is called Jacky's, the other is Jilly's, and they're located just about a block apart. Both say there's plenty of room for everyone, and so far they've been right. The younger is **Jacky's Bistro** (2545 Prairie Street, Evanston; 847–733–0899), and while decor and menu come direct from the classics, it's also the kind of convivial place where you'll know if the next table is celebrating a birthday. Try a wine flight to browse their list, and don't forget to save some room for those pots de crème.

Things are a tad more formal—tables farther apart, conversa-tion more private—at **Jilly's** (2614 Green Bay Road, Evanston; 847–869–7636). But the service is no less friendly and the kitchen is every bit as able, turning out seasonal changes on bistro fare for lunch and dinner. (In fact, if you choose Jacky's for dinner, you get another chance at Jilly's for a Sunday Champagne brunch—a coup at $18.95 each.) Either bistro will send you out well fed for less than $100; to tell the truth, if asked to choose, I'd flip a coin and be very happy either way.

If you're willing to spend more, you can hand your palates over to chef Grant Achatz at the wildly acclaimed **Trio** (1625 Hinman, Evanston; 847–733–8746). An all-degustation menu in versions ranging from $75 to $175 (yes, that's per person) aims to stimulate all five senses: A lobster dish, for example, arrives cradled in a larger dish holding rosemary-infused water, for the scent of the herb with-out its prickly texture. Cerebral, yes; but delicious, too, and just a short walk from the Orrington.

Or dine back down on earth at the **Lucky Platter** (514 Main Street, Evanston; 847–869–4064), a funky, fabulous spot for awesome pumpkin soup, jambalaya, even tofu fajitas—and a BYOB haven that won't run more than $10 or so for each of you. No reser-vations, so be patient.

After dinner, consider driving north along Sheridan Road, the closest road to Lake Michigan. Its twists and turns force drivers to slow down and enjoy the view of lush vegetation and glacier-carved ravines that makes this some of the nation's priciest real estate. Be sure to watch for the fantastic sight of the **Baha'i House of Worship** (100 Linden Avenue, Wilmette; 847–853–2300), on the west side of Sheridan Road, just as you travel from Evanston to the next town north. This stunning edifice, which reminds many of the wildly romantic Taj Mahal, is open to the public daily (10:00 A.M. to 5:00 P.M. during the winter, to 10:00 P.M. during the summer) without charge, whether for strolling its beautifully kept grounds or ascending an imposing stairway to enter and contemplate.

DAY TWO: morning/afternoon

You can spend the morning luxuriating in your room, or you can get outdoors and stroll around the Northwestern campus, which is just to the Orrington's north and is the perfect place for a pleasant morning ramble. If you head in this direction, you'll be able to get Starbucks coffee at every turn *and* have no trouble spotting the crowds to follow to the Saturday afternoon game.

Also near the hotel are some of Evanston's shopping areas, with the quaint boutiques the town treasures alongside such chain giants as the Gap and Barnes & Noble. Just to the east of the Orrington is Lake Michigan and a lovely public park along the shore. The beach is great, too, and though you may think football season isn't ideal for a dip, late summer and even early fall often are surprisingly steamy here. In any case, try to find time to enjoy a visit to the lake during your stay.

You can get a pregame snack at the Orrington's own **Coaches Cafe**. Weekdays it's mostly business-type lunching, but evenings and weekends it becomes a student spot. Just make sure you're at Ryan Field (1501 Central Street) before game time. It's a very doable walk from the Orrington, so the inevitable dense traffic needn't bother you. And don't forget to pack something purple if you're cheering on the 'Cats.

Even approaching Ryan is a little spine-tingling, with flags flying and the band playing and throngs on their way in. No matter how you feel about football, once you're here, you're sure to be caught up in the mood of the day.

"Going to a game is a great date," says Northwestern alum Fern Schumer Chapman, whose Texan husband, Steve, adores college football. "Until the '95 season, you never expected the team to win, so we would just go for the spirit of it. And you do get the goosebumps when they play the Northwestern fight song!"

If you find your goosebumps are weather-induced, snuggle under a cozy blanket and sip some hot chocolate together as you watch the action, which even in the 'Cats's worst doldrums always included some fine plays. Then get with the crowd, clapping and cheering and stomping. "It's really exuberant," says Fern. "Believe me, you don't have to know much about football to have a good time."

DAY TWO: evening

DINNER

The Bridges of Cook County

As you drive north along Sheridan Road, watch for a succession of lovely little stone bridges that you'll see toward northern Wilmette and as far north as Highland Park. Many bridges don't actually cross anything, and the road is too narrow to be conducive to pulling over and taking a moment to smooch. No matter—these bridges are so sweet and scenic, you'll be glad you kept an eye out.

After the game, make your way back to the Orrington and get ready for a swell evening at **Va Pensiero** (1566 Oak Avenue, in the Margarita Inn, Evanston; 847–475–7779; www.vapensierorestaurant.com). Ask for recommendations of romantic restaurants on the North Shore, and Va Pensiero is one you'll hear frequently. (*I* certainly did!) This small room is housed in a pensione-style hotel that originated as a home away from home for young women who went to work during the late nineteenth century and, naturally, needed a respectable place to stay and a chaperone to look out for them.

Today, its first floor holds a restaurant decorated in soothing shades of peach; ask for a cozy booth when you reserve. The menu is Italian, but with an eye toward lightness and beautiful presentation. You'll notice some dishes that incorporate *agrodolce* (sweet-sour) flavors. The kitchen is attentive to the smallest detail, as you'll see from the butter that comes

Let Your Love Blossom

As you leave Va Pensiero, ask the staff to head you in the right direction for a visit to **Merrick Park** (at the corner of Lake Street and Oak Avenue in Evanston). This lovely haven is a riot of roses in season, but even when the blooms are faded, its graceful fountain and shady benches offer a serene spot to sit or wander. The only note of civic sternness is a posted sign informing you that ceremonies are allowed only by permit—so if you're choosing the perfect spot for a wedding, be sure your papers are in order!

with your predinner bread. A touch of cream cheese and some subtle seasoning elevate this spread from tasty butterfat to true ambrosia.

Entrees at Va Pensiero include wonderful pastas and expertly prepared fish, seafood, and meats. It's also a good place to make your dinner from a half order of pasta and an appetizer or two—but don't forget to save room for a cappuccino custard. Va Pensiero's dinner tab should weigh in at perhaps $80 for the two of you. If you don't recognize the (admittedly slightly obscure) origin of the restaurant's home, remember to ask; it'll lift your spirits, no matter who won that football game earlier.

DAY THREE: morning/afternoon
BREAKFAST

Here's a dilemma: If you start the day with a brisk walk along the lakefront, or a stroll through Evanston's beautiful residential areas, you'll feel virtuous and entitled to the whipping cream you'll get with your coffee at **Walker Bros. Original Pancake House** (153 Green Bay Road, Wilmette; 847–251–6000). On the other hand, if you eat first and walk later, you're likely to arrive earlier and thus have a shorter wait for your table at this densely populated spot. Whatever your decision, it's true you'll have to cool your heels before placing an order at this North Shore landmark. But who else gives you a gorgeous array of elaborate stained-glass windows to contemplate in the meantime? Bring the Sunday paper and exchange sections while you're not discussing the windows, and before long you'll be glad you were patient. Pancakes and waffles are the favorites in this family-friendly restaurant (it's just down the block from the popular Kohl Children's Museum), but everything else here is delicious, too. It's a lip-smacking way to blow the final whistle on your Wildcats weekend.

FOR MORE ROMANCE

The true-blue football fanatic is sure to swoon for a weekend that also includes a **Chicago Bears** game. Season ticket holders have a lock on home-game tickets, but a ticket broker can help, especially when chilly weather is forecast and/or the Bears aren't playing as well as Chicago fans wish they would (which is usually—it's been mostly downhill since they won Super Bowl XX in 1985). Try for tickets through the Bears office (847-615-2327). If you have no luck, call a bonded, licensed ticket broker, such as **Looks Like the Front Row** (800-525-3380), which is run by former White Sox baseball player Eric Soderholm.

When your tickets are set, arrange a tailgate party for two from **A La Carte** (111 Green Bay Road, Wilmette; 847-256-4102), a charming take-out place located a few doors south of Walker Bros. They'll create a yummy, sturdy feast that stands up to the journey to Soldier Field, which is most easily reached by car. Drive south on Green Bay Road to Chicago, where the street's name changes to Ridge Avenue, and stick with its twists and turns—including another name change, to Bryn Mawr Avenue, just before you reach Lake Shore Drive. The Drive, as locals call it, takes you directly to Soldier Field, where there's plenty of parking and you can enjoy your repast before the game.

Wrigleyville Weekend

THERE ARE LIFELONG CHICAGOANS WHO DON'T CARE a bit about sports but love to go to a baseball game at Wrigley Field. And Wrigley is ideal for romance. "It's perfect for a date," explains a fan of the park (not necessarily the game). "The game's going on, so you have something to talk about. And you *can* talk, unlike a movie, or pay attention to the game when you don't feel like talking. Plus, if you don't know much about baseball, fans love to explain things."

Whether you're getting acquainted or long past dating, you'll love relaxing in the verdant, venerable "friendly confines." And even if you're not a baseball fan, you probably know that the Chicago Cubs are baseball's perennial—there's no nice way to say it—losers. But Chicago loves them anyway, partly because their home field is a baseball legend. Wrigley Field is small and comfortable in an old-shoe way. Its outfield walls are covered with lush ivy, and its scoreboard has the distinction of being the last one in which humans post the numbers by hand. After a game ends, a W or L flag (telling whether the Cubs won or lost) flies above the park for the benefit of commuters passing by on the El train.

Another secret of Wrigley Field's charm is that it's in one of the city's hottest residential-plus-entertainment neighborhoods. Most of its homes and apartment buildings are as old as the park (which dates to 1914) but beautifully restored. And its nightlife is superb: good restaurants, lots of music, and plenty of coffeehouses for the morning after.

So join the fabled Bleacher Bums for a weekend that starts and ends with the Cubbies, packing tons of fun in between. Go Cubs!

Romance AT A GLANCE

◆ Bask in the sunroom of your suite at a neighborhood treasure, the **Majestic Hotel** (528 West Brompton Avenue; 773–404–3499 or 800–727–5108); or revisit the '30s at the **City Suites** (933 West Belmont Avenue; 773–404–3400 or 800–248–9108).

◆ Stroll to the "friendly confines" of **Wrigley Field** (1060 West Addison Street; for tickets call 800–843–2827) to enjoy an afternoon of cheering on the Cubbies in the famous bleachers.

◆ Go halfway 'round the world—no airfare needed—for an exotic dinner at **Tibet Cafe** (3913 North Sheridan Road; 773–281–6666) or next door at the West African **Ofie** (3911 North Sheridan Road; 773–248–6490).

◆ Lose yourselves in an old-fashioned movie matinee at the **Music Box** (3733 North Southport Avenue; 773–871–6604).

◆ Yuck it up at **Improv Olympic** (3541 North Clark Street; 773–880–0199). Remember, Chicago is the home of improvisational comedy!

PRACTICAL NOTES: This weekend can and should be done on foot. Wrigleyville is relatively safe and friendly, and destinations are close enough to walk to everything.

DAY ONE: afternoon

Check into a great little neighborhood hotel. The hard part is choosing between a pair, both under the same ownership and with similar rates (rooms start at $139; suites are $159). The **Majestic Hotel** (528 West Brompton Avenue; 773–404–3499 or 800–727–5108) nestles on a quiet little block, all its neighbors residential; yet it's only steps from the lakefront and Lincoln Park and just about 6 blocks east of Wrigley Field. Decorated to resemble an English inn, the Majestic boasts a large lobby that's really more a clubby sitting room, with comfy chairs, built-in bookshelves, and a gorgeous pink marble fireplace. It's an excellent place to linger over the complimentary morning coffee and cinnamon rolls (from Ann Sather, yum), or over the civilized tea that takes over (tastefully, of course) every afternoon.

Rooms and suites at the Majestic are big enough to be comfortable but small enough to be cozy, with warm decor, queen-size beds, and huge old mirrors in the bathrooms. Try to get a sunroom suite, among the most inviting I've seen: The sunroom area is all windows, looking out onto leafy trees and, to the east, Lincoln Park. Suites offer kitchenette convenience, with microwaves, minifridges, and place settings. For maximum romance ask about the bridal suite.

If the Majestic Hotel is quiet and English, the **City Suites** (933 West Belmont Avenue; 773–404–3400 or 800–248–9108) is Roaring Twenties and all-American. Opened in the 1920s as a hotel for vaudeville performers, the hotel is on a busy thoroughfare, just 4 blocks south of Wrigley Field and a few doors down from a major stop on the elevated rapid-transit system. You might find the block slightly seedy, with its tattoo parlor across the street and foot traffic that isn't all yuppies—but other neighbors include very respectable Japanese shops and restaurants, so don't be intimidated.

Besides, the atmosphere changes immediately as you step into the front hallway and look to your left, where a huge black-and-white photo of a citified smooching couple titled *Romance Circa 1930s* meets your eye. The lobby is all soft lighting and soothing, gray-and-brown decor highlighted by a beautiful green marble fireplace. A lovely antique sideboard holds complimentary morning coffee and delicious cinnamon rolls (Ann Sather is next door; its full menu is available through room service), which you can sink into a comfy chair to enjoy.

Rooms aren't much for views, but who cares when they're so nicely renovated and offer such a comfortable sofa in which to cuddle and channel-surf? Try to get the largest suite, with its two full rooms separated by doors and double-size living area with a big dining-room table.

Once you're settled in, head for **Wrigley Field** (1060 West Addison Street). It scarcely needs be said that you want an afternoon game. After a major battle to install lights in 1988, the Cubs have played a minimum of night games, and, anyway, you can't beat baseball in the sunshine. Tickets often are available on game day, but it's safer to order in advance by calling (800) 843–2827 or visiting www.cubs.com, starting in late February for the season. Bleacher seats—which offer no cover from the sun but give a good view and are the home of the legendary Bleacher Bums (on whom there is more below)—are $24, and remember to bring your sunscreen. Terrace and upper-deck boxes are $26 but are available only for weekday games. Reserved terrace seats and upper-deck reserved seats are $20 and $26, respectively.

Come to Wrigley before game time so you can stroll hand in hand throughout this venerable old park as you find your seats. Bleacher seats are unnumbered, so you may want to arrive well before the first pitch to stake out a spot you like. In years past bleacher seats never were sold until game day and cost just a few bucks. This policy allowed maximum flexibility for the persons of leisure known as the Bleacher Bums—retired folks, night-shift waitresses or factory workers, and codgers of every stripe who were immortalized by the Organic Theatre's long-running hit play named for them. Today's "bums" are a little more upscale, but there's still no shortage of opinion in the bleachers, which will give you plenty to talk about later.

DAY ONE: evening

DINNER

Of course you'll have eaten lunch at Wrigley—a hot dog and beer, naturally—and you'll probably be ready for a walk as you leave. Clark Street is a major entertainment strip, so it's easy to stay right here for dinner, music, dancing, or whatever. For an inexpensive dinner, consider **Matsuya** (3469 North Clark; 773-248-2677), a local fixture where the sushi was great before most Americans ever heard of it. Squid, chicken, and beef teriyaki are tasty, too. Prices at Matsuya are low—probably not more than $15 or so per person. Similarly inexpensive Thai food is at **PS Bangkok** (3345 North Clark; 773-871-7777), which makes an excellent satay (plain grilled meat or chicken on a skewer) as well as more complex, authentic dishes. Or line up at **Mia Francesca** (3311 North Clark; 773-281-3310), where people don't mind waiting for pastas, pizzas, and specials that rarely cost more than $20 per person at dinner. It tends to be noisy and busy, but this restaurant's fans are as devoted as they are numerous.

If you've both got a rock 'n' roll heart, dance the night away at **Metro** (3730 North Clark Street; 773-549-0203; www.metrochicago. com), where the audience and the bands tend toward black leather. But this is where you'll hear some of the best rock around, and at low rates—generally not more than $30 admission for the two of you—this could let you experience a very happening band before their record deal. Call beforehand to find out who's booked. Also, don't overlook **Cubby Bear** (1059 West Addison Street; 773- 327-1662), kitty-corner from Wrigley and home of an incredibly eclectic booking policy that runs from jazz performers to country stars to rock bands.

Or yuck it up at **Improv Olympic** (3541 North Clark Street; 773-880-0199; www.improvolympic.com), home of the Harold. What's the Harold? Funny you should ask, although the answer turns out to be even funnier. It's a uniquely Chicago theater game involving comic improvisation on the Second City model, which requires audience participation to feed the onstage proceedings. Tickets are $8.50, and Friday and Saturday shows are at 8:00 and 10:30 P.M. In the Second City tradition, the later show tends to be more freewheeling.

To the north on the strip is one of the younger generation of Chicago theaters that offer provocative shows, sometimes comic, sometimes serious. **Live Bait Theater** (3914 North Clark Street; 773-871-1212; www.livebaittheater.com) is a staging ground for avant-garde shows by various artists, and its annual "Fillet of Solo" is a performance-art smorgasbord. There's even a militantly *non*-sports bar, **Ginger Man** (3740 North Clark; 773-549-2050), a bit to the north; you'll recognize it by its publike outdoor sign.

Perhaps you'd like to venture from Clark Street. Do it for dinner, and you can choose between two cuisines you won't find on every corner. From the Wrigley Field corner of Addison and Sheffield, walk a few blocks north on Sheffield to Byron Avenue. Here, in one of those urban quirks, the street's name changes from Sheffield to Sheridan Road. Cross Byron, and you're just steps away from a pair of exotic, inexpensive restaurants: **Ofie** (3911 North Sheridan Road; 773-248-6490) and **Tibet Cafe** (3913 North Sheridan Road; 773-281-6666).

Probably the easiest way to choose between these culinary excursions is to peruse the menus posted in their windows. To the south, Ofie—the name, pronounced OH-fee-ay, means "home" in the Ghanian language—helpfully color codes the menu into mild, spicy, and vegetarian selections from West African nations including Nigeria, Ghana, and Sierra Leone. Consider one of the Nigerian stews accompanied by a starchy ball of fufu—a mix of plantains and yams that looks something like mashed potatoes and serves, like bread, as a noncutlery tool in eating. Or go with what you know in a familiar catfish steak—though it's wise to remember that West African food can be fiery. Ask about heat levels, be adventurous when you order, and be prepared to share—though with entrees topping out around $17, Ofie won't break anyone's bank.

Run by a couple of refugee monks, Tibet Cafe is a happy home for vegetarians; though beef and chicken are also on the menu, the kitchen does best with curries, dumplings, soups, and other preparations in which vegetables star. Stick with a super-safe sauté of broccoli and mushrooms, or try a more intriguing salad of cauliflower and potatoes with a spicy kick. Tibet Cafe is even less expensive than Ofie, the high end being just $8.75 for entrees.

For after-dinner entertainment, back in the Belmont-Sheffield area, you really can't beat the neighborhood itself—a panoramic pedestrian's delight that will reward you with sights you'll recall together for years to come.

DAY TWO: morning/afternoon

After enjoying your hotel's complimentary continental breakfast, get ready for an old-fashioned treat: the Saturday movie matinee. It's alive and well at the **Music Box** (3733 North Southport Avenue; 773-871-6604), a neighborhood theater lovingly renovated and intelligently booked by a movie-loving management. Saturday matinees start at 11:30 A.M. and include short subjects before a double feature that pairs a great oldie with something contemporary—anything from the classic *Citizen Kane* plus the supermodel saga *Catwalk*, to the definitive western, *The Searchers*, plus the Oscar-winning *Anne Frank Remembered*. (Lighter titles have included *Breakfast at Tiffany's* and the Carmen Miranda epic *The Gang's All Here*.)

Admission is $8.00 per person (not bad for two movies), and if you might be back, pick up a five-admission card for $28.00. For a schedule that covers thirteen weeks of programs, call the theater. To hear an old-fashioned movie organist hold forth on the Music Box instrument, come on a weekend evening, when Dennis Scott plays during intermissions.

The Music Box area is, again, a very congenial place for strolling and chatting, with lots of little shops to browse. Vintage clothes are worth a look at **Wisteria** (3715 North Southport Avenue; 773-880-5868), and **Fourth World Artisans** (3440 North Southport Avenue; 773-404-5200) offers gifts aplenty for the folks back home. As you stroll, notice this area's many examples of new homes (lots of town houses) that are being built with an eye toward fitting gracefully in with the existing older buildings.

DINNER

When you're ready for dinner, stay on the street and go Italian. Reservations aren't essential at **Red Tomato** (3417 North Southport Avenue; 773-472-5300), so if you're hungry early, go on over. You can relax with a drink while looking forward to veggie lasagna or another selection from an always-fresh menu that changes every few weeks. Prices hover in the $9.00 to $17.00 range for entrees, and owner Joe DiVenere is always happy to take culinary requests.

Or try pasta with a sense of humor at **Strega Nona** (3747 North Southport; 773-244-0990). Named for the wise witch of children's literature, Strega Nona calls its menu "global Italian," which means the cheese on your fettucine with veggies might be feta. Or try the popular penne-veggies combination under a creamy garlic sauce. You shouldn't miss the bruschettone (looks like bread, tastes like a million lire). Dinner here should come in less than $50 total. Again, reservations aren't accepted, but appetizers and drinks are available while you wait. If the weather cooperates, there's a nice outdoor area, too.

Not up for noodles? Try the inexpensive tapas at **Twist** (3412 North Sheffield Avenue; 773-388-2727), a fiesta of a restaurant whose popularity means a fairly high noise level—but it's all in the name of fun and a great bargain for dinner. Sample lots of little bites, wash 'em down with sangria, and see if you don't get out for less than $20 each.

After dinner, ramble back toward Clark Street and make another choice from yesterday's array (aforementioned). Or, if the Cubbies' outing left you depressed, cheer up with comedy in Old

Town at **Zanies Comedy Club** (1548 North Wells Street; 312–337–4027). Later, stop in at **Pepper Lounge** (3441 North Sheffield Avenue; 773–665–7377), where you can sip a chocolate martini.

DAY THREE: morning

BREAKFAST

For an unusual breakfast alternative, walk over to **Uncommon Ground** (1214 West Grace Street; 773–929–3680), which offers the genuine Chicago dish of steamed eggs. Said to have originated in the coffeehouses of Hyde Park (home of the University of Chicago), steamed eggs are made in an espresso machine. They're a creamier, smoother version of scrambled and well worth a try; many fans feel they can never go back to the old frying pan. Uncommon Ground's coffee is fine, too, and a huge cup of mocha and a croissant provide a sweet wake-me-up.

Or check out **Deleece** (4004 North Southport; 773–325–1710), where Sunday brunch offers such treats as a breakfast pasta tossed with tomatoes, goat cheese, scrambled eggs, garlic, and herbs. Wow!

Wherever you eat, get a couple of fat Sunday papers to linger over. Then stroll back to Wrigley Field for the second part of your doubleheader weekend. As you cheer on the Cubbies, remember that we love 'em, win or lose. And don't forget to look for the scoreboard flag, W or L, as you head for home.

FOR MORE ROMANCE

Another baseball game? Absolutely, and especially if you're an American League fan. The **Chicago White Sox** (333 West Thirty-fifth Street; 312–674–1000) are the pride of the South Side, now playing in a pristine stadium younger than anyone on the field. I've been to the shiny, modern Comiskey Park several times, and here's my advice: Stay low. The lower your seat, the closer you are to the action and the less likely you are to suffer the vertigo that afflicts poor souls in the park's upper reaches. Adding insult to that injury is the amazing fact that *you can't even follow the ball from up there.*

A Little Taste of London

Amaze your sweetheart by finding a little bit of London tucked in the hustle and bustle of Wrigleyville. Go to the corner of Grace Street (3800 north, 2 blocks from the ballpark) and Seminary Street (1100 west, just east of Clark Street). Walk a block north on Seminary to Byron Street, then east on Byron to **Alta Vista Terrace.**

This quiet residential street exists for exactly 1 block—and a beautiful one it is. Lined up along its narrow length are beautiful brick rowhouses that mimic those of London's nicer neighborhoods. They're so lovely, yet so un-Wrigleyville, that a stroll on Alta Vista makes a wonderful mini-getaway in the middle of your weekend escapes.

Alta Vista is nicknamed "the street of forty doors," and if you look carefully, you'll see that each door has a twin, across the street and at the other end. The houses come honestly by their century-old look, having been built between 1900 and 1904—and it's a hint of their original character that, in some, the third floor was a ballroom. Their lovingly kept exteriors have changed little since then, and in the early 1970s, the entire street was named one of Chicago's very first official landmarks.

If you happen to be here at Christmas, your consolation prize for missing base-ball could be a visit to Alta Vista Terrace. Beautifully decorated individually to a harmonious whole, these lovely homes are one of my favorite things about Christmas in Chicago.

On the park's plus side are creature comforts: clean washrooms and plenty of 'em; lots of snack stands; secure and abundant parking; and even reasonably safe public transportation to and from the Loop. Just be sure your tickets place you well below the nosebleed section, where you'll pay a "bargain" $12. Top price is $26, but there's plenty in between. The trip from the North Side Wrigleyville to South Side Comiskey will take some time—a solid hour if traffic snarls—so you'll be able to quiz each other on sports trivia at length.

Hoop Lovers' Holiday

HEN CHICAGOANS TALK ABOUT ROMANCE, about love and devotion and putting someone on a pedestal, they may not be talking about a personal romantic relationship. We are just as deeply committed to cherishing the memory of the 1980s and '90s Chicago Bulls dynasty. The city was lucky in love during the reign of His Airness, Michael Jordan—also known as MJ, Michael, or simply as the finest basketball player ever.

What we loved—still do—about Michael is the way he stood first among equals while remaining a gentleman. He always was—still is—polite with fans and the media, generous to charities (especially for children), and patient about the relentless attention he attracts. Before and after retiring from the Bulls, Michael lived—still does—in a quiet northern suburb with his wife, Juanita, and their three rarely photographed children.

MJ's now with the Washington Wizards, but a high level of Michael worship continues to prevail here in town and, we are confident, worldwide. Really, no visit to Chicago is complete without a nod to the Bulls. Why not make it a full bow and spend some time at the sites that Michael made famous?

PRACTICAL NOTES: The basketball season starts in October and runs into April, with playoffs in May and June. Bulls tickets go on sale in September (Chicago Bulls: 312–455–4000), and the silver lining behind a merely mortal team is that now you can almost always get tickets.

Romance
AT A GLANCE

♦ *Plunge into sports mania with a visit to the Magnificent Mile's shrine to sports—**Nike Town** (669 North Michigan Avenue; 312–642–6363).*

♦ *Enjoy a pregame dinner in Greektown at **Santorini** (800 West Adams Street; 312–829–8820).*

♦ *Snap pictures of yourselves next to the famous Michael Jordan statue at the **United Center** (1901 West Madison Street; 312–455–4500), then get in there and cheer for the **Chicago Bulls.***

♦ *Savor a Michael-icious supper at **One Sixtyblue** (160 North Loomis Street; 312–850–0303) or stargaze at **Millennium** (832 West Randolph Street; 312–455–1400).*

DAY ONE: morning/afternoon

LUNCH

Start your Bulls bash with lunch and a few baskets at **ESPN Zone** (43 East Ohio Street; 312–644–3776). At this glitzy sports shrine, you can catch the big game du jour on a 16-foot screen surrounded by a dozen 36-inch video monitors carrying other events. Seating is even more the stuff of fantasy: a row of leather recliners, each equipped with its own audio controls, in which you can relax while watching. And you're definitely allowed to eat in this living room when you order from an all-American, moderately priced menu of burgers, sandwiches, salads, and extravagant desserts that beg to be shared.

Better yet, get active by testing your own skills—noncompetitively, of course. In ESPN Zone's Sports Arena, you can stick to shooting baskets if you like, or try your hands at a couple of other sports—quarterback passing for football fans, a slap-shot binge for the hockey crowd. The Zone's pay-for-play arrangement involves buying game cards, in various increments, that give you a specific number of points. Cards start at just $6.00 with a good deal in the $21.00 card, which offers one hundred points.

After lunch, you can discuss the beauty of the game of basketball during a stroll over to the Magnificent Mile, where you'll find a tourist attraction that's something of a temple to the commercial aspects of modern sports. You might think of **Nike Town** (669 North Michigan Avenue; 312-642-6363) as the house that Michael Jordan built. Indeed, at its entrance you'll see a replica of the Jordan statue whose original, a tourist attraction itself, stands outside the Bulls' home, the United Center. Inside at Nike Town there's even more Michael, along with other Nike-identified star names such as Spike Lee, to promote the label's shoes and gear.

When the multimedia Nike bombardment palls, get some fresh air by walking a couple of blocks north to the very antithesis of North Michigan Avenue's retail fixation. Right across from Water Tower Place itself, pause to refresh your spirits in the lovely, secluded little courtyard garden at the **Fourth Presbyterian Church** (866 North Michigan Avenue; 312-787-4570). A pleasant fountain helps muffle the noise of traffic, and you can sit together on any of several sets of steps to rest up for the next stop on your basketball pilgrimage.

DAY ONE: evening

DINNER

Soon it's time for a pregame dinner, and you're both likely to be in an even better mood after an *opaa* or two down in the old Greektown neighborhood. Gentrification has transformed what once was a fairly seedy strip along South Halsted Street, and nowadays there are at least as many upscale restaurants as there are gyros joints. A beauty, at the corner of Halsted and Adams Streets, is **Santorini** (800 West Adams Street; 312-829-8820), a name that evokes the sunny, whitewashed feeling of an island just for you. This newer breed of Greek restaurant serves sea bass as well as lamb, tiramisu, and baklava—and you really don't have to holler *opaa* when the saganaki flames.

A big plus of eating in Greektown is that it places you just a short cab ride—less than a couple of miles—from the United Center. Be sure to let your waiter know that you're heading for a Bulls game, so you'll be out in plenty of time to catch a cab and make your way with orientation time to spare.

Classic Chicago Couples:
MJ and JJ

They met when he was practically unknown, a tall young athlete who still recalls how this attractive young woman impressed him by paying her own way at the restaurant where her bunch of friends ran into his.

Now the parents of three, Juanita and Michael Jordan live a remarkably low-key life in the suburbs, where they've built a big house with plenty of room for extended family. They've seen more ups and downs than Michael has comebacks, but at this writing they're still together. And if we know everything we want to know about Michael, here's a telling story about Juanita: On the day the entire country watched her husband make his huge-ly hyped comeback to the Chicago Bulls, she skipped the game. It was out of town, and she had promised the kids they'd go see "Disney on Ice."

First things first. You can see why Michael married her.

When you reach the **United Center** (1901 West Madison Street; 312–455–4500), be sure to get a good look at the famous statue of Michael Jordan that went up after he returned to the Bulls from his foray into pro baseball. It's the sort of landmark people love to have their pictures taken in front of, so bring the camera and go ahead.

After a day on the Bulls beat, you might think you're jaded. But just wait and see: When the stadium lights go down, you'll fall for the thrill of the deep organ music, swinging spotlights, and the Bulls' announcer's tension-filled voice heralding "*your* Chicago Bulls!" The two of you are sure to feel a chill as the starting lineup is introduced.

Even the completely ignorant can follow the basic action in basketball and get caught up in the excitement of the game. The show that accompanies the game is eye-catching, too, what with wacky fans, cheerleaders, team mascots, and whatever else the marketing mavens have concocted. At halftime you can browse the lobby souvenir stands for a keepsake. (Your ticket stub would do, too, of course.)

Win or lose, Bulls fans—and many of the players—like to party after a game. Often they wind up at one of the fashionable restaurants on West Randolph Street, an old warehouse district that's rehabbing as fast as building permits can be procured. (It's also near Oprah Winfrey's offices and studio, Harpo Inc., which improves the stargazing prospects.)

One good Bulls bet is **Millennium** (832 West Randolph Street; 312-455-1400), a trendy spot where everything—chairs, tables, plates, portions—is a little larger than life, making things comfortable for those very tall guys. Even when crowded, it's a welcoming place for drinks, dinner, or dessert. The menu is dominated by prime steaks that don't come cheap, but there's plenty of variety.

Or stop farther west on Randolph—not far from the United Center, in fact—at **One Sixtyblue** (160 North Loomis Street; 312-850-0303), one of the most sophisticated, New York-ish spots in town. The design is stunning; the menu is eclectic; the prices are high; and the silent partner is—you guessed it—Michael. Cigar smoke may clog the air by late night, but that's power smoke you're inhaling.

FOR MORE ROMANCE

Time for equal time! Women's collegiate basketball gives you the chance to holler yourselves hoarse among fans just as passionate as the pros'. Several formidable women's teams play locally, but for convenience, you can't beat the UIC Pavilion (525 South Racine Avenue; 312-413-8421), where the **University of Illinois Chicago Flames** regularly burn up the court against stiff NCAA Division 1 Competition. Their location is logistically fantastic: minutes from downtown, accessible by any expressway as well as CTA, and close to the wonderful restaurants of Little Italy. Take in an afternoon match and you'll have plenty of time for a leisurely dinner just steps from the Pavilion at **Rico's Cafe La Scala** (626 South Racine Avenue; 312-421-7262). "They're so nice, they'll even make my favorite pasta when it's not on the menu," says veteran Flames fan Sabryna Cornish, referring to Rico's angel-hair pasta with fresh mozzarella and tomatoes.

Another nice plus: Women's collegiate basketball is affordable! Tickets for Flames' home games are just $10, and they're easily obtained through the school's Web site (www.uic.edu), or by calling (312) 413-8421.

Romantic Holiday on Ice

WHAT COULD BE MORE ROMANTIC THAN GLIDING on the ice, smooth and graceful, almost floating as you go? Cold and discomfort fade away as you zip along, and the only thing that could make it all even better is doing it with your sweetheart.

In Chicago, you can—right along the lakefront. We're lucky to have an excellent ice rink downtown, and hockey fans are even luckier: Chicago also has not one, but two pro hockey teams. The veteran Blackhawks of the National Hockey League trade time with the basketball Bulls in the United Center, while the upstart Chicago Wolves play at the northwest suburban Allstate Arena.

All in all, you're looking at a slippin', slidin' day of fun on ice. And it's a good chance to surprise your significant other with a mystery date: Get hockey tickets, make sure your companion knows how to stay up on the ice, then announce an expedition to a secret destination where you'll pull the laces tight and glide away together.

PRACTICAL NOTES: It's absolutely essential to call and check on whether outdoor ice is thick enough for skating. Also find out whether group lessons or an entertainment program is scheduled for the day and time you plan to skate.

Tickets to a Chicago Blackhawks game are easiest to get by mail. Get a schedule by calling (312) 943–7000 or by visiting www. chicagoblackhawks.com, and choose the game you want to attend. Send the team office a note with a check, and your tickets will be set aside *before* single-ticket sales begin. Single-game Blackhawks tickets

Romance
AT A GLANCE

◆ Take your skates downtown—or rent 'em on site—at the **Daley Bicentennial Plaza Ice Rink** (337 East Randolph Street; 312–742–7648).

◆ Warm up Cajun-style at **Heaven on Seven** (111 North Wabash Avenue; 312–263–6443).

◆ Peruse another kind of ice at the shops of the **Jeweler's Center at the Mallers Building** (5 South Wabash Avenue; 312–739–1606), or be kids again at **Navy Pier** (600 East Grand Avenue; 312–595–7437).

◆ Watch the pros in a game featuring the **Chicago Blackhawks** (at United Center, 1900 West Madison Street; tickets: 312–559–1212) or the **Chicago Wolves** (at Allstate Arena, 6920 North Mannheim Road, Rosemont; tickets: 312–559–1212).

◆ Get cozy over a postgame bowl of red at **Cheli's Chili Bar** (1137 West Madison Street; 312–563–9032).

range from a very affordable $15 to $250. Sales start in September for the first third of the schedule; the second and third parts go on sale in December and February, respectively. Tickets also are available through Ticket Master (312–559–1212), whose service charges can really add up.

Tickets to a Chicago Wolves hockey game range in price from about $9.00 to $40.00 and are available at the Allstate Arena box office or through Ticket Master (312–559–1212). The Wolves' staff is happy to help fans arrange all sorts of romantic surprises—whether it's booking a limo to whisk you to and from the game or helping to plan something more life-altering. "We have guys proposing here all the time," says account executive Andy Madden. To get your personal plan under way, call the Wolves at (800) 843–9658 or visit www.chicagowolves.com.

Most of this winter itinerary is easy to negotiate, even without a car. If you're staying downtown, you can walk to some destinations; others are an easy cab ride.

DAY ONE: morning

Start your day of wintry pleasures with a workout on ice. The slickest surface in town, as you'll soon see, is not on some City Hall pol's palm, but atop a stretch of downtown parking. The **Daley Bicentennial Plaza Ice Rink** (337 East Randolph Street; 312–742–7648) is the nice, flat top of the underground Grant Park parking garage, and its location gives you a wonderful view of Lake Michigan, Grant Park, and the skyline. The rink is open from 10:00 A.M. to 3:45 P.M. and from 6:00 to 10:00 P.M. weekdays; weekend hours are 10:00 A.M. to noon, 12:30 to 2:30 P.M., and 3:00 to 5:00 P.M. Admission is $1.50, which covers the whole day during the week or one of the two-hour sessions on Saturday or Sunday. (Senior citizens get in free.) Skate rental is $1.50 for adults, and the rink's amenities include music, a warm-up area, and vending machines.

LUNCH

When you've skated as long as you like, you're sure to be ready for lunch. One option is to slip out of skates and grab a cab into the Loop for lunch in a civic institution. At **Marshall Field and Co.** (111 North State Street; 312–781–1000), lunch is more than a meal; it's a Chicago tradition. The Walnut Room has been favored by generations of hungry shoppers, especially for its famous chicken potpie. The turkey club is good, too, and no matter what you have, save room for a dessert made with the store's signature Frango mints. Prices run from about $7.00 to about $12.00, and you can even get a beer or a glass of wine. *Caution:* Reservations are accepted only for groups of five or more, so you may have to wait. Try to come early or late; hours are 11:00 A.M. to 4:00 P.M. daily (noon to 3:00 P.M. on Sunday). *Extra caution:* If you're here around Christmas, the wait is interminable because of another tradition: lunch around the massive, beautiful Christmas tree.

You might prefer to go a block east to **Heaven on Seven** (111 North Wabash Avenue; 312–263–6443), a Cajun enclave in an otherwise nondescript office building. Two menus list "normal" food and such Cajun standards as red beans and rice as well as po'boy sandwiches. Regulars always check out the daily specials. Best of all, nothing costs more than $9.95. Heaven is open from 8:30 A.M. to 5:00 P.M. weekdays and from 10:00 A.M. to 3:00 P.M. on Saturday.

DAY ONE: afternoon

Once you're on Wabash Avenue, it's tough not to notice its abundance of great shopping. If you want to join the Chicago cognoscenti in searching out exquisite jewelry, stroll a little south to the **Jeweler's Center at the Mallers Building** (5 South Wabash Avenue; 312-853-2057; www.jewelerscenter.com). This art deco building, recently renovated to its original burnished splendor, is home to dozens of jewelers, importers, and dealers in gems and metals. From Shalom Wholesale Jewelry to Korea Gems to Bobby Precious Metals, someone here speaks your language. And they'll be happy to design your own piece, repair your watch, appraise a family heirloom, or sell you the engagement ring you thought you couldn't afford. Go ahead—it can't hurt to look.

Another option, and one that keeps you along the lakefront, is spending the afternoon at **Navy Pier** (600 East Grand Avenue; 312-595-7437). Take a cab over from the ice rink and get an eyeful of the weatherproof Crystal Gardens, a plant-filled atrium complete with trick fountains that's certain to help you forget Chicago winter.

The nice thing about Navy Pier—apart from the pleasure of being on the lake, no matter what the weather—is that there's so much to do. The Pier, once a crummy collection of warehouses, is now a beautifully renovated tourist destination with its own landmarks. You'll enjoy a pair of carnival beauties: a grand merry-go-round and a tall, tall Ferris wheel that, when lit in the evening, suggests the same faraway, wistful quality as the green light on Jay Gatsby's pier.

Tub for Two

For couples who need a rest after ice skating—who doesn't—here's a midday break your honey will never forget. Pamper your aching leg muscles, along with the rest of you, in a luxurious private hot tub at **Great Lakes Spa Suites** (15 West Hubbard Street; 312-527-1311). This very clean, perfectly respectable operation offers patrons a cozy little suite of their own in which to soak in a hot tub and shower afterward. Bathing suits optional, and towel service is available from the spa. Rates are $43 per hour for two, with VIP or presidential suites that also have a sauna at $53 or $63 per hour. Reservations are recommended, and there are special rates for weekday visits.

On a more practical note, remember that the Pier is home to the **Chicago Children's Museum** (312-527-1000). This is a terrific place to visit even if you're not a kid, and its presence means that Navy Pier is a consciously family-friendly place. (In other words, if you're kid-phobic, be forewarned!)

The Pier is also loaded with pleasant little shops, plus an IMAX theater if you'd like to experience a slam-bang film—perhaps on space travel, volcanoes, or the exploits of Michael Jordan. The Pier's food court has deli, Chinese, hot dogs, and the like. For a more upscale meal, grab a cab and head west—the general direction you'll be going in to head for hockey—and beat the trendies with an early dinner at **Watusi** (1540 West North Avenue; 773-862-1540). This hyper-hip spot does snappy takes on Latin American food—even the bread is spicy—and shows off nicely with a house special of roasted suckling pig. Dining early means you'll avoid the crowds that gather late, allowing you to focus on each other—or maybe on the value in atmosphere and attitude that comes with Watusi's moderate prices (dinner shouldn't run more than $60 for both of you).

If you're going to a Blackhawks game, consider taking the bus to the United Center (1900 West Madison Street). The Grand Avenue bus will take you west to Damen Avenue, where you can ride south to Madison Street. You'll want to take a cab back afterward, though, perhaps stopping to line up with other fans at **Cheli's Chili Bar** (1137 West Madison Street; 312-563-9032), a sports bar owned by former Hawk Chris Chelios that serves up a very warming bowl of red for only $3.50. (It's open only during the season—late after Hawks and Bulls home games—and Chelios is said to visit often.)

The CTA also can get you to Rosemont for a Chicago Wolves game. Take the Grand Avenue bus to the rapid-transit station at Grand and Dearborn, where you can catch the train that connects with the O'Hare line. Get off at River Road, then take the Pace bus to the Horizon. This may sound complicated, but, honestly, it's simple.

But enough about transportation: Let's talk about the game! We all know hockey is rough and prone to violence, but there's no denying the excitement of its fast-moving action and the players' spectacular skills. If the fights and fairly routine bloodshed bring on a squeamish spell, keep in mind that these guys are padded for protection and looking to win. Meanwhile, appreciate the speed and dexterity that are even more essential to hockey than strategy. Add the electricity of an intensely partisan crowd, and you've got your-selves a thrilling spectacle.

The crowd makes it easy to get caught up in the game, and you'll find yourselves hollering with abandon. Between periods, take a welcome break from screaming to browse the souvenir stands and maybe buy a keepsake. At the United Center, you'll find a good one that's not expensive if you pick up a Hawks puck (about $7.00).

Whether the home team wins or loses, you're both likely to feel exhausted from shouting and sweating. But you'll perk up nicely after a song at the **Redhead Piano Bar** (16 West Ontario Street; 312–640–1000; www.redheadpianobar.com), one of the friendliest of an all-too-rare breed. As you head homeward, devote your last bit of energy to cuddling up against the cold and enjoying some instant-replay reminiscence about your holiday on ice.

For MORE ROMANCE

If you'd like to surprise your sweetie with ice skating in July, head for the Chicago Park District's own **McFetridge Sports Center** (3843 North California Avenue; 312–742–7585), where year-round skating is interrupted only at the end of summer for refurbishing the ice. Call for information on open-skate times. Admission is $2.50 for adults; skates rent for $2.00, and the skate shop will sharpen your blades for only $4.00.

Out of this World

Stealing Away at Starved Rock

OMETIMES LEAVING THE CITY is the most romantic way for you to make time for each other. When you're interested in someone and want to know more; when you're in love and looking for a special interlude together—these are moments when you should consider getting out of town.

The area offers lots of getaway places, but not many of these lie in close proximity to the city. And you certainly don't want to spend half your time behind the wheel. So pick up the phone and start planning your escape to Starved Rock.

PRACTICAL NOTES: You'll need to drive to Starved Rock State Park. Remember to look ahead as you consider a Starved Rock getaway. If you have the flexibility, make it a midweek interlude; bookings are much more sparse at that time and the cabin you want more likely available. Also try for an off-season period; summer is the most popular, but the fall leaf-watching season is huge, too. Come in spring when it's muddy or in winter when it's snowy. The park is beautiful anytime. Don't forget to book dinner reservations at the Red Door Inn (815–223–2500) in Peru when you book at Starved Rock.

DAY ONE: morning/afternoon

Before you even hit the road, you'll have reserved a room or cabin at **Starved Rock State Park Lodge** (800–868–7625; www.starvedrocklodge.com). Plan well in advance; the lodge is very popular, especially in the summer and fall months. Reservations are

♦ *Steal away to **Starved Rock State Park's** rustically romantic lodge (815–667–4211).*

♦ *Book your own cabin—king-size bed, fireplace, and privacy.*

♦ *Surrender to the splendor of waterfalls, glacier-formed canyons, and stunning rock formations.*

♦ *Hike, fish, swim, ride horseback, play tennis.*

♦ *Dress up and indulge in an elegant dinner at the **Red Door Inn** (1701 Water Street, Peru; 815–223–2500).*

accepted two years in advance, and the most popular rooms are snapped up earliest.

To avoid such a wait, why not consider a getaway when you *really* need it—in the dead of winter? That's the time to rent cross-country skis by day and sink into a comfy couch by night. Or come in the spring, when early wildflowers bloom—as early as March, if the weather cooperates.

When you reserve, be aware that there's quite a bit of variation in accommodations. Romantically inclined visitors often like one of the lodge's private cabins, which feature their very own fireplaces and super-comfortable king-size beds. At $69 to $100 a night, they're an incredible bargain (subsidized by Illinois residents' tax dollars, so if you live in-state, don't be too grateful).

They are on the small side, however—basically a comfortable, self-contained hotel room—so if you want to spread out, try to get what many consider the best quarters in the place: a lovely room whose bay window looks out over the park (excellent for a rainy weekend) and whose sitting area offers a couch that's just right for two.

The lodge's other rooms are wonderful, too, although they don't offer the degree of privacy you'll have in your own cabin. But at $91 per night for a double, not many guests are complaining—even though meals are separate. Soothing green and mauve tones are featured in all the rooms' decor, and except for the rustic Pioneer cabins, each room and cabin has a television and VCR if you want to while away a couple of hours in seclusion.

To arrive at Starved Rock, you'll drive about 90 miles from downtown along I–80, out into the cornfields that tell you you've left the city behind. As you arrive and check in, be sure to make reservations at the lodge restaurant for lunch, dinner, and tomorrow's breakfast and lunch.

Take a moment to notice the lodge's classic woodsy look. In fact, if you've ever stayed in a rustic, northwoods lodge, you're likely to be struck by déjà vu. Unlike the many deluxe hotels and citified bed-and-breakfast homes elsewhere in this book, Starved Rock State Park Lodge offers the timeless lodge look of a rugged 1930s building—appropriately, since the lodge was a product of the Depression-era Civilian Conservation Corps, which put jobless men to work on public projects. Half a century later, a late-1980s renovation brought updating and the addition of more rooms to the main wing.

An excellent result of the renovation is the lodge's terrific swimming pool, complete with sauna and whirlpool, to let you take a delightful dip even in the midst of winter. Better yet, it's open until 10:00 P.M. (11:00 P.M. weekends), so you don't have to swim in daylight hours.

And there's the Great Room, which is just what a lodge should be: roomy yet cozy, welcoming guests to its central feature—a huge, double-sided stone fireplace that's the very image of outdoorsy. It's the kind of place that looks as if an out-of-the-way table ought to be devoted to the jigsaw puzzle everyone's been working on. (Well, why not bring your own?)

The Great Room can be a tad crowded on busy weekends; the Starved Rock lodge has a total of ninety-four rooms and cabins and is a family-friendly place. Again, that suggests an off-peak getaway if you want to be sure of getting one of those comfy Great Room couches to yourselves.

Depending on the weather, your mood, and your energy level, you'll want to settle into your cabin before choosing an activity. A swim might be inviting, or maybe you'd rather stroll the grounds for as long as it takes both of you to unwind. Or you could just warm up your cabin—maybe with the champagne you requested when reserving.

In any case, you're sure to wonder about the park's name. It comes from a tall sandstone butte that, according to legend, was the last stronghold of an Indian band at war with another tribe during the eighteenth century. Surrounded by their enemies, the group starved rather than surrender.

Staying Upright Together

Come to Starved Rock in January, and you can learn to cross-country ski together. The park's annual Winter Wilderness Weekend adds basic ski lessons to the usual ski rentals. If you learn together, you'll have a terrific aerobic activity you can continue together. Ask at the lodge for information, including dates and prices.

But that's the only grim note to this getaway. Your time at Starved Rock will be filled with outdoor fun or indoor relaxation. Ask at the desk for details on fishing, canoe rental, cross-country skiing in season, or going into the park on horseback. Tennis is an option in summer, and don't overlook the park's status as a naturalist's haven. With hundreds of species of plants and plentiful birds and other wildlife, the park is a joy for those who always pack their nature guides.

DAY ONE: evening

DINNER

Like its accommodations, Starved Rock's restaurant is a bargain you'd be happy to get at a much higher price. Prime rib tops the menu at $18, but fried chicken, fish, and other selections are less. And for vegetarians, lots of salads and a veggie stir fry are a nice accommodation. At these prices, your budget won't notice if you pop for one of the kitchen's excellent desserts at every meal.

Walk off the calories with an evening stroll or swim, then retire to the privacy of your cabin, where you don't need any hints on how to entertain yourselves.

DAY TWO: morning/afternoon

BREAKFAST

Breakfast in the lodge restaurant is an event in itself, especially for busy people who rarely enjoy a full spread of eggs, meats, and all the old-fashioned trimmings. And at $25 or less for both of you, it's tempting to indulge—especially in the Sunday brunch.

No matter what you choose for breakfast, be ready to walk it off as you explore the countryside. A stop at the park's Visitors' Center will get you oriented, with take-along brochures showing the park's trails and highlights. Marked trails total about 12 miles, with some trails as short as ¾ of a mile. Most of the trails cover easy ground, with sand surfaces and even a bit that's paved. The park's terrain makes stairs inevitable, but if you prefer to skip the strain, trails make it easy to arrange your walk so you'll arrive at stairs to go down instead of up.

Visitors are allowed just about everywhere in the park, so you can get up close to the park's namesake, as well as its canyons and rock formations. Hiking trails are so clearly marked, you won't get lost unless you want to be alone together. Be sure to try the one that leads to Lovers' Leap. It goes from the top of Starved Rock, down stairs, and through a left fork at a four-way intersection of trails. You'll zigzag through woods, climbing gradually to a T-intersection where you turn left and walk another 30 yards or so to another left fork. Down this way is Lovers' Leap, a good spot for smooching and schmoozing.

Eventually you'll make your way back to the lodge for lunch in the restaurant. Spend the afternoon outdoors again, or make it a sinfully lazy spell of doing absolutely nothing. You wouldn't be the first high-powered couple to come all the way to Starved Rock and spend most of your weekend sleeping, relaxing, or otherwise using your quarters.

DAY TWO: evening

DINNER

By dinnertime, maybe you're ready to stir. Take a drive—half an hour or so—to the little town of Peru, where the beautiful, quaint **Red Door Inn** (1701 Water Street; 815–223–2500) is the nicest restaurant around. Dating to 1850, the Red Door was built along the Illinois River, then, as now, a thriving commercial route. Today, restored by the charming local couple who run it, the Red Door serves informal lunches and elegant dinners to customers who come from many miles around.

The restaurant's choicest seating is in its lovely atrium, which overlooks the river (and makes a fine haven for nonsmokers). It's a wonderful spot to sip a before- or after-dinner drink together. The dinner menu is strictly fine-dining, with seafood, chicken, and many other entrees—but the house specialty, well worth trying, is a posh steak Diane cooked tableside. Best of all, the Red Door's prices leave Chicagoans smiling in relief—about $70 for both of you. Remember to make reservations, and to ask for specific directions at the Starved Rock Lodge desk.

DAY THREE: morning/afternoon

Enjoy another hearty breakfast in the lodge restaurant, then decide how much time you can devote to another hike before heading back to the city. You can also explore the neighboring **Mathiessen State Park,** just southeast of Starved Rock, where waterfalls tumble into the Vermilion River. Mathiessen's trails tend to be more challenging than those at Starved Rock. And Mathiessen is where you'll go during a winter visit to rent cross-country skis or ice skates—or even snowshoes, if you're really adventurous.

As you head for home, savoring the midwestern landscape, detour about 20 miles to the west and look for the town of Princeton. Here, at 1863 Highway 26, is a sweet reminder of nineteenth-century Illinois: a red covered bridge that's the last one in the state still open to traffic. Whether or not you're fans of *The Bridges of Madison County,* there's no denying the romance of this simple, sturdy structure.

DAY THREE: evening

DINNER

You'll know you're back in civilization if you stop for dinner at **Tallgrass** (1006 South State Street, Lockport; 815–838–5566). A century-old setting graced with exquisite breakables provides the backdrop for one beautiful presentation after another from the kitchen's thoroughly modern menu of up-to-date French cuisine. Your only decision is whether to go with the four-course dinner (at $45) or the five-course one ($55). Tallgrass serves dinner Wednesday through Sunday and is located north of I–80, about 35 miles southwest of downtown Chicago; ask for a map when you make dinner reservations.

FOR MORE ROMANCE

Look for farmers' markets or roadside stands as you make your way back to the city. Often there's more for sale than fresh fruits and vegetables. If you run across one that offers such other items as jams and jellies or handicrafts, make these your souvenirs of the weekend. Every time you butter your toast and open that jam, you'll think of each other—not to mention the warm feeling of curling up close under an afghan you bought together.

Romance and the Business Traveler
HOW TO SAVOR THE O'HARE AREA

OME VISITORS TO CHICAGO SEE no more of the city than can be glimpsed from a taxicab window. Technically, of course, they're in Chicago as soon as they land at O'Hare International Airport—but they get off the plane, check in at a hotel, and plunge into a round of meetings or presentations or sales calls. When it's finished, these all-work, no-play travelers turn around and fly back out again.

Not a bit of local color in the picture, and not a bit romantic—but it *could* be. Many business travelers have the clout and/or the frequent-flier miles to bring a sweetheart if they want to. Trouble is, they know in advance that there won't be time for a fun trip downtown, and why bother traveling with a cherished partner if you're certain business won't leave you a moment alone together?

Here's why: because it's *very* romantic to jet off anywhere with your partner. Because it's very romantic to plan a special evening together that will bring a sweet and soothing end to a hard day's work. Because it's very romantic to share a fabulous dinner and see a memorable show in the most pedestrian of places—Rosemont, Illinois, the community surrounding O'Hare. (*Note to Chicagoans:* Couples seeking weekend getaways could go here, too.) Although all the activity takes place in the course of one day and one evening, you and your partner presumably are already checked in at a hotel because of the business that brought you here, and you

Romance AT A GLANCE

◆*Book a swanky suite at* **Marriott Suites** *(6155 North River Road; 847–696–4400 or 800–228–9290) or* **Rosemont Suites Hotel** *(5500 North River Road; 847–678–4000 or 888–476–7366) near O'Hare.*

◆*Play golf at the* **Ramada Plaza Hotel O'Hare** *course (6600 North Mannheim Road, Rosemont; 847–827–5131).*

◆*Travel in style via* **Ace Limousine** *(773–549–5550).*

◆*Dine sumptuously at* **Nick's Fishmarket** *(10275 West Higgins Road, at Mannheim Road, Rosemont; 847–298–8200);* **Morton's, the Steakhouse** *(9525 West Bryn Mawr Avenue, Rosemont; 847–678–5155); or* **Carlucci** *(6111 North River Road, Rosemont; 847–518–0990).*

◆*Take in a musical at the* **Rosemont Theater** *(5400 North River Road, Rosemont; 847–671–5100) or a "big show" at the* **Allstate Arena** *(6920 North Mannheim Road, Rosemont; 847–635–6601).*

will probably return to the hotel to sleep rather than catching the red-eye out of town.

PRACTICAL NOTES: Plan, plan, plan! And note that while this itinerary covers an entire day and evening, you may take advantage of only parts.

Many business travelers are able to choose their own hotels. If you can, consider a suite for maximum comfort when you work. Two good choices in Rosemont are the Rosemont Suites Hotel at O'Hare and the Marriott Suites-O'Hare.

If business takes you to the Rosemont Convention Center, the connecting walkway from the **Rosemont Suites Hotel** (5500 North River Road; 847–678–4000 or 888–476–7366) will keep you out of the elements. Each suite opens onto a bright, art-filled central atrium where breakfast and a complimentary cocktail hour are offered daily. The hotel is decorated in Frank Lloyd Wright's Prairie style, which carries over into the suites' squared stained-glass lamps and muted red-and-white colors. Living rooms are smallish but somehow fit in a refrigerator, coffeemaker, microwave oven, and minibar. And the television is situated so that you can cuddle up on a comfy couch to watch. Beds are king size, but be sure to specify that (rather than two separate beds!) when you reserve. A machine-equipped exercise area overlooks the indoor pool. The hotel's fairly formal restaurant, **Basil's Kitchen,** has plush booths; choosing a corner booth makes you feel quite private. Suites start at about $109 nightly for weekend packages.

At the **Marriott Suites** (6155 North River Road; 847–696–4400 or 800–228–9290), light fills the large rooms of a suite when the elegant French doors separating bedroom (with king-size bed) from living room are opened. A writing table has its own little nook for quiet; baths are downright luxurious, and a refrigerator and coffeemaker are provided. Downstairs, a sunny outdoor deck extends the indoor pool's recreational space during summer. The hotel's restaurant, Allie's, is informal and pleasant; and one of the area's best restaurants, Carlucci, is next door in a connected building. Marriott rates vary, with weekend packages available for as little as $109 per night.

Another O'Hare-area hotel of special note is the **Ramada Plaza Hotel O'Hare** (6600 North Mannheim Road, Rosemont; 847–827–5131). Right in the heart of airport country, this foresightful hotel put in a nine-hole golf course. It's open when the weather is favorable (unfortunately, there's no planning for *that*) and is open to the public. Ask about tee times and other information.

DAY ONE: morning/afternoon

Making your romantic getaway as posh as possible is likely to mean a limousine. One reliable company is **Ace Limousine** (773–549–5550), which specializes in chauffering people around the O'Hare area. Available cars range from a Lincoln Town Car to a full-blown stretch limousine, and the wheels can meet you at the airport or hotel on as little as a couple of hours' notice. Charges are calculated on a trip-by-trip basis, which means that each time you're transported from one point to another, a separate trip will be calculated. For a special touch, they'll arrange to have a bottle of champagne waiting for you in the limousine (and charge you only for the price of the bubbly).

Before you pop the cork, however, at least one of you has some work to do. How to pass that time comes down to what the nonworking partner feels like doing solo. If you're limo-happy or are renting a car, you might want to spend the day shopping at one of the area's major malls. **Woodfield Mall** (at Golf Road [Highway 58] and Highway 53 in the farther-northwest suburb of Schaumburg; 847–330–1537) is one of the world's largest, with hundreds of stores under one roof. **Oakbrook Center** is in the tony suburb of Oak Brook (at Highway 83 and Twenty-second Street; 630–573–0700), and its outdoor grounds are as beautifully kept as its upscale shops. Hotel staff can guide you to either mall, and both offer first-run movies as well as shopping.

One unusual attraction in Rosemont is the **Donald E. Stephens Museum of Hummels.** Named for the village mayor, this museum features more than 1,000 of the little ceramic figures in the world's largest public display. Housed in the Rosemont Convention Center (5555 North River Road, Rosemont; 847–692–4000), the museum is open from 8:00 A.M. to 3:00 P.M. weekdays, and admission is free.

Don't neglect the pleasures of a lazy day spent working out, swimming, or just catching a cable movie at the hotel. All the better to help your hard-working honey relax when the day ends!

DAY ONE: evening

DINNER

As befits an airport-centered town, Rosemont offers a wide range of restaurants, so you'll be able to choose a cuisine (and an atmosphere) you both enjoy. Just remember: Many restaurants are accustomed to serving businesspeople, so you should mention when reserving that your focus is romantic. Let the restaurateur help you make the evening magical.

Romantic is just the word that comes to mind when people suggest **Cafe La Cave** (2777 Mannheim Road, Des Plaines; 847–827–7818), where the service is just wonderful and the continental menu goes for the kind of old-fashioned opulence that follows rack of lamb with a rich dessert. The big, formal dining room aspires to the Palace of Versailles, but the smaller "cave" room is where you'll find your own little world at an intimate corner table. (Mention "romantic" when you reserve, and they'll take care of it.)

At **Nick's Fishmarket** (10275 West Higgins Road, at Mannheim Road; 847–298–8200), fish and seafood are obviously the order of the day, as suggested by the big, beautiful saltwater aquariums (which some might feel bring dinner rather close while it's still swimming). Snuggle into one of those broad booths and feel the day's work drift away. When you get around to ordering, consider some of the Hawaiian specialties that are favorites of owner Nick Nickolas. If you're not the fishy type, you'll be pleased with chicken, steak, or pasta. Dinner for two will total about $100.

Morton's, the Steakhouse (9525 West Bryn Mawr Avenue, Rosemont; 847–678–5155) is located a short stroll from the Rosemont Suites Hotel, and it's where *Home Improvement* dad Tim Allen might take his sons to study the art of manly dining. Thick, toothsome steaks are the big draw, with prime rib and lobster also popular. Depending on the size of your steaks—they range from reasonable to cardiac alert—dinner may cost anywhere from $100 to $120 for the two of you.

The rustic cooking of Tuscany is the basis for the menu at **Carlucci** (6111 North River Road; 847–518–0990), where there's a bottle of olive oil on each table for dipping the delicious bread that will come your way as you're seated (again, mention when you reserve that you're looking for cozy; this room doesn't have many nooks). The delicious scent of a wood-burning fireplace in the open kitchen should put you in the mood for something roasted—maybe chicken, maybe mushrooms or other veggies—and of course there are pastas, too. Dinner should total around $80 to $100.

For your postdinner pleasure, Rosemont has two large-scale entertainment venues that are worth checking for the dates of your visit. The giant one is the **Allstate Arena** (6920 North Mannheim Road, Rosemont; 847–635–6601), which seats 18,500 people and holds the very biggest acts, from Bruce Springsteen to Luciano Pavarotti. Obviously this is not the place for an intimate romantic experience, but it may be a great opportunity to see a show you'd never be able to catch back home. The Allstate schedule also is of interest to sports fans, since it provides the home court for DePaul University's Blue Demons basketball team and the home ice for hockey's bad boys, the Chicago Wolves.

If you decide to take in a concert or other event at the Allstate, expect the attire and attitudes to be casual, and be prepared for lines at every turn (especially the women's bathrooms). On the other hand, the facility is clean and well kept, and people generally are polite, so a show here can make for a pleasant or even outstanding evening. Ticket prices vary enormously, from $10 for a college basketball game to $75 for such big names as Janet Jackson.

The cozier—and, let's face it, much classier—of this area's venues is the **Rosemont Theater** (5400 North River Road, Rosemont; 847–671–5100), which seats 4,200 and is elegantly decorated with glass, marble, and lots of shine. Accessibilty and variety in music are valued at the Rosemont, where crowd-pleasing fare like *Cats, Carousel,* and *Lord of the Dance* share the calendar with mainstream music from Barry Manilow, Luther Vandross, Amy Grant, and Michael Feinstein. You also could catch edgier acts, such as the Cranberries or Pink, as well as big-name comedy by Bill Cosby, George Carlin, or Jeff Foxworthy.

Rosemont probably has as many bars as it has restaurants, but the most satisfying spot for an after-show drink is likely to be your hotel bar—or even the cute little minibar up in your room, where dress is casual or even optional. It's the surest way to give your fellow businesspeople the slip and keep the end of the evening to yourselves.

FOR MORE ROMANCE

Bottom line: You're stuck at the airport, frazzled and in need of privacy. Search out these secluded spots, suggested by Monique Bond, who as spokesperson for the city's Department of Aviation knows every corner of O'Hare. In the relatively quiet Terminal 2, near the exhibit about airport namesake Butch O'Hare (a World War II airman), you'll find benches facing out the window for that public anonymity that suits lovers. At the end of the United Airlines C concourse, crowds thin and you can watch taxiing planes while you wait for yours. United's dimly lit "neon tunnel" is a little eerie yet romantic, especially with its permanent sound track, Gershwin's *Rhapsody in Blue.* And there's almost nobody riding the two-car tram that connects Terminals 3 and 5. Claim a car for yourselves, and you'll feel a lot better about waiting for your flight.

Un-Conventional
A Chance for Romance at McCormick Place

VERY YEAR MILLIONS OF PEOPLE come to Chicago for conventions or meetings at McCormick Place. It's big, it's sterile, it's crowded, and it's busy. It's built for hordes, not for couples. Yet many of these visitors are in desperate need of a romantic break. Maybe they've just met someone and hit it off—or they *would*, if they could just get away for a moment to focus on each other. Then there are couples who are partners in work as well as love and who find their only respite from glad-handing and deal-doing at McCormick Place when they're too exhausted to notice. Believe it or not, however, even the vast indifference of McCormick Place can provide stolen moments that lovers treasure. Romance in the face of adversity is perhaps the truest romance—so indulge yourselves.

TAKING A BREAK at McCormick Place

When you're in the thick of doing business at McCormick Place, a quick break may be the best one you'll get. So stop for coffee in the **Chicago Room** restaurant, which is on the East Building's mezzanine level, near the entrance from the Soldier Field parking lot. It's off the beaten path. "Most people don't find us right away," said the friendly woman who rang up my order ($3.00 for a twelve-ounce bottle of spring water; bring plenty of money when you visit McCormick Place). Better yet, this restaurant's walls are not glass; get a back corner booth or rear-wall banquette for privacy.

If you must get something done while making time for your beloved, head for the same East Building mezzanine area, opposite the escalators, or for the North Building's first-floor escalator area, around the corner from McDonald's and across from the Visitors' Information area. In both these locations, you'll find **shoeshine stands** where you can sit comfortably, hold hands, and whisper to each other as experts spiff up your footwear. (Remember to tip generously; a stingy sweetheart is a former sweetheart.)

The best way to escape the peculiarly time-suspended feeling at McCormick Place is to go outdoors. At the far south end of the East Building, look for the ramp to the underground garage and exit through the glass doors beyond it. (Don't go down; you'll wind up among the cars.) Just to your left is a grassy area set with rustic stone benches and circles of various sizes that look as if they're waiting for modern-day Druids—or modern-day lovers. They seem to invite you to sit down and enjoy the lake, which is practically at your feet. There's a sidewalk for strolling next to the water and a thicket of trees for atmosphere. Even the dim buzz of Lake Shore Drive's traffic sounds has a lulling effect.

It's also possible to get close to the lake upstairs in the East Building. Doors in the building's east wall of windows open to loading docks that overlook the lake. Usually a couple of chairs happen to be out there, too. It's worth slipping out if you can.

One other way to enjoy some of your time at McCormick Place is to take in a show at the East Building's **Arie Crown**

Theater (312-791-6000). When the Arie Crown isn't booked for convention-related programs, it often hosts popular-music programs and touring companies of Broadway shows. Check before you come to find out if there will be a show here that you'd like to see together.

GETTING out

Perhaps the greatest challenge of McCormick Place is leaving it. Avoid deadly cab lines—and impress your sweetheart—by arranging beforehand to be whisked away by limousine. Both the East and North Buildings provide a separate entrance for limos to pick up their passengers, and it's worth every penny to get out that easily. Remember, you don't need a giant stretch limo for just the two of you, which means you needn't spend a fortune; check on whether your company has a recommendation on which service to use. A good one is **Ace Limousine** (773-549-5550), which charges about $50 to zip from McCormick Place to your destination.

Whether you leave by taxi or limo, you can avoid possible construction tie-ups on Lake Shore Drive by *not* going north on the Drive. Instead take time to visit the nearby **Prairie Avenue Historic District,** along South Prairie Avenue from Eighteenth to Twentieth Streets, where the city's oldest building, the Greek Revival Widow Clarke House, stands. Here, too, the Pullman, Armour, and Field families built opulent nineteenth-century mansions, including noted architect H. H. Richardson's 1887 Glessner House. Regular tours are available Wednesday through Sunday, and you can arrange custom tours, too; call (312) 326-1480 for information.

Near both McCormick Place and Prairie Avenue is **Chinatown,** with its abundance of shops and restaurants. Perhaps the most romantic place to dine is the **Emperor's Choice** (2238 South Wentworth; 312-225-8800), with linen tablecloths and napkins, soft lighting, and a tank of tropical fish for serenity. Seafood entrees are popular here, and prices are low—less than $20 per person for dinner.

Another way to make a quick exit from McCormick Place is to take the South Shore Metra train to Van Buren Street and Michigan Avenue or to its terminus, at Randolph Street and Michigan. The train platform is at the North Building; go to the escalator area and

Ten Places to Steal a Kiss
at McCormick Place

It can—and should!—be done. In the North Building, look into the telephone area just beyond the Level 2 Business Center. The corner at the outside door is relatively secluded. Kitty-corner to this, all the way across the lobby and on either side of McDonald's, are two little nooks holding nothing but a few vending machines. Upstairs, overlooking the North Building's main convention floor, a deck is accessible by stairs on either side; more than a few conventioneers have strolled up there for a little light necking. And in the adjacent South Building, comfy chairs abound near the lobby's spouting sculptural fountain; go a level or two up, and you'll be alone.

Between the East and North Buildings, gaze out the windows of the long corridor spanning Lake Shore Drive traffic and, when you're sufficiently oblivious, kiss right in front of passersby. Or, in good weather, take the outdoor route below, with its flower-filled planters and inviting benches.

As you enter the East Building from the North, you're in a heavily trafficked lobby. But if you walk across the lobby, toward the Soldier Field parking lots, just beyond the crowds you'll notice an area where half walls around several vending machines create a private oasis. Downstairs, on the mezzanine level near the escalators, a space given over to phone facilities offers some semi-booths just big enough for two. Back upstairs, at the east end of the building, there's a low-walled area with change machines, vending machines, and padded benches; doors on the east wall, if unlocked, will let you sneak outdoors. A "Staff Only" area along this wall is likely to be deserted. And walking to the south brings you to the best bet of all: a stretch of small meeting rooms, usually open and often empty, where dim lighting and soft carpeting are a welcome change.

There. That's eleven places. Enjoy them.

look for signs to the platform. Signs may be makeshift due to construction, but pay attention, and they'll direct you there. The platform is outdoors, at the bottom of a steep stairway, and a must to avoid if it is deserted.

Leaving the train at Van Buren places you a couple of blocks south of the **Art Institute of Chicago** (Michigan Avenue at Adams Street; 312-443-3600). Stop in if there's time for a visit. (The Art Institute is described in greater detail in the chapter "Art and Soul:

Classic Chicago Couples:

Oprah and Steadman

Talk about broadcast communications: Here's a power couple. Oprah Winfrey, of course, is one of the nation's richest women, wildly successful in her television talk show, Harpo production company, and magazine venture. Her longtime squeeze, sports promoter Steadman Graham, is a terrifically handsome former athlete who is pretty darn successful himself. There is no rush to the altar for these two grown-ups, nicknamed "steady-as-you-go" for their long, long courtship. It works for them—so here's to love before marriage.

The Art Institute and More.") Or stay on the train to Randolph Street, and you'll emerge at the **Chicago Cultural Center** (78 East Washington Street; 312–346–3278). This civic treasure, noted for its Tiffany dome and light fixtures, once was the downtown library; now it holds a daily schedule of programs and exhibits and is home to the **Museum of Broadcast Communications** (open from 10:00 A.M. to 4:30 P.M. Monday through Saturday and noon to 5:00 P.M. Sunday; 312–629–6000).

DINNER

If you're in the mood for dinner, right across Michigan Avenue is **La Strada Ristorante** (151 North Michigan Avenue; 312–565–2200), an elegant, New York–style Italian restaurant where reservations are a must, and entrees range from about $18 to about $26. Or you might prefer to catch a cab for a trip about a mile north on Michigan to such top-of-the-line spots as the seafood lovers' **Cape Cod Room** (140 East Walton Place, in the Drake Hotel; 312–440–8486) or the **Ritz-Carlton** (160 East Pearson, in the Ritz-Carlton Hotel; 312–266–1000). There's even a relative bargain to be had at the **Ritz-Carlton Cafe,** where dinner for two comes in at about $60 to $70.

 Still have some energy left? Take the El or a cab up to **Pops for Champagne** (2934 North Sheffield Avenue; 773–472–1000;

www.popschampagne.com), a delightful wine bar that offers dinner by appetizer and live jazz every night. You needn't spend much more than $20 or $30 here to have a great time, especially if the weather is conducive to sitting outdoors in the garden. If the weather's that friendly, you may want to take an after-dinner stroll in the neighborhood as well.

Or heat up the night at **Chicago Firehouse** (1401 South Michigan Avenue; 312–786–1401), a much-talked-about spot in the far south Loop's newest nightlife area. For the hungry, dinner here offers comfort-food familiarity with a fresh-as-tomorrow twist. There's entertainment most nights, too, sometimes by the beloved jazz pianist Judy Roberts—who, coincidentally, also performs at Pops, above.

Asian Appreciation Weekend

I F YOU AND YOUR COMPANION LOVE the thrill of travel, you're in the right place. One of the wonderful things about Chicago is its incredible ethnic diversity. While this is more and more true of other cities nationwide, Chicago's ethnic angle is special. Here, there's some sort of critical mass that allows immigrants from all over the world to thrive while retaining their identities, customs, and languages. I've seen it among Poles, Hispanics, Chinese, Italians—you name it, there's a neighborhood grocery catering to it and parents praying that their children will continue to treasure it.

The Asian portion of this ethnic territory is especially fascinating because it's more than immigrants clinging to home. It's generations of Chinese who have created a community so independent and successful, its firehouse and banks and street signs carry Chinese characters as well as English. It's Vietnamese, Thais, Laotians, Koreans, and others pursuing the American dream by way of little restaurants where one family member—the one waiting tables—speaks English.

Asian Chicago is a great place to visit and to share the excitement of exploring another culture together. Here's how to go about it.

PRACTICAL NOTES: Although this itinerary's destinations are accessible by public transportation and cabs, it's more practical to use a car to reach the Chicago Botanic Garden in Glencoe and the two Evanston locations. And it should be pointed out that the exoticness of Asian Chicago is as seen through the eyes of a couple who are not of Asian descent.

Romance AT A GLANCE

♦ Sample sake and sushi at **CoCoRo** (668 North Wells Street; 312–943–2220), or try Taiwanese at **Mei Shung** (5511 North Broadway Avenue; 773–728–5778).

♦ Explore everyday life in the shops of **Little Vietnam** along West Argyle Street.

♦ Balance mind and body with a massage at **Ohashiatsu Chicago** (825 Chicago Avenue, Evanston; 847–864–1130).

♦ Savor the subtleties of Thai food at a four-star restaurant, **Arun's** (4156 North Kedzie Avenue; 773–539–1909).

♦ Meditate during Sunday-morning services at the **Midwest Buddhist Temple** (435 West Menomonee Street; 773–943–7801).

DAY ONE: afternoon/evening

Easing into your Asian-inspired weekend starts with booking yourselves into the most serene bed-and-breakfast I've ever seen. Represented by **Bed & Breakfast Chicago** (800–375–7084), this self-contained garden apartment is located on Fullerton Avenue, one of the North Side's busiest streets—yet to step into the apartment is to enter a sanctuary of quiet and grace, a home-away-from-home in which you're sure to feel an instant calm, no matter how chaotic things are outside.

Just approaching the apartment's outdoor entrance is an event, as you open your own little European-style gate and walk down a narrow passageway. Indoors, says the hostess, "I've kept things very simple—very clean, straight lines, really almost spare." That means soothing off-white walls, lights that don't glare, and low-pile carpet (perfect for sitting on the floor while you meditate). The furniture throughout is functional and comfortable: in the living room, a comfy sofa, bookshelves, a small television and VCR; in the adjacent dining area, just a table and chairs. The bedroom holds a nice big bed and not much else. The kitchen is Western, with enough work space for any meals you care to prepare, plus a dishwasher and washer and dryer for the practical side of life. The atmosphere throughout is as peaceful and inviting as you could want; the apartment rents for $135 to $155 per night for two people.

DINNER *option one*

Now that you've eased yourselves into a serene, pan-Asian state of mind, you can choose a specific country's cuisine when you're ready to head out for dinner. You can focus your evening on Japan by reserving a table at the chic **CoCoRo** (668 North Wells Street; 312–943–2220), where you'll see that there's much more to Japanese food than sushi. That's not to say you shouldn't try the sushi, of course, and an easy way to do it is by settling in at the restaurant's sushi bar, to the rear of the house. Here you'll also find kushi—nibbles of meats, seafood, and vegetables, popped onto a skewer and grilled simply, with little adornment.

These more familiar foods are a good way to keep your head while sampling another Japanese specialty: sake, the ancient and potent rice wine. CoCoRo has a wide selection of sakes that will start you off in educating your palates while you sip. Ask your server for guidance, and be careful not to overindulge; sake is serious drinking, and you might need your wits later. Your server also can help when it's time to choose an entree and you're faced with such difficult decisions as deep-fried soft-shell crab versus delectable Japanese beef.

CoCoRo is moderately priced, not more than $60 for both of you; if you finish dinner in a mood to wander, head a few blocks south to the Chicago River and a little east to La Salle Street. Just beyond the building that houses the city's traffic court, at 321 North La Salle Street, you'll find one of the more secluded, lesser-known spots in town to steal a kiss. Hide away and smooch immediately north and east of the bridge that spans the river at La Salle.

If you can tear yourselves away from necking, take a contemplative minute to gaze both east and west along the riverfront. Until recently, despite the pioneering presence of Marina City's landmark corncob towers, this now-developed expanse was a weedy netherland used mostly by tourists boarding sight-seeing boats. Today, as is evident wherever you look, it's a peaceful, pretty piece of downtown, with its own plazas, walkways, and gardens to explore.

This area also places you near plenty of nightlife, in which you can give yourselves over to the appreciation of American music that flourishes all over the world, including Asia. There's jazz at **Andy's** (11 East Hubbard Street; 312–642–6805), an institution among those who work in the area. Weekend evenings, the crowd comes in especially for the music, which goes on till after midnight at a modest cover charge (and a two-drink minimum on Saturday). Or go a little north to **Blue Chicago** (in two venues: 736 North Clark Street, 312-642-6261; and 536 North Clark Street, 312-751-2433), a slice of the South Side where many local veterans perform. Despite its locations, Blue Chicago doesn't feel like uptown, which is its appeal. Music starts at 9:00 P.M.; again, cover charges vary.

For a radical change of pace, stay with your Japanese theme and cut loose the way the Japanese do: with karaoke. **Hidden Cove Karaoke Bar** (5336 North Lincoln Avenue; 773-275-3955) is an undistinguished neighborhood bar—OK, perhaps a tiny bit seedy—but the mike is open nightly for the no-holds-barred sing-along that is karaoke. Sure, you'll make complete goofs of yourselves. But you'll do it together, and that's the whole point. If you're driving, don't bother looking for street parking; there are spaces behind the building.

DINNER *option two*

A completely different way to spend your evening is exploring one of Asian Chicago's ethnic enclaves, the area that has evolved into **Little Vietnam.** This stretch of several blocks along Argyle Street, right in the middle of the tough Uptown neighborhood, is a brightly lit, reasonably safe, bustling oasis of restaurants, grocers, and little storefront businesses. One of the best restaurants is **Hau Giang** (1104-6 West Argyle Street; 312-275-8691), where the decor is minimal, the better to focus on the food, and you'll have to bring your own beer or wine (from the liquor store down the block). If you're familiar with Vietnamese food, you know your hotness tolerance; if not, try spring rolls, satays, and a low-intensity beef, shrimp, or chicken entree. Or ask one of the servers for help; their English is fine, and they're very pleasant, although the efficiency level varies from speedy to snail-like. Relax and concentrate on Hau Giang's oh-so-reasonable prices, which make it difficult to hit $50 for two.

If you're willing to spend a bit more, go upscale to do it at what many consider the best Vietnamese restaurant in town. With its leafy palms, wicker furniture, and slowly whirling fans, **Pasteur**

(5525 North Broadway Avenue; 773-878-1061) evokes the languid atmosphere of an old French-owned plantation. The French influence peeks through in the menu, which carries the French seafood stew, bouillabaisse, as well as such Saigon specialties as an appetizer of crepes filled with chicken, shrimp, and mushrooms. Dishes from the northern capital of Hanoi include banh tom ngu, an appetizer of fried shrimp and yams, and pho, a soup that's finished with a flourish tableside. Entrees include the popular clay-pot chicken, Saigonese curry broth, and a sautéed whole Dungeness crab; vegetarians can choose happily from possibilities combining coconut milk, tofu, Asian eggplant, lotus root, and more. Prices are a bit higher than at other Vietnamese restaurants in the area, but you'll still be able to eat well for about $60 or $70.

For a Chinese dinner, try **Mei Shung** (5511 North Broadway Avenue; 773-728-5778), where the menu encompasses Taiwanese specialties as well as the more familiar Mandarin dishes. This is the place to try tofu (c'mon, park your attitude at the door), which is prepared with coriander and a zippy oyster sauce. I like the basil chicken, always a safe choice, but why not enlist your server's help in exploring the menu's more exotic selections? Mei Shung has no liquor license, but you're welcome to bring your own bottle. Here, again, prices are relatively low at about $30 or $40 for two, and you'll do well to take a patient attitude toward leisurely paced service.

Wherever you go for dinner, allow some time to browse through the grocery stores on Argyle Street. They're full of foodstuffs you probably never heard of; my Vietnamese sister-in-law makes a beeline here whenever she visits from her Florida home. Afterward, head back toward your quiet B&B and, perhaps, one of the nightlife spots mentioned earlier.

DAY TWO: morning/afternoon

Breakfast in your own little kitchen can be as Western as you want it to be, so stop to fortify yourselves before you head out for a day at the **Chicago Botanic Garden** (Lake-Cook Road at I-94, Glencoe; 847-835-5440). About 30 miles and a world away from downtown, this serene expanse of flora is a wonderful way to escape whatever you want to escape. In keeping with the weekend's Asian theme, you'll find a true respite in its Sansho-En garden, a three-island Japanese enclave.

Briefly, here's a bit of the garden's symbolism. Its pine trees represent long life, its lanterns represent water, and the rounded lines of its sculpted bushes stand in for hills and mountains. Even the rocks and gravel have meaning: Boulders represent islands, and gravel is arranged around them to suggest the motion of waves breaking on shore. One of the islands represents Horaijima, the island of everlasting happiness reserved for the immortals. (Including you and your sweetheart, of course!)

There's much more at the Botanic Garden, including a lovely English garden. But don't feel you must come during the summer. The Japanese garden keeps its character year-round, its evergreens pruned for winter with an eye to helping them catch falling snow. I've been here on bleak fall days, when there's neither foliage nor snow, and still felt much better for it. Admission is free, but parking is $7.00; the garden is open daily except Christmas from 8:00 A.M. till sunset. You needn't leave the garden to get some lunch, although the Gateway Center is more gift shop than gourmet haven.

LUNCH

If you prefer to eat Asian, head back south from Glencoe toward Evanston, the first suburb north of Chicago, where several Chinese and Japanese restaurants can give you a dandy lunch. **Kuni's** (511 Main Street, Evanston; 847–328–2004) offers some of the area's best sushi, sashimi, and maki. Noodle dishes are good, too, if you're not up to speed on the raw stuff. For maximum variety, order an assortment plate and share. Kuni's is open for lunch every day except Sunday and Tuesday (although dinner is available on Sunday), and prices, again, are reasonable: definitely less than $40 total for a very substantial lunch for the two of you.

Evanston also is the home of **Ohashiatsu Chicago** (825 Chicago Avenue, Evanston; 847–864–1130), where you can experience another Asian pleasure—the ohashiatsu massage. Combining Asian medicine with a gentle touch, this technique aims to achieve balance among body, mind, and spirit while tuning up your energy flow and balance. To schedule an appointment and learn more about ohashiatsu, call and leave your telephone number; your call will be returned.

When all your kinks are worked out, head back into the city and a dress-for-dinner stop at your B&B before dinner. In fact, now that you're practically stress-free, a nap might even be in order before you strike out for the North Side, where an out-of-the-way Albany Park restaurant will give you a memorable Thai meal.

DINNER

Arun's (4156 North Kedzie Avenue; 773–539–1909) isn't just a local favorite. It's one of the nation's finest Thai restaurants, offering regional specialties that go way beyond the satay circuit. Ask for help in putting together a dinner of compatible choices, or make it easy by opting for the Chef's Design menu, which offers an opulent array of six appetizers, four entrees, and two desserts. Even the rice is special here, its jasmine scent giving another note to everything. You won't have to bring your own liquor; try the Singha beer, which goes beautifully with this complex food, or choose from a wine list that has collected honors from *Wine Spectator*.

Like any fine restaurant, Arun's is pricey—the Chef's Design menu is a relative bargain at $85 per person when an a la carte dinner could creep into three digits—but it's one of a kind. Monday is the day off here, and make sure you reserve well in advance.

DAY THREE: morning

BRUNCH

Roll out of bed for brunch at **Garden Buffet** (5347 North Lincoln Avenue; 773–728–1249), a Korean spot that's short on atmosphere but long on authenticity. Open from 11:00 A.M. to 11:00 P.M. daily, Garden Buffet stocks its namesake buffet with everything from kimchee to sushi for an all-you-can-eat extravaganza that's a bargain at $16.99 per person. But you might want to consider an option you won't get back home: cooking your own entree on a charcoal-fueled

China in Chicago

If you only have time for a brief visit to Chicago's Asian community, head for the Near South Side corner of Cermak Road and Wentworth Avenue. You'll know you've found Chinatown when you see the pagoda-like buildings and huge red and green gate spanning Wentworth. Prepare to be startled by the feeling that you've suddenly landed in another country. From street signs to restaurant menus, architecture to ambient music, absolutely everything here is Chinese.

You'll enjoy strolling south on Wentworth, browsing through souvenir shops and comparing restaurant menus posted in windows. As you explore, you'll realize that Chinatown is more than a tourist destination. This compact, self-contained neighborhood holds banks, schools, grocery stores, churches, a firehouse, dozens of businesses, and hundreds of homes. Sure, it's touristy—but it's also a genuine community in which you can live long and comfortably without speaking English.

*Restaurants are Chinatown's major attraction, so arrive hungry. The most spiffy restaurant here is **Emperor's Choice** (2238 South Wentworth Street; 312–225–8800), where the table linens are linen and the service is pleasant. Try the lobster-centered dinner for two, which will make you feel quite sumptuous for a thrifty $40.*

If you'd like souvenirs that outclass T-shirts, look for jade. There's plenty here, in designs you might not see anywhere else, and the prices are good. Coolest souvenir: If each of you has at least one pierced ear, buy and split a pair of jade earrings.

brazier that's brought to your table. Many fans never vary from the tangy short ribs, but others choose chicken, pork, beef, or shrimp. If you're feeling *very* wide awake, the restaurant has a karaoke room, too.

A different Sunday morning option—and a good choice if you'd like to go deeper into the Asian spirit than a surface-skimming weekend—is joining the nonmembers who are welcome to visit Sunday services at the **Midwest Buddhist Temple** (435 West Menomonee Street; 773–943–7801). The morning starts early, with a meditation service at 8:00 A.M. The service contains several sections, with sitting, walking, and a brief talk, then a question-and-answer period. At 10:00 A.M., there's a service proper in English, which is followed by a Japanese-language service at 11:45 A.M. Be sure to dress appropriately—a skirt, dress, or nice-looking slacks for women, neat slacks for men. Shorts, sport shirts, and similarly casual attire are out.

Afterward, continue a couple of miles farther north to visit the Asian shops along Belmont Avenue. (If you want to take the El, the Fullerton stop is a few blocks west and north of the temple, and you'll be right where you want to be when you exit at Belmont.) The largest is **Toguri Gifts and Mercantile Co.** (851 West Belmont Avenue; 773–929–3500), where the staff is friendly and chatty, and the merchandise is authentic. Check out various kinds of Japanese slippers, including the ones that you wear anchored between second and third toes. They're actually comfortable, and you can get special cotton socks to accommodate them. One item to check out is a Salux "beauty skin cloth," a yard of textured nylon that seems expensive at $4.95. But take a chance and take it home. It's the greatest for scrubbing your back in the shower, as you'll learn if you buy one and try it on each other.

Other intriguing stuff: beautiful paper kites in many sizes, all brightly decorated and ready to fly; delicate porcelain tea sets and sake sets; all sorts of incense; pretty wrapping paper and stationery; exotic candies and cookies; and all sorts of children's accessories decorated with Hello Kitty, the wide-eyed feline that's more insipid than Barney. It's all pretty cool and fun to look at.

LUNCH

To take in another experience that lets you know you're not in Kansas anymore, go west to the major intersection of Lawrence Avenue and Western Avenue, which is in the Lincoln Square neighborhood. Then go a few blocks farther west to the **Korean Restaurant** (2659 West Lawrence Avenue; 773–878–2095), a nondescript spot where decor is hardly the point. This round-the-clock restaurant serves a huge variety of Korean specialties, from grilled meats and fish to still more selections you won't know how to pronounce. But try anyway, especially if you notice something you'd like that can be cooked at your table on a gas grill. You'll get plenty of food at a minimal price—not more than $20 or so total.

For more romance

If you'd like to explore the Asian art of meditation, consider signing yourselves up for a five-week beginners' minicourse at the **Peace School** (3121 North Lincoln Avenue; 773–248–7959). Usually held on Monday evenings, the minicourse teaches students a breathing-based meditation technique that also uses visualization to start participants on the way to emptying their minds of life's stresses. With its promise of relaxation and *myung sahng,* or "bright thinking," the technique offers an optimistic outlook that's bound to be a plus for anyone. The minicourse costs $50, and completing it qualifies students to attend free half-hour sessions every Monday, Wednesday, and Friday evening at the school.

Love in the Hot Zone
A TROPICS-INSPIRED WEEKEND

WHETHER YOU DO IT IN THE HEAT OF SUMMER or the chill of winter, a warmed-up weekend in Chicago is the next best thing to visiting the tropics—on four continents. The city's Hispanic and Indian populations each support a vibrant cultural life that welcomes others to join in; so does a sizable community of islanders, Jamaican and others, whose special foods and hypnotic music have seduced many a northerner. Chicago has Turkish steam baths, Middle Eastern nightclubs, Ethiopian restaurants, and more. It's a melting pot indeed, one in which each ingredient retains its own zesty flavor. Whether you revel in your own ethnic link to one of these cultures or delight in the exploration of ethnicities outside your own, this round-the-world, all-over-town weekend will heat up your all-American love life.

PRACTICAL NOTES: This itinerary takes in some far-flung destinations, so it's most practical to drive. If you prefer cabs, they should be plentiful.

DAY ONE: evening

Stay in the hottest new hotel in town, **W Chicago Lakeshore** (644 North Lake Shore Drive, 312–943–9200; www.whotels.com), where the lakefront view is breathtaking, especially from the Altitude lounge. This rooftop room takes the top-of-the-world feeling a step further by putting you in motion—revolving so slowly that you're not quite aware of moving unless you look out the windows that surround you. Some find it disconcerting, some enchanting, but there's no disputing the fabulous view.

♦ Wake up to a tropical brunch at **La Fonda** (5350 North Broadway; 773–271–3935).

♦ Luxuriate in a Turkish steam bath at the century-old **Division Street Russian Baths** (1916 West Division Street; 773–384–9671).

♦ Play with your food—it's polite to eat Ethiopian food with your fingers—at **Addis Abeba** (3521 North Clark Street; 773–929–9383).

♦ Just a few doors down, "lively up yourself" with reggae at the **Wild Hare & Singing Armadillo Frog Sanctuary** (3530 North Clark Street; 773–327–4273); then applaud late-night belly dancing at **Al Khayam** (2326 West Foster Avenue; 773–334–0000).

♦ Shop the subcontinent in the Indian grocery stores, sari boutiques, and jewelry shops along **Devon Avenue** (6400 north, west from Western Avenue).

Of course, you're here for a room, too, and that view is available from many of the W Chicago Lakeshore guest rooms. Ask when you book—you won't be surprised to learn that rooms with lake views cost a bit more than those overlooking the city—and be prepared for rates on the high side (perhaps $250 a night). Then again, The W Chicago Lakeshore offers every comfort in addition to that view, from king-size beds to a "Munchie Box" of snacks for when you need a little something to go with the local microbrew you'll find in the minibar.

As you head into the night—or perhaps on your way back—stop in at the hotel's restaurant, **Wave,** which has generated a high level of nightlife buzz among the fashionistas. Head for the raised level that surrounds the main dining area and see if you can't score one of the little nooks that let you snuggle in near secrecy.

DINNER

Head out to begin the evening with mai tais at a downtown spot so retro, it's hot again. **Trader Vic's** (in the Palmer House Hilton, 17 East Monroe Street; 312–726–7500) is an over-the-top, bamboo-bedecked Polynesian paradise of the sort that never existed except in Western imaginations—but go for it anyway! Pull up a potent fruit concoction and, if you have the luck to be here between 4:30 and 6:30 P.M. on a weekday evening, help yourselves to the complimentary Tiki Time buffet. No matter what the hour, nibble as you sip; and do take a moment to discuss the charms of the Tiki aesthetic.

When you're ready to move on to a late dinner—in the tropic-zone manner, surely not before nine—switch seas from South Pacific to Caribbean at **Nacional 27** (325 West Huron Street; 312–664–2727). You'll be greeted with rhythm-drenched music that heralds a wide-ranging, strictly festive celebration of Latin America's twenty-seven nations, from Cuba to Argentina. If the weather's suitably sultry, you can get in the swing by dining outdoors—Chicago's climate certainly swelters on many a summer night. Indoors or out, Nacional 27's menu offers creative fish and lighter-side entrees alongside classics like ropa vieja and, for dessert, a creamy flan; spicing it all is music to get you up and dancing. Prices hover at the high end of moderate.

Friday and Saturday evenings, you can salsa up a storm or make merengue your own at Nacional 27—but if you want to shake it till the really wee hours, head for a Hispanic haven that pulses until 4:00 A.M., even on Tuesday. **Club 720** (720 North Wells Street; 312–397–0600) is an intoxicating swirl of Latin musical styles, with live salsa bands upstairs from thumping Spanish-language rock or downstairs from DJ-driven dancing. It's frantic, it's friendly, and it's definitely not boring.

DAY TWO: morning

BREAKFAST

Start the day—not too early, of course—on a full stomach, courtesy of **La Fonda** (5350 North Broadway; 773–271–3935), a little Colombian storefront in the classic family-run model. This one's a cut above many, though, with a charmingly rustic look and warm, friendly service that belies its low prices. A weekend brunch buffet offers all you can eat of all kinds of specialties; I always want arepas, a corn cake filled with mushrooms and cheese. (The deluxe version has shrimp and a red-pepper aioli, too.) My friends Julie and Jose Riesco don't always agree in the kitchen—she's Mexican, he's Cuban—but they both adore La Fonda's sancocho de res, a beef soup that will fortify you for absolutely anything.

You might enjoy exploring this polyglot area, where practically everyone seems to be from an exotic homeland—Pakistan, Africa, Haiti, or somewhere you can only guess at. Keep in mind that it's off the beaten track for out-of-towners, so you'll want to be big-city careful.

Back south, prepare to relax at **Division Street Russian Baths** (1916 West Division Street; 773-384-9671), where men have gone to escape home and hearth since 1906. Happily, the baths have moved into the twenty-first century with the addition of facilities and hours for women, who are welcome on Wednesday, Friday, Saturday, and Sunday from 10:00 A.M. to 10:00 P.M. In the only "hot room" of its kind in the city, a large granite stone keeps dry heat going; there's a vapor room to improve the skin, a whirlpool for tired muscles, and massages (from masseuse or masseur) to promote relaxation.

Visitors pay $20.00, which includes a refundable $1.00 deposit on a lock for the locker where you'll store your clothes. Two towels, a sheet, and soap are provided. You'll find diversity aplenty in your fellow bathers, who may be Russian, Hispanic, African-American, or young Americans who live in Ukrainian Village, the regentrifying neighborhood you're in.

The only drawback is that men and women are separated while in the baths, so you'll have some time apart. When you get back together, you might want to spend some time exploring the area around your B&B, which is its own kind of "hot zone"—a neighborhood where relatively cheap housing has attracted the artists who then attract other, more moneyed residents. If you happen to come during September, try to catch the Around the Coyote festival of local art and artists.

DAY TWO: evening

DINNER

Or maybe you'd like to follow the time-honored tradition of hot countries everywhere by taking an afternoon siesta. Either way, when it gets to be dinnertime, tackle a new kind of dining at **Addis Abeba** (3521 North Clark Street; 773-929-9383), where Ethiopian food offers both new flavors and the delightful experience of eating with your fingers. People often try to come here with a group, the better to sample as much as possible, but don't hesitate to

A Shoe-In

Looking good for love in the hot zone can be a challenge. I, for example, wear a size 4 shoe, and the high heels that a truly sultry look requires are very, very hard to find. But even I can choose from a variety of little platforms and very high heels at Skyscraper Heels (2202 West Belmont Avenue; 773-477-8495), where they carry platforms, boots, and sandals in every imaginable style, and color, up to a whopping size 15. There are a few corsets, too, but the shoes are likely to keep you busy for a good long time. Enjoy!

be adventurous in a group of just the two of you. If more exotic selections seem a trifle too off-beat, stick with vegetarian entrees from the inexpensive-to-moderate menu.

To dance another night away, stroll down the block to the **Wild Hare & Singing Armadillo Frog Sanctuary** (3530 North Clark Street; 773-327-4273), a Chicago institution for folks who love reggae—and that's not just Jamaicans. The Wild Hare is crowded nightly with fans of this hypnotic, languid beat that's perhaps the easiest in the world to dance to. Cover charges vary, depending on the entertainment; or weekend evenings there's usually a band. Let your bodies sway to the rhythms of the islands. (Don't be surprised if you notice the distinct aroma of Jamaica's most famous—if illicit—cash crop.)

To wrap up your evening in astonishing style, head a little north and west to **Al Khayam** (2326 West Foster Avenue; 773-334-0000), where things don't really get going until after midnight. When they do, your senses will be awakened by a Middle Eastern mix of music, dance, and drink, highlighted by a belly dancer and singing that might be in Arabic, Hindi, Kurdish, Greek, or Assyrian. You can join in the dancing if you like; don't bother being self-conscious, but don't feel you have to dance, either.

DAY THREE: morning/afternoon

BRUNCH

Do you have to be told to sleep in today? Probably not, so brunch is a natural instead of breakfast. Sample one more exotic region by

driving to the **Devon Avenue** Indian neighborhood, a center of
Indian and Pakistani life for the entire city. At **India House
Restaurant** (2548 West Devon Avenue; 773–338–2929), Sunday
brunch is served from 11:30 A.M. to 3:00 P.M. and includes food and
drink you may not be able to pronounce, let alone recognize—so
feel free to ask the staff for guidance. Plenty of vegetarian dishes are
available, as are mango shakes (yum!) and the yogurt drink, lassi,
for the health-conscious. There's also chicken, seafood, and meat if
you're up for a full meal.

After brunch, step outside, look around, and you'll see that once
again, you're in a fascinating neighborhood. Venture into a "sari
palace" and look through the hundreds of bolts of exquisite fabrics,
perhaps choosing something irresistible for yourself or your partner.
Get yourselves buzzed into a jewelry store and find stunning neck-
laces, ankle bracelets, and earrings, intricately worked in twenty-
two-karat gold and precious stones. And don't miss **Patel Bros.**
(2610 West Devon Avenue; 773–262–7777), a grocery that could
change your life in the kitchen. Floor-to-ceiling shelves on an entire
wall hold neat stocks of so many spices, your nose will spin. More
varieties of rice and lentils than you ever dreamed possible are here,
too, as well as canned goods you won't find at the supermarket back
home. If you enjoy cooking together, be sure to look through an
Indian cookbook before you come and bring a shopping list. On
the way out, pick up a purple can of delicious passion-fruit soda.

City Slickers' Western Weekend

Y*EE-HA!* CHICAGO'S A BIG CITY, but it's got a country heart—if you know where to look. And the funny thing is, you'll find it all over town.

A friend once told me that she liked Chicago because it's a place where you can reinvent yourself without having to leave town. If you've ever harbored a secret wish to be a cowpoke (and what red-blooded kid didn't?), this here's the place, right now's the time, and look who you've got to ride with!

So git along and saddle up for a weekend that's a little bit country, a little bit western, a little bit Mexican, and a whole lotta fun. Bring your drawl, if you have one. If not, just bring the sweetheart of your personal rodeo. Y'all are all you need anyway.

PRACTICAL NOTES: You'll need a car for some of this weekend's stops, most notably the rides to FitzGerald's and Forest View Farms. City destinations can be reached by cab, but not those two.

DAY ONE: evening

Luckily for all us comfort-lovin' city folk, this countrified weekend doesn't mean tossing the ol' bedroll on the ground in Grant Park. You can keep to the western theme (at least nominally) at the **Best Western Inn of Chicago** (162 East Ohio; 312–787–3100). Located in the heart of city-slicker land—on the posh Gold Coast, just off Michigan Avenue—the Best Western dates back to the early years of the twentieth

◆ Hang your hats on the Gold Coast, pardner—at the **Best Western Inn of Chicago** (162 East Ohio; 312–787–3100).

◆ Sample a sophisticated cuisine you never knew existed at the finest Mexican restaurant north of the border: Rick and Deann Bayless's' **Frontera Grill** (445 North Clark Street; 312–661–1434).

◆ Stomp up a storm while you learn line dancing at **Willowbrook Ballroom** (8900 South Archer Avenue, Willowbrook; 708–839–1000).

◆ Find authentic cowboy hats, embroidered shirts, genuine snakeskin boots, even rodeo gear—everything you'll need to outfit yourselves at **Alcala Western Wear** (1733 West Chicago Avenue; 312–226–0152).

◆ Saddle up for a canter-guided along tenderfoot-friendly trails—at **Forest View Farms** (5300 West 167th Street, Tinley Park; 708–560–0306).

century, when it was the St. Clair, one of those independent little hotels that regular guests treasure. Refurbished for today, with cool grays, glowing greens, and health-club facilities next door, it retains a friendly ambience at Michigan Avenue rates (starting around $99, or $175 for a suite). A sibling hotel, **Best Western River North Hotel** (125 West Ohio; 312–467–0800), is just west of State Street in the fashionable district from which it takes its name. With similar rates and accommodations (River North does boast its own indoor pool), either offers a comfortable home from which to explore the West—Chicago-style.

DINNER

To dine like gauchos, head for the Brazilian **Fogo de Chao** (661 North LaSalle Street; 312-932-9330), where staggering slabs of grilled meat are an all-you-can-eat carnivore's fiesta. Or take a fine-dining drive to **Courtright's** (8989 South Archer Avenue, Willowbrook; 708-839-8000), where an emphasis on the freshest local foods means entrees like farm-raised rabbit and house-aged beef. Ask about the tasting menu, which lets the chef's choices shine at a reasonable price.

Courtright's is less than a hoot and a holler from **Willowbrook Ballroom** (8900 South Archer Avenue; 708–839–1000;

www.willowbrookballroom.com). Every other Friday, this old-fashioned wooden floor rings with boot-stompin' steps as country line
dancers gather from all over town to kick up their heels. The fun runs
till midnight, and if you can make it during the week, there's a line-
dancing lesson every Monday and Tuesday. At $6.00 per person for
either dancing or a three-hour lesson, Willowbrook is a bargain that's
worth the travel. To get there, take Lake Shore Drive south to I–55 and
exit the highway at La Grange Road. Continue south on La Grange till
you see the turnoff for Archer Avenue and take that for a couple of
miles, when you'll spot Willowbrook on the right side of the road.
(Of course, the same directions will get you to Courtright's.)

DAY TWO: morning

BRUNCH

Start your day with a brunch to tell the folks back home
about. As you'll learn at the **Frontera Grill** (445 North Clark
Street; 312–661–1434), Mexican food is much more than
margaritas and mole. Chef-owner Rick Bayless is a former student of
anthropology who lost his objectivity by falling in love with the
food of the nation he studied. With his wife, Deann, Bayless has
become one of the nation's most accomplished students of Mexican
food; the couple have made Frontera and its fine-dining sibling,
Topolobambo, destinations for serious connoisseurs from all over.

Saturday brunch goes on from 10:30 A.M. to 2:30 P.M., and since
Frontera accepts reservations only for groups of five or more, you
have to wait. Be cheerful about it, and your reward will be subtle,
delicious dishes you'll never even hear of beyond the villages of
Mexico. Frontera is one of those restaurants you can tell friends
back home about, and if they know anything about restaurants,
they'll be impressed with your sophisticated selection. Better yet is
the modest price: Expect brunch for two to run about $30.

DAY TWO: afternoon

Even the roughest rider gets a kick out of approaching **Alcala
Western Wear** (1733 West Chicago Avenue; 312–226–0152), where
the full-size horse out front lets you know this is the place. Browsing

indoors, you'll find absolutely everything for the well-dressed cow-poke of either sex. The aisles are filled with boots and hats, fancy shirts and real jeans, silver accessories, and leather everything. There's genuine riding gear, too, and it's western, not English—chaps, spurs, short crops, saddles, and more. Don't miss the tore-ador outfits in the rear and the glass display cases throughout the store, in which turquoise jewelry and elaborate belt buckles are art-fully arranged around real rattlesnakes (dead, thank you).

Another authentic aspect to this Tex-Mex haven is its bilingual whoopin' and hollerin'. There's no problem if you speak only English, but Spanish is at home here, too. And nobody minds if you want to spend your time just looking.

As you head back to the Best Western temporary homestead, you might take some time to enjoy all-American art at the **Terra Museum of American Art** (664 North Michigan Avenue; 312-664-3939). Or check out the hallway near the lower-level cafeteria at the **Art Institute of Chicago** (Michigan Avenue at Adams Street; 312-443-3500), where several examples of Frederic Remington's Western work are on display.

DAY TWO: evening

DINNER

This is a day whose only appropriate dinner is a succulent steak, and Chicago—a meat-and-potatoes town if ever there was one—does not disappoint. There are several top-notch steak houses not far from the hotel, and your main decision is likely to be based on atmosphere.

The traditional steak house is a rowdy place, so if you prefer somewhat quieter surroundings, make reservations at **Eli's the Place for Steak** (215 East Chicago Avenue; 312-642-1393). Eli's is a Chicago institution, the kind of place that pops up regularly in the newspaper gossip columns. From local socialites to Sinatra himself, Eli's has always been a favorite among discerning carnivores. Prices are reasonable: A sirloin will run about $28, and many a regular wouldn't dream of skipping a side of potato pancakes. Save room for dessert, too; Eli's cheesecake is famous all over town.

Another institution is **Morton's The Steakhouse of Chicago**

Classic Chicago Couples:
Potter and Bertha Palmer

Chicago was not long past its own days as a wild, woolly western outpost when Mr. and Mrs. Potter Palmer became its first and perhaps finest "power" couple. Potter was an enormously influential real estate baron; his Palmer House hotel carries on today, and he was the first to build a palatial home on what eventually became Lake Shore Drive—still the finest address in town. His equal in moving and shaking was Bertha Honore Palmer, who was one of the prime organizers of the World's Columbian Exposition in 1893 and an early fan of French Impressionism, especially the work of Claude Monet and of her own friend, Mary Cassatt. If you go to the Art Institute (one of her great beneficiaries), look for the portrait of her that I always think of as "the fairy princess." And by the way, in the twenty years between her husband's death and her own, this twinkling beauty more than doubled the fortune Potter had left.

(1050 North State Street; 312–266–4820; www.mortons.com), where part of the draw is maître d' Raki Mehra, a smooth professional who, when asked, can help assure your evening will be special. The steaks alone would do it, of course; Morton's stood fast during the lean years when steaks were out of fashion (actually, the Morton's crowd never noticed steaks were out of fashion), and its gigantic double porterhouse is still a standard. This 48-ounce stunner costs about $60 and, need it be mentioned, definitely will feed both of you.

A newer spot that's favored by the stretch-limo set (meaning you just might spot a hungry celeb) is **Gibsons Steak House** (1028 North Rush Street; 312–266–8999). While hardly a soothing experience, the hustling, bustling Gibsons delivers a superb sirloin at about $64 for two. If your romance is rock-solid, get a side order of garlicky sautéed spinach.

With a belly-bustin' steak dinner finished, your major decision for the remainder of the evening is whether you're up for a drive. If so, go west on I–290 about twenty minutes to the suburb of Berwyn—the home of one of the area's very best music clubs. **FitzGerald's** (6615 Roosevelt Road, Berwyn; 708–788–2118) has provided countrified Chicagoans with a steady stream of shows by many of the current crop of Texan singer-songwriters, including Butch Hancock and Jimmie Dale Gilmore. The club's eclectic booking policy embraces jazz, blues, and some rock, too, so check on who's booked during your stay. Tickets are in the $5.00 to $15.00 range and often are available in advance. FitzGerald's is a bar, though, so if you want to sit right up front, you should arrive early.

Prefer to stay in the city limits? There are plenty of places to hear a twangy guitar not far from the Near North Side steak houses mentioned earlier. One is the remarkable **Cubby Bear** (1059 West Addison; 773-327-1662), a bar kitty-corner from Wrigley Field that has showcased acts ranging from Johnny Cash to Jo Carol Pierce. It's crowded and can be smoky, but imagine seeing the Man in Black up close in a neighborhood bar. Tickets to that show were $30 apiece, but prices that high are rare. Like FitzGerald's, the Cubby Bear books a wide range of acts, so you'll want to check on who's playing when you visit.

Several other clubs book a broad range of country and western, rockabilly, Tex-Mex, and similar musical styles. One great spot is **Schubas** (3159 North Southport Avenue; 773-525-2508), a friendly bar that is favored by many discerning fans of country and its relations, and where cover charges won't set you back much. Check on who's playing, and be open-minded. You may be lucky enough to catch a performer you both adore, or maybe you'll take a chance on someone you don't even recognize. Either way, it could be an experience that gives you and your country cutie a memory to treasure.

DAY THREE: morning/afternoon

BRUNCH

Skip the hardtack-and-bad-coffee part of down-home livin' and start your day with a Sunday-mornin' barbecue brunch. **Brother Jimmy's BBQ** (2909 North Sheffield Avenue; 773-528-0888) opens at 11:00 A.M. on Sunday to serve geographically distinguished barbecue, northern being sweet-sauced and southern vinegary. There's also fried chicken and, of course, *good* coffee to wash down a pecan-pie dessert. Brother Jimmy's is sometimes crowded and can be casual to a fault, but it's a great place to get your rib fix at reasonable rates. In fact, if you want to pull up a chair and stay put, a Sunday all-you-can-eat deal covers ribs and beer for just $18.95 per person.

Or tear yourself away from that barbecue and head out (about an hour's drive) to the southwestern suburb of Tinley Park. Here you can saddle up for real at **Forest View Farms** (5300 West 167th Street, Tinley Park; 708–560–0306). Set near the extensive recreational holdings of the Cook County Forest Preserve, Forest View is a stable that rents horses for guided trail rides along the forest preserve's system of trails. The stable is as friendly to the tenderfoot as the experienced rider, says stable hand John Meyers. "If you don't want to run or gallop, you don't have to," he says. "We'll make sure the ride is nice and easy if that's what people want."

Forest View Farms is open from 8:00 A.M. to 5:00 P.M. daily (weather permitting; no riding in the rain), and guides usually take riders out in groups. The least busy times are weekdays, Meyers says, and early arrivals are less rushed, too. No reservations are accepted, but guides will take a couple out by themselves if a group hasn't assembled within a reasonable period after you arrive. An hour-long ride costs $15.00 per person, with an extra $2.00 fee for an annual equestrian license (similar to a fishing license).

FOR MORE ROMANCE

If you're in the area during fall or winter and can pull together at least eighteen other adventurous people, take 'em on a hayride or sleigh ride at Forest View Farms. Hayrides are offered through the fall, for a minimum of twenty people at $7.00 each. There's also the Haunted Hayride, Meyers says, "basically a hayride, with a spooky theme." When you're in town to visit family and everyone needs to get out, remember: Dress warm, snuggle up, and celebrate! If it's just the two of you, and there's enough snow on the ground, choose a wildly romantic sleighride for two. At just $25 for a half hour, you'll jingle with delight all the way.

Hauntingly Romantic
HALLOWEEN WITH YOUR HONEY

HALLOWEEN MAKES EVERYONE LONG FOR somebody to love—and hug when the lights get dim. When you're lucky enough to have each other, it's a fabulous time to seek out thrills and chills together. Here's a sampling of ways to do that.

PRACTICAL NOTES: A downtown hotel offers good transportation to the Far North Side and the Near South Side. Driving is a good way to go, too, but then you'll have parking fees downtown.

DAY ONE: morning/afternoon

Check into a downtown hotel that may not be haunted—but who's to say? The **Palmer House Hilton** (17 East Monroe Street; 312-726-7500) is the nation's oldest continuously operating hotel, and there just have to be a few skeletons rattling around there somewhere. Ghosts or no, you'll enjoy its red-velvet atmosphere of a bygone era. The Beaux Arts ceiling alone, restored by an artisan who also worked on the Sistine Chapel, is more of an eyeful than you'll find in many new hotels.

The Palmer House's recently redone rooms offer a cozy home away from home, and suites let you spread out in style. Also consider the deluxe Towers, which whisks guests skyward via private elevator to a Towers lobby and lounge. Continental breakfasts are free here, as are cocktail-hour hors d'oeuvres and the services of a concierge. And all the Palmer House guests have access to a fitness club featuring a pool, steam room, sauna, whirlpool, exercise equipment, and even computerized equipment to measure your body fat.

Romance AT A GLANCE

♦ Snuggle up to the opulent atmosphere of the nation's oldest continuously operating hotel, the **Palmer House Hilton** (17 East Monroe Street; 312–726–7500).

♦Ride the El to the north end of town and find a dress-up bonanza at **A Lost Era** (1511 West Howard Street; 773–764–7400).

♦ Entertain your inner children by painting or carving pumpkins at **Oz Park** (601–733 West Webster Avenue; 312–742–7898).

♦ Go ghost-hunting all over town with Richard Crowe during the **Chicago Supernatural Ghost Tour** (708–499–0300).

♦ Delve into the Dia de los Muertos exhibit at the **Mexican Fine Arts Center Museum** (1852 West Nineteenth Street; 312–738–1503).

♦ Explore your inner lives with Chicago's favorite psychic, **Sonia Choquette** (773–989–1151).

♦ Laugh it all off at the world-famous cradle of improvisational comedy, **Second City** (1616 North Wells Street; 312–337–3992).

Regular room rates start at $199 for a double, but ask about the special rate of $139 for a double, or $184 in the Towers (both are based on availability).

From the hotel you can take the Howard elevated train (which stops right under the Palmer House) to its terminus on Howard Street. Here, **A Lost Era** (1511 West Howard Street; 773–764–7400) is an absolute classic: an old-fashioned, slightly dusty jumble of antiques, clothing, and assorted stuff that would make a perfect setting for a suspense novel—maybe a *Bell, Book and Candle* romance involving witch and mortal.

If you and your mortal mate are planning to attend Halloween festivities that call for a costume, this is the place to look. There are old coats, capes, suits, dresses, accessories, shoes, even wigs and makeup. There is knowledgeable help and enough space to try on. You can rent or buy props as well as costumes, so even if you don't need a getup this year, think ahead. Next year, after all, you might be throwing your own party.

Some people just know that a gorilla suit, not vintage duds, is what they really need. For them, **Broadway Costume** back downtown (1100 West Cermak Road; 312-829-6400) is ready to help. Founded in 1886, Broadway does many shows' costumes and offers the wonderful extra of having seamstresses on hand to help fit what you want. Here, too, you can buy or rent, and it's worth a visit just to browse through the dozens of hats and accessories you'll find here.

If you're not into dress-up, here's a low-key Halloween project your inner children can enjoy together. Get some felt-tip markers (or small cans of black, white, and red paint, plus several little sponge brushes), spray can of shellac, and a bunch of miniature pumpkins. Then settle down in the park for a jack-o'-lantern session. See which of you can create the scariest face, the funniest face, the face that looks most like your sweetheart. It's an entertaining, inexpensive way to play together.

Which park to pick? That depends mostly on the weather and where you're starting from. If it's pleasant and you're on the North Side, head for the magical realm of **Oz Park** (601-733 West Webster Avenue; 312-742-7898), where the entrance is marked by a statue of the Tin Man and there's even a yellow brick road. The park and trappings commemorate L. Frank Baum, who lived in Chicago while writing *The Wonderful Wizard of Oz*. Or, if you're downtown on a beautiful day, establish yourselves down by the river: specifically, on the north bank of the Chicago River, east of Michigan Avenue. This is where Sandra Bullock strolled with Bill Pullman in *While You Were Sleeping*, the Chicago-made romance in which the underdog guy gets the girl (yes!). Secluded, it's not . . . but there is the privacy city people allow each other in public. And how romantic to create your own little world here as you draw and giggle.

LUNCH

Oz Park is conveniently near a good spot for lunch. The **Red Lion Pub** (2446 North Lincoln; 773-348-2695) is a restaurant-bar that calls itself "the next best thing to being in England." At Halloween time, the Red Lion's big draw is its reputation as the haunted home of a woman whose death upstairs is said to have left a lingering lilac scent. Order a burger and decide for yourselves if there's any smell but beer in this cozy pub's atmosphere.

Do the Halloween thing with a dignified touch by strolling together through one of the city's most interesting cemeteries—so interesting, in fact, that the Chicago Architecture Foundation offers tours. **Graceland Cemetery and Chapel** *(4001 North Clark Street; 773–525–1105) is the resting place of many wealthy Chicagoans whose graves are nearly as ornate as their earthly homes were. Look for the beautifully decorated Getty Monument, which was designed by famed Chicago architect Louis Sullivan, and Lorado Taft's sculpture of a hooded figure, titled* Eternal Silence. *Money continues to talk at Graceland—and please, no Elvis jokes.*

If you'd like to take a tour of the cemetery with the Chicago Architecture Foundation, call (312) 922–3432 for information. If you want to go on your own, the cemetery is open daily.

Then head to the Near South Side neighborhood of Pilsen, where an artists' colony coexists with a predominantly Mexican population. Both influences are evident at the **Mexican Fine Arts Center Museum** (1852 West Nineteenth Street; 312–738–1503), which features an annual Dia de los Muertos (Day of the Dead) exhibit. This traditional Mexican version of All Souls' Day is celebrated on November 2, as families build *ofrendas,* or altars, that salute and/or evoke the spirit of a dead relative or friend. Of course, the spirit is welcome to pay survivors a visit; and some daring or humorous altars suggest a teasing invitation to death itself.

The museum's altars are created by artists, with a different theme each year. One year, for example, the theme was grandmothers, and it's no work to imagine how heartfelt and touching those *ofrendas* were. The show's popularity kept it in place until December as thousands of artists and regular folks came to see a sophisticated brand of folk art. Although some images look macabre to non-Mexicans—grinning skeletons are everywhere—it's an eye-opening look at another culture's attitude toward death. The museum is open from 10:00 A.M. to 5:00 P.M. Tuesday through Sunday, and admission is free.

DAY ONE: evening

DINNER

Feeling sufficiently spooked? Shake it off by stepping into another culture that honors its elders at **Le Colonial** (937 North Rush Street; 312–255–0088). The Vietnamese menu bears a slightly French accent; as for atmosphere, I have never heard anywhere described so consistently as both elegant and exotic. Before ordering, sip cocktails in the upstairs lounge, or at the popular outdoor tables if weather permits, for a full measure of fashionability.

The Irish say that the one thing the devil can't stand is laughter, so scare off the spooks by taking in a show at **Second City** (1616 North Wells Street; 312–337–3992). Over the years, this Chicago institution has nurtured many of the *Saturday Night Live* performers and writers, as well as actors and writers whose accomplishments run the cultural gamut, from Mike Nichols's highbrow directing career to later members' hit movies, such as *Ghostbusters*, *Animal House*, and *Caddyshack*.

Second City's improvisational approach to comedy gets a workout in the latter part of the show, and many people prefer the 11:00 P.M. shows on Friday and Saturday because they believe the later hour leads to greater wackiness. No matter what show you catch, the satire is wicked and the laughs are plentiful. Ticket prices range from $6.00 (on Monday, for a live "best of" show spanning thirty years of sketches) to $15.00. This also is the place for an after-dinner drink while you chuckle.

DAY TWO: morning/afternoon

BREAKFAST *or* LUNCH

 Make it a late breakfast or early lunch as you prepare for a full afternoon of thrills, chills, and "maybes." You'll begin the afternoon at **Goose Island Brewing** (1800 North Clybourn Avenue; 312-915-0071), where an early lunch might skip a brew but certainly includes one of the brewery's great sandwiches.

Finish up by noon, when you'll board the bus for the **Chicago Supernatural Ghost Tour.** Skeptics may doubt "professional ghost-hunter" Richard Crowe, who has offered these tours for twenty-five years, but there's no question he's got every local ghost story down. From Resurrection Mary—a ghostly girl often spotted hitchhiking along South Archer Avenue, trying to reach a long-ago dance—to sightings of Clarence Darrow's promised return to the spot near the Museum of Science and Industry where his ashes are scattered, Crowe is brimming with tales and possibilities.

The tour, which is offered from noon till 5:00 P.M. weekends and from 7:00 P.M. till midnight daily during the Halloween season, covers a wide slice of the metropolitan area and costs $40 per person. Crowe reports at least one wedding uniting a couple who met on a ghost tour, and it's doubtless his stories will make you cuddle a little closer to your safe, secure sweetheart. The only snag is that tours fill quickly during October and November, so Crowe encourages people to sign up early. Write P.O. Box 557544, Chicago, IL 60655-7544 with the date you want, or call him at (708) 499-0300.

DAY TWO: evening

As you leave the tour, you're sure to have more than enough to talk about! Do it over a brew at Goose Island, which really is a must for any beer lover. Then have a wonderful dinner and bring your evening to a close under yet another spell—the kind a wonderful musician can cast. At **Palette's** (1030 North State Parkway; 312-440-5200), the arty atmosphere is strictly for looks; the menu is a friendly list of steaks, seafood, pastas, and trendy pizzas ranging from about $10 to about $30. (Sample the snappy lemon tart—wow!) And the entertainment is sophisticated and timeless, provided by veteran piano man Bobby Harrison, who tickles the ivories in what *Chicago* magazine has lauded as the best piano bar in town. At this time of year, he probably doesn't have to be asked to do "Bewitched, Bothered and Bewildered" or "Witchcraft"!

FOR MORE ROMANCE

Give your sweetheart—or both of you—a peek into your inner self with Chicago's favorite psychic, **Sonia Choquette.** Sonia's impeccable reputation among intelligent people rests on her way of exploring what she calls your "soul path." There's no "you'll meet a tall, dark stranger" here; rather, she'll focus on your hopes and dreams, obstacles and strengths. She works in hour-long consultations, in which her tools include I Ching, tarot cards, and astrology (no crystal balls, thank you!).

Sonia will meet with a couple after seeing each of you individually, and you can get a gift certificate for a consultation. Call far ahead, since Sonia is booked months in advance; or call on the spur of the moment to see whether a cancellation will let you in sooner. Meanwhile, check out her writings in *The Psychic Pathway* and *Your Heart's Desire*. To book a consultation or arrange a gift certificate, call (773) 989-1151. Looking deeper isn't cheap—Sonia charges $375 for a consultation—but her legions of fans swear she's worth every penny. Judge for yourselves!

General Index

A

A La Carte, 177
Accent Chicago, 57
Ace Limousine, 209, 210, 216
Active Endeavors (sports equipment), 18
Addis Abeba (restaurant), 231, 233–34
Air & Water Show, 39
Al Khayam (restaurant), 231, 234
Alcala Western Wear, 237, 238–39
Allegro Hotel, 137
Allstate Arena, 193, 209, 212–13
A Lost Era (antiques), 244
Alta Vista Terrace, 186
Ambria (restaurant), 93, 96
Ancient Echoes (objets d'art), 18
Andersonville, 3–12
Andy's (jazz), 140, 222–23
Ann Barzel Dance Collection, 148, 150
Ann Sather (restaurant), 4–5
Anna Held Flower Shop, 5
Anna Kay Skin Care Salon, 56
Apple Tree Theater, 162
Argyle Street, 223, 224
Aria, 35
Arie Crown Theater, 215–16
Armitage Avenue, 13, 14
Army & Lou's (restaurant), 47, 51
Art Institute of Chicago, 126–28, 165, 217, 239
    Garden Restaurant, 127, 128–29
    Restaurant on the Park, 127, 129
    Thorne Rooms, 166
Arthur Heurtley House, 107–8
Artists' Restaurant, 126, 160
Arturo Express, 55
Arun's (restaurant), 221, 226
Auditorium Building, 110
Auditorium Theatre, 112, 155, 159

B

Baby Doll Polka Club, 24, 26, 149
Baha'i House of Worship, 172, 174
Barbara's Bookstore, 118
Barneys New York, 55
Basil's Kitchen, 210
Beau's Bistro, 59
Bed & Breakfast Chicago, Inc., 14, 93, 139, 155, 221
Ben & Jerry's Ice Cream Parlor, 20–21
Berghoff (restaurant), 111–112
Best Western Inn of Chicago, 236–37
Best Western River North Hotel, 237
Betsey Johnson, 55
Big (bar), 35
Big Chicks, 7
Big Shoulders Cafe, 22
Billy Goat Tavern, 38–39
Bin 36 (restaurant), 84, 87
Biograph Theater, 96–97
Bite Cafe, 96
Bloomingdale's, 43
Blue Chicago, 223

B.L.U.E.S., 140, 142

Bocaditos (restaurant), 98

bookstores, list of, 118–19

Breakfast Club, 152

Brent Books and Cards, 118

Brew & View at the Vic, 120

Broadway Costume, 244–45

Bronzeville, 47–48

Brookfield Zoo, 93, 97
 Indian Lake, 98

Brother Jimmy's BBQ, 241–42

Buckingham Fountain, 76, 78

Buckingham's (restaurant), 138

Buddy Guy's Legends (blues club),
 127, 131

Bughouse Square, 117

Bulls, Chicago, 187–91

Cafe Ba-Ba-Ree-Ba!, 164, 166–67

Cafe Brauer, 94

Cafe Iberico, 117–18

Cafe La Cave, 211

Cafe Matou, 53, 58

Cafe Olé, 98

Cafe Pyrenees, 70, 71–72

Cafe Selmarie, 124–25

Cafe Spiaggia, 65

Caliterra (restaurant), 60

Calo (restaurant), 6

Cape Cod Room, Drake Hotel,
 53, 54, 218

Carlucci (restaurant), 209, 212

Carson Pirie Scott & Co., 110–11

Centuries & Sleuths (bookstore), 118

Champagne Flights (balloon
 rides), 70, 71

Chanel Boutique, 56

Charlie Trotter's (restaurant),
 13, 14, 15

Charlie's Ale House, 87

Chatto (salon), 56

Checkerboard Lounge, 142

Cheli's Chili Bar, 193, 196

Cheney House Bed and Breakfast,
 104, 105

Chez Joel, 115, 119

Chiasso, 57

Chicago Academy of Sciences
 Peggy Notebaert Nature Museum,
 93, 95

Chicago Architecture
 Foundation, 110
 River Cruise, 104, 113

Chicago Bears, 177

Chicago Bee Building, 48

Chicago Blackhawks, 192–93

Chicago Botanic Garden,
 76, 79, 224–25

Chicago Bulls, 187, 188

Chicago Children's Museum, 196

Chicago Cubs, 178–81, 185

Chicago Cultural Center, 142–43, 218

Chicago Dance and Music Alliance,
 147, 150

Chicago Diner, 73, 96

Chicago Firehouse (restaurant), 219

Chicago Flower & Garden
 Show, 82

Chicago from the Lake, 86

Chicago Historical Lake and River
 Cruise, 84, 86

Chicago Historical Society, 14, 22, 49,
 164, 166

Chicagoland Canoe Base, 72–73

Chicago Opera Theater, 138

Chicago Presents Chamber Music and Early Music Series, 24

Chicago River, 70

Chicago Shakespeare Theater, 130, 162

Chicago Sportfishing Charters, 84, 89

Chicago Summer Dance, 153

Chicago Sun-Times Building, 34

Chicago Supernatural Cruise, 89

Chicago Supernatural Ghost Tour, 244, 248

Chicago Symphony Orchestra, 140, 145

Chicago Transit Authority (CTA), xiv the El, xiv, 118

Chicago White Sox, 185

Chicago Wolves, 193

Chinatown, 216, 227

Choquette, Sonia (psychic), 244, 249

City Suites (hotel), 179, 180

Civic Opera House, 132–34

Claridge Hotel, 115

Club 720, 232

Coaches Cafe, 174

CoCoRo (restaurant), 221, 222

Coffee & Tea Exchange, 17

Colleen Moore's Fairy Castle, 164–65

Comiskey Park, 185–86

Continental Airport Express, xiv

Convito Italiano, 70

Coq d'Or, 55

Corner Bakery, 91

Cotton Club (dancing), 148, 150

Court Theater, 24, 29, 158–59

Courtright's (restaurant), 237

Cousins (restaurant), 10

cruise ships
Odyssey, 38, 90
Spirit of Chicago, 84, 88
Windy, 84, 87

Cubby Bear, 182, 241

Cubs, Chicago, 178–81, 185

Currents (restaurant), 37

Cynthia Rowley (boutique), 16

Daley Bicentennial Plaza Ice Rink, 193–94

Dance Connection (dance instruction), 153

David and Alfred Smart Museum of Art, 30

Davis Theater, 124

Deleece (restaurant), 185

Des Plaines River, 69, 70
Offshore Marine, 70

Devon Avenue, 231, 235

Dick's Last Resort, 140, 144

Division Street (nightclub), 35

Division Street Russian Baths, 231, 233

Dixie Kitchen & Bait Shop, 24, 25

Documentary Films, 26

Do-It-Yourself Messiah, 60

Donald E. Stephens Museum of Hummels, 211

Double Door, 143

Drake Hotel, 52, 53, 137

DuSable Museum of African-American History, 47, 49

Edgewater Beach Apartments, 5

Edgewater Beach Hotel, 5

Eighth Regiment Armory, 48

Eli's the Place for Steak, 239

Emperor's Choice
(restaurant), 216, 227

Empty Bottle, 96, 143–44

Ernest Hemingway Museum, 108

Escada USA, 56, 57

ESPN Zone, 188

eta Creative Arts
Foundation, 47, 51

Evanston, 171–77

Everest (restaurant), 133, 135

F.A.O. Schwartz, 57

F.A.O. Schweetz, 57

Facets Cinematheque, 65–66

Faded Rose (furnishings), 17

Farm in the Zoo, 94

Festival Theater Shakespeare
in the Park, 109

5th Province (bar), 66

Findables (boutique), 19

Fireside Restaurant, 4, 12

Fischer, 16

Fish out of Water (B&B), 93

FitzGerald's, 240–41

Fogo de Chao (restaurant), 237

Foreign Affairs (restaurant), 115

Forest View Farms (stable), 237, 242

Four Seasons Hotel, 40–45, 137

Fourth Presbyterian
Church, 59, 189

Fourth World Artisans, 184

Frank Lloyd Wright, 103–10, 209
by Bus, 106
Home and Studio, 106

Prairie School of Architecture
National Historic District, 106

Frank W. Thomas House, 108

Frivolity, 17

Frontera Grill, 237, 238

Gamma Photo Labs, 19

Garden Buffet (restaurant), 226–27

Garden Restaurant, 127, 128–29

Geja's Cafe, 14, 19–20

Gethsemane Garden Center, 9

Gibsons Steak
House, 35–36, 116, 240

Ginger Man (bar, restaurant), 182

Ginkgo Tree Bookshop, 106

Gioco (restaurant), 151

Gladys' Luncheonette, 47, 48

Godiva Chocolatier, 57

Gold Coast Guest House, 76

Goodman Theatre, 53, 58, 130

Goose Island Brewing, 248

Gourmet Cabinet, 8

Graceland Cemetery and
Chapel, 246

Grandmother Gardens, 78–79

Grant Park, 31, 75, 76, 80

Grant Park Music
Festival, 76, 135

Great Lakes Spa Suites, 195

Great Train Story, 164

Green Dolphin Street (jazz club),
58–59

Green Mill Jazz
Club, 115, 123, 144

Griffin Theatre, 9, 11

Gucci, 43, 56

H

Harold Washington Library Center, 115, 120–21, 142
  Wintergarden, 121
Hau Giang (restaurant), 223
HeartBeat, 16
Heartland Cafe, 7
Heaven on Seven (restaurant), 193, 194
Hermès of Paris, 55
Hidden Cove Karaoke Bar, 223
Hills-DeCaro House, 108
Hilton Chicago, 137–38
Hot House (nightclub), 144
Hot Tix, 155, 157
Hotel Inter-Continental, 53, 54, 109
House of Blues, 139
House of Blues Hotel, 113
Hubbard Street Dance Theater, 149–50
Hyde Park, 23–30

I

IBM Building, 111
Illinois Center, 32
Improv Olympic, 179, 182
India House (restaurant), 235
Indian Lake, 98
Inn on Early, The (B&B), 4
Instant Ravinia, 80
Inter-Continental Hotel, 53, 54, 109
Irish American Heritage Center, 66
Isis on Armitage (boutique), 19
Italian Cultural Center, 62–63
Italian Village (restaurant), 133, 137

J

Jackson Harbor Grill
  (restaurant), 27, 90

Jackson Park, 24, 27, 75
  Wooded Island, 28
Jalapeño's (restaurant), 28
Jacky's Bistro, 173
Jane's (restaurant), 160
Jazz Showcase, 145–46
Jeweler's Center at the Mallers
  Building, 193, 195
Jilly's (bar/restaurant), 36
Jilly's (bistro), 173
Jimmy's (The Woodlawn Tap and
  Liquor Store), 29
John Hancock Building, 111
  Signature Room on the Ninety-
  Fifth Floor, 112
Joffrey Ballet, 148, 151
Jordan, Michael, 187–91

K

Kan Zaman (restaurant), 10–11
Kathy Osterman Beach, 5
Kingston Mines, (nightclub), 142
Kitty O'Shea's (bar), 138
Kiva (salon), 56
Kopi, A Traveler's Cafe, 4, 8
Korean Restaurant, 228–29
Kuni's (restaurant), 225
Kustom (dance nightclub), 148, 152

L

La Bocca della Verita
  (restaurant), 125
La Cantina (restaurant), 137
La Colonial (restaurant), 247
La Donna Restaurant, 6
La Finestra (restaurant), 6
La Fonda (restaurant), 231, 232
Lake Michigan, xi, 38, 39, 50, 70, 72

Odyssey (cruise ship), 38, 90

Odyssey jazz brunch, 90

Windy (cruise ship), 84, 87

Lakeshore Links, 37

Landmark of Andersonville, 8

La Petite Folie (restaurant), 28–29

La Sardine (restaurant), 164, 167

La Strada Ristorante, 215–18

Lava Lounge, 160

Le Bouchon (restaurant), 155, 156–57

Lifeline Theater, 162

Light Opera Works, 138

Lincoln Park, 4, 5, 13, 75

  Grandmother Gardens, 78

Lincoln Park

  Conservatory, 78, 95

Lincoln Park Zoological

  Gardens, 14, 21–22

Lincoln Park Zoo, 92–95

  Cafe Brauer, 94

  Farm in the Zoo, 94

Little Vietnam, 221, 223

Live Bait Theater, 182

Loew's House of Blues

  Hotel, 139–40

Lookingglass Theater

  Company, 130

Looks Like the Front Row, 177

Lord & Taylor, 56

Los Manos (gallery), 8

Lower Wacker Drive, 32, 38

Lucky Platter, 173

Lutnia (restaurant), 70, 73

Lyric Opera, 132–34, 136

M

Magnificent Mile, 52–61

Streeterville, 54

Majestic Hotel, 179–80

Manny's (restaurant), 66

Marianne Strokirk (salon), 55

Marilyn Miglin (salon), 55–56

Marina City, 111

Marquette, 86–87

Marriott Suites, 209, 210

Marriott Theater in

  Lincolnshire, 155–56

Marshall Field's, 56, 59–60, 110, 194

Martyrs (bar), 144

Mathiessen State Park, 206

Matsuya (restaurant), 181

Maud Travels (B&B), 155

Mayet Bead Design, 16

McCormick Place, xiii, 214–19

  Chicago Room (restaurant), 214

McFetridge Sports Center, 197

McGuane Park, 63, 64

Medici's Pan Pizza, 29–30

Mei Shung (restaurant), 221, 224

Mercury cruise, 39

Merrick Park, 176

Merz Apothecary, 124

Metro, 140, 143, 181–82

Metropole Lounge, 35

Metropolis (restaurant), 18

Mexican Fine Arts Center

  Museum, 244, 246

Mia Francesca (restaurant), 181

Michigan Avenue, 34, 53, 109

Michigan Avenue

  bridge, 32, 34, 88

Midway Airport, xiv

Midwest Buddhist Temple, 221,

  227–28

Millennium (restaurant), 188, 191

Mitchell Tower, 30
Monadnock Building, 110
Montrose Harbor, 6
Monument to the Great
    Migration, 47
Morton Arboretum, 76, 81
Morton's The Steakhouse of Chicago,
    239–40
Morton's, the Steakhouse, 209, 212
Mrs. Park's Tavern, 56
Mrs. Thomas Gale House, 108
Museum of Broadcast
    Communications, 218
Museum of Contemporary
    Art, 155, 157
Museum of Science and Industry, 24,
    26–27, 53, 164
    Christmas Around the World, 61
    Colleen Moore's Fairy
        Castle, 164–65
    Finnigan's Ice Cream Parlor, 27
    Great Train Story, 164
Music Box (movie
    theater), 179, 183–84
Myopic Books, 118

Nacional 27 (restaurant), 149, 232
Nathan Moore House, 108
National Heritage Corridor
    Cruise, 91
Navy Pier, 32, 35, 37, 86, 88, 193, 195
Neo-Futurarium (theater), 9–10, 11
Next Theater Company, 162
Newberry Library, 115, 116–117,
    148, 150
Nick's Fishmarket, 209, 211–12
Nike Town, 188, 189

900 North Michigan Cinemas, 43
No Exit (coffeehouse), 7
Noble Horse (carriage rides), 53, 54
North Lake Shore Drive
    (building), 111
North Pier, 32
North Pond Restaurant, 94
Northlight Theater, 162
Northwestern University, 171
Northwestern University
    Wildcats, 172

Oak Park, 106–7
Oak Street, 53, 55
Oak Street Beach, 39
Oakbrook Center, 211
Odyssey, 38, 61, 90
Offshore Marine, 70, 72
Ofie (restaurant), 179, 182–83
O'Hare International
    Airport, xiv, 208–210, 213
Ohashiatsu Chicago (massage),
    221, 225–26
Old Town School of Folk Music, 18,
    140, 141–42
Omni Ambassador East, 147, 148
Omni Orrington, 172, 174
One Sixtyblue (restaurant), 188, 191
Organic Theater Company, 162
Oriental Institute Museum, 30
Orly's (restaurant), 28, 30
Outpost (restaurant), 142
Oz Park, 244, 245

Palette's, 248
Palm, The, (restaurant), 37

Palm Court, 53, 58

Palmer House Hilton, 243, 244

Park Avenue Cafe, 59

Park West (nightclub), 20

Pasteur (restaurant), 223–24

Patel Bros., 235

Pauline's (diner), 11

Peace School, 229

Pegasus Players, 162

Pepper Lounge, 185

Peter A. Beachy House, 108

Petersen's Restaurant & Ice Cream
    Parlor, 108

Petterino's (restaurant), 130

Philander's Oak Park
    (restaurant), 109

Phoenix (restaurant), 164, 165

Piccolo Mondo (restaurant), 27

Picnic Express, 80

Pioneer Court, 34

Piven Theater, 162

Pizzeria Due, 63–64

Pizzeria Uno, 63–64

Pleasant Home Mansion, 108

Poor Phil's Shell Bar, 109

Pops for Champagne (wine
    bar), 215, 218–19

Prairie (restaurant), 121–22

Prairie Avenue Bookshop, 118

Prairie Avenue Historic District,
    215, 216

Printers Row (restaurant),
    127, 129–30

Printers Row Book Fair, 124

Promontory Point, 24, 28

PS Bangkok, 181

Pump Room, 148, 149

Ramada Plaza Hotel O'Hare, 209, 210

Ravinia Park, 80

Red Door Inn, 202, 205–6

Redfish (restaurant), 88–89

Redhead Piano Bar, The, 197

Red Light (restaurant), 93, 96

Red Lion Pub, 245

Redmoon Theater, 161

Red Tomato (restaurant), 184

Restaurant on the Park, 127, 129

Reza's (restaurant), 10

Rico's Cafe La Scala
    (restaurant), 191

Ritz-Carlton Cafe, 218

Riva (restaurant), 37

Rivers (restaurant), 135

Rockefeller Memorial Chapel, 24, 29

Rogers Park, 7

Rookery Building, 110

Rosa's Blues Cruise, 145

Rosehill Cemetery, 4, 11–12

Rosemont, 208–13

Rosemont Convention Center, 209

Rosemont Suites Hotel, 209–10

Rosemont Theater, 209, 213

Rush Street, 35

Russian Tea Time (restaurant), 130,
    155, 159

S

Saks Fifth Avenue, 56

Salon 1800, 17

Sandemeyer's Bookstore in Printers
    Row, 119

Santorini (restaurant), 188, 189

Savoy Truffle, 115, 116

Savvy Traveler, The (bookstore), 118

Schubas (bar, music), 241

Sears Tower, 111

Seasons (restaurant), 41–42

Second City, 244, 247

Shakespeare Garden, 76, 82

Shallots (restaurant), 66

Shaw's Crab House, 34–35

She She (restaurant), 141

Sheraton Chicago Hotel & Towers, 83–84

Sidney Marovitz Golf Course, 6

Simplon Orient Express (restaurant), 141

Skokie Park District Northshore Sculpture Garden, 77

Skyscraper Heels, 234

Soldier Field, 171, 177

South Shore Cultural Center, 47, 50

Spertus Museum, 66

Spiaggia (restaurant), 63, 65

Spirit of Chicago (cruise ship), 84, 88

Square One (dance club/restaurant), 152

Starbucks, 17

Stars of Lyric Opera, 135

Stars Our Destination, The, (bookstore), 118

Starved Rock State Park, 201–4

Steppenwolf Studio, 160–61

Strega Nona (restaurant), 184

Studio 90 (boutique), 7

Studio 910 (boutique), 16

Sugar Magnolia (boutique), 55

Sulzer Regional Library, 123–24

Summer Sunset Cruise, 88

Supreme Life Insurance, 48

Sutter House (B&B), 14

Swedish American Museum, 4, 7

Swedish Bakery, 7

Swissotel, 32–34

Hideaway Lounge, 37

Symphony Center, 140, 145

T

Tabula Tua (gifts), 17

Tallgrass (restaurant), 206–7

Tarantino's (restaurant), 21

Taste of Chicago (event), 32, 36–37

Teatro Vista, 161–62

Terra Museum of American Art, 239

theaters, 158, 162

Think Small by Rosebud (dollhouses), 164, 167

3rd Coast (cafe), 144

Tibet Cafe, 179, 182, 183

Tiffany & Co., 56

Tizi Melloul (restaurant), 122–23

Toguri Gifts and Mercantile Co., 228

Tomboy (restaurant), 6

Tony 'n' Tina's Wedding, 63, 64–65

Trader Vic's (restaurant), 231

Transitions Bookplace/Cafe, 118

Tribune Tower, 34

Trio, 173

Tucci Benucch (restaurant), 43

Twist (restaurant), 184

U

Uffa (restaurant), 21

Ultimo, 55

Unabridged Books, 119

Uncle Fun, 167

Uncommon Ground, 185

Union Station, xiv

United Center, 188, 190, 196, 197

Unity Temple, 104, 107

University of Chicago, 24, 25
    Rockefeller Memorial Chapel, 24, 29

University of Illinois Chicago Flames, 191

Urban Gardener, 16–17

USA Rainbow Roller Center, 10

U.S. Amateur Ballroom Dancers Association, 153

Va Pensiero (restaurant), 172, 175–76

Venetian Night (event), 39

Victory Gardens, 162

Village Arts Theater, 22

Vinci (restaurant), 155, 161

Vivere, 137

W Chicago Lakeshore (hotel), 230–31

Wabash YMCA, 48

Walker Bros. Original Pancake House, 176–77

Walk of Fame, 47–48

Walnut Room, Marshall Field & Co., 194

Washington Park, 48–49

Water Tower Place, 56

Watusi (restaurant), 196

Wave (restaurant), 231

Waveland Bowl, 37

Welles Park, 124

Wheeler Mansion (B&B), 24–25

While You Wait (boutique), 8

White Sox, 185

Whole Foods Market, 72

Wikstrom's (deli), 5

Wildflower Works garden, 77

Wild Hare & Singing Armadillo Frog Sanctuary, 231, 234

Williams-Sonoma, 56

Willowbrook Ballroom, 148, 149, 152–53, 237

Windward Sports, 74

Windy, 84, 87–88

Windy City Inn, 139, 140

Wintergarden, 121

Wishbone (restaurant), 120

Wisteria (clothing), 184

Women & Children First (bookstore), 7, 118

Woodfield Mall, 211

Woodlawn Tap and Liquor Store, 29

Wright, Frank Lloyd, 103–10, 209

Wrigley Building, 34

Wrigley Field, 178, 179, 180–81, 185

Wrigleyville, 178

Yoshi's Cafe, 161

Zanies Comedy Club, 185

Zoom Kitchen, 78

Special Indexes

ROMANTIC RESTAURANTS

Restaurant price categories in this index, represented by one to three dollar signs, reflect the cost of an appetizer, an entree, and dessert for each person. Under "Tea and Desserts," the cost indicators are only for tea and a dessert. The approximate price for each category is indicated in the following key:

Inexpensive ($): Less than $20
Moderate ($$): $20 to $40
Expensive ($$$): $40 and up

African/African-American

Addis Abeba ($), 3521 North Clark Street, 233–34

Army & Lou's ($), 422 East Seventy-fifth Street, 47, 51

Gladys' Luncheonette ($), 4527 South Indiana Avenue, 47, 48

Ofie ($) 3911 North Sheridan Road, 179, 182–83

American

Aria ($$$), 2909 Fairmont Hotel, 35

Brother Jimmy's BBQ ($$), 2909 North Sheffield Avenue, 241–42

Cafe La Cave ($$$), 2777 Mannheim Road, Des Plaines, 211

Chicago Firehouse ($$), 1401 South Michigan Avenue, 219

Courtright's ($$$), 85 South Archer Avenue, 237

Dixie Kitchen & Bait Shop ($$), 5225 South Harper Avenue, 24, 25

Fireside Restaurant ($$), 5739 North Ravenswood Avenue, 4, 12

Heaven on Seven ($), 111 North Wabash Avenue, 193, 194

Mrs. Park's Tavern ($$$), Doubletree Hotel and Suites, 57

North Pond Restaurant ($$), 2610 North Cannon Drive, 94

Pump Room ($$$), 1301 North State Parkway, 148, 149

Red Door Inn ($$), 1701 Water Street, Peru, 202, 205–6

Restaurant on the Park ($$), Art Institute, 127, 129

Ritz-Carlton Cafe ($$), Ritz Hotel, 218

Riva ($$), Navy Pier, 37

Rivers ($$), 30 South Wacker Drive, 135

Seasons ($$$), Four Seasons Hotel, 41–42

Signature Room on the Ninety-Fifth Floor, John Hancock Building ($$), 112

Tallgrass ($$$), 1006 South State, Lockport, 206–7

Walnut Room ($), Marshall Field's State Street store, 194

Asian

Arun's ($$$), 4156 North Kedzie Avenue, 221, 226

CoCoRo ($$), 668 North Wells Street, 221, 222

Emperor's Choice ($), 2238 South Wentworth Avenue, 216, 227

Hau Giang ($), 1104–6 West Argyle Street, 223

India House ($), 2548 West Devon Avenue, 235

Korean Restaurant ($), 2659 West Lawrence Avenue, 228–29

Kuni's ($), 511 Main Street, Evanston, 225

La Colonial ($$$), 937 West Rush Avenue, 247

Matsuya ($), 3469 North Clark Street, 181

Mei Shung ($), 5511 North Broadway Avenue, 221, 224

Pasteur ($$), 5525 North Broadway, 223–24

PS Bangkok ($$), 3345 North Clark Street, 181

Red Light ($$$), 820 West Randolph Street, 96

Tibet Cafe ($), 3913 North Sheridan Road, 179, 182, 183

For Breakfast

Ann Sather ($), 5207 North Clark Street, 4–5

Breakfast Club ($), 1381 West Hubbard Street, 152

Pauline's ($), 1754 West Balmoral Avenue, 11

Walker Bros. Original Pancake House ($), 153 Green Bay Road, Wilmette, 176–77

For Brunch

Dick's Last Resort ($), 435 East Illinois Street, 140, 144

Garden Buffet ($$), 5347 North Lincoln Avenue, 226–27

Jane's ($), 1655 West Cortland Street, 160

Medici's Pan Pizza ($), 1327 East Fifty-seventh Street, 29–30

Odyssey Jazz Brunch ($$), off Navy Pier, 90

Orly's ($), 1660 East Fifty-fifth Street, 29, 30

Park Avenue Cafe ($$), 199 East Walton, 59

Casual/Cafes

A La Carte ($), 111 Green Bay Road, Wilmette, 177

Artists' Cafe ($), 412 South Michigan Avenue, 126, 160

Arturo Express ($), 919 North Michigan Avenue, 55

Big Shoulders Cafe ($), Chicago Historical Society, 22

Billy Goat Tavern ($), 430 North Michigan Avenue, 38–39

Bite Cafe ($), 1039 North Western Avenue, 96

Cafe Brauer ($), Lincoln Park Zoo, 94

Cafe Chicago (aka Chicago Room, $), McCormick Place, 214

Cafe Selmarie ($), 2327 West Giddings Street, 124–25

Cheli's Chili Bar ($), 1137 West Madison Street, 193, 196

Chicago Diner ($), 3411 North Halsted Street, 96

Coaches Cafe ($), Omni Orrington Hotel, Evanston, 174

Corner Bakery ($$), 516 North Clark Street, 91

Garden Restaurant ($), Art Institute, 127, 128–29

Goose Island Brewing ($$), 1800 North Clybourn Avenue, 247–48

Jackson Harbor Grill ($), 6401 South Coast Guard Drive, 27, 90

Kopi, a Traveler's Cafe ($), 5317 North Clark Street, 4, 8

Lucky Platter ($), 514 Main Street, Evanston, 173

Manny's ($), 1411 South Jefferson Street, 66

Metropolis ($), 924 West Armitage Avenue, 18

Starbucks ($), 1001 West Armitage Avenue, 17

3rd Coast ($), 29 East Delaware Place, 144

Uncommon Ground ($), 1214 West Grace Street, 185

Whole Foods Market ($), 1000 West North Avenue, 72

Wishbone ($$), 1001 West Washington Street, 120

Zoom Kitchen ($), 923 North Rush Street, 77–78

For Dessert

Ben & Jerry's Ice Cream Parlor ($), 338 West Armitage Avenue, 20–21

Finnigan's Ice Cream Parlor, Museum of Science and Industry, 27

Petersen's Restaurant & Ice Cream Parlor ($), 1100 Chicago Avenue, Oak Park, 108

Swedish Bakery ($), 5348 North Clark Street, 7

Eclectic

Bin 36 ($$$), Marina City, 339 North Dearborn Street, 84, 87

Charlie Trotter's ($$$), 816 West Armitage Avenue, 13, 14, 15

Deleece ($$), 4004 North Southport Avenue, 185

Geja's Cafe (fondue, $$), 340 West Armitage Avenue, 14, 20

One Sixtyblue ($$$), 160 North Loomis Street, 188, 191

Outpost, ($$), 3438 North Clark Street, 142

Palette's ($$), 1030 North State Parkway, 248

Printers Row ($$$), 550 South Dearborn Street, 127, 129–30

Savoy Truffle ($$), 1466 North Ashland Avenue, 115, 116

Shallots ($$), 2324 North Clark Street, 66

She She ($$), 4539 North Lincoln Avenue, 141

Tomboy ($$), 5402 North Clark Street, 6

Watusi ($$), 1540 West North Avenue, 196

Yoshi's Cafe ($$), 3257 North Halsted Street, 161

French

Ambria ($$$), 2300 North Lincoln Park West, 93, 96

Cafe Matou ($$), 1846 North Milwaukee Avenue, 53, 58

Cafe Pyrenees ($$), River Tree Court, Milwaukee Avenue at Route 60, Vernon Hills, 70, 71–72

Chez Joel ($$), 1119 West Taylor Street, 115, 119

Everest ($$$), 440 South La Salle Street, 133, 135

Jacky's ($$$), 2545 Prairie Street, Evanston, 173

Jilly's (bistro) ($$), 2614 Green Bay Road, Evanston, 173

La Petite Fole ($$), 1504 East Fifty-fifth Street, 28

Le Bouchon ($$), 1958 North Damen Avenue, 155, 156–57

Seasons ($$$), Four Seasons Hotel, 41–42

German/Middle European

Berghoff ($$), 105 West Adams Street, 111–112

Lutnia ($$), 5532 West Belmont Avenue, 70, 73

Russian Tea Time ($$), 77 East Adams Street, 130, 155, 159

Simplon Orient Express ($$), 4520 North Lincoln Avenue, 141

Greek

Santorini ($$), 800 West Adams Street, 188, 189

Italian

Calo ($$), 5343 North Clark Street, 6

Carlucci ($$$), 6111 North River Road, Rosemont, 209, 212

Convito Italiano ($$), Plaza del Lago, 1515 Sheridan Road, Wilmette, 70

Gioco ($$), 1312 South Wabash Avenue, 151

Italian Village ($$), 71 West Monroe Street, 133, 137

La Bocca della Verita ($$), 4618 North Lincoln Avenue, 125

La Donna ($$), 5142 North Clark Street, 6

La Strada Ristorante ($$$), 151 North Michigan Avenue, 215, 218

Mia Francesca ($$), 3311 North Clark Street, 181

Piccolo Mondo ($$), Windermere Hotel, 1642 East Fifty-sixth Street, 27

Red Tomato ($$), 3417 North Southport Avenue, 184

Rico's Cafe La Scala ($$), 626 South Racine Avenue, 191

Spiaggia/Cafe Spiaggia ($$$/$$), 980 North Michigan Avenue, 63, 65

Strega Nona ($$), 3747 North Southport Avenue, 184

Tarantino's ($$), 1112 West Armitage Avenue, 21

Tucci Benucch ($$), 900 North Michigan Avenue, 43

Uffa ($$), 1008 West Armitage Avenue, 21

Va Pensiero ($$$), Margarita Inn, Evanston, 172, 175–76

Vinci ($$), 1732 North Halsted Street, 155, 161

Latin American/Spanish

Cafe Ba-Ba-Ree-Ba! ($$), 2024 North Halsted Street, 164, 166–67

Cafe Iberico ($$), 739 North La Salle Drive, 117–18

Fogo de Chao ($$$), 661 North La Salle Street, 237

Frontera Grill ($$), 445 North Clark Street, 237, 238

La Fonda ($), 5350 North Broadway, 231, 232

Nacional 27 ($$), 2748 North Lincoln Avenue, 149, 232

Middle Eastern

Al Khayam ($$), 2326 West Foster Avenue, 231, 234

Cousins ($$), 5203 North Clark Street, 10

Kan Zaman ($$), 5204 North Clark Street, 10–11

Reza's ($$), 5255 North Clark Street, 10

For Pizza

Medici's Pan Pizza ($), 1327 East Fifty-seventh Street, 29–30

Pizzeria Uno ($$), 29 East Ohio Street, 63–64

Pizzeria Due ($$), 619 North Wabash Avenue, 63–64

Seafood

Cape Cod Room ($$$), Drake Hotel, 53, 54, 218

Nick's Fishmarket ($$$), 10275 West Higgins Road, 209, 211–12

Philander's Oak Park ($$), Carleton Hotel, Oak Park, 109

Poor Phil's Shell Bar ($$), 139 Madison Street, Oak Park, 109

Redfish ($$), 40 North State Street, 88–89

Shaw's Crab House ($$), 21 East Hubbard Street, 34–35

Steak Houses

Buckingham's ($$$), Chicago Hilton and Towers, 138

Eli's, the Place for Steak ($$$), 215 East Chicago Avenue, 239

Gibsons Steak House ($$$), 1028 North Rush Street, 35, 36, 116, 240

Millennium ($$$), 832 West Randolph Street, 188, 191

Morton's The Steakhouse of Chicago ($$$), 1050 North State Street, 239–40

Morton's, the Steakhouse ($$$), 9525 West Bryn Mawr Avenue, Rosemont, 209, 212

Palm, The, ($$$), Swissotel, 37

Vegetarian-Friendly

Bite Cafe ($), 1039 North Western Avenue, 96

Chicago Diner ($), 3411 North Halsted Street, 73, 96

Heartland ($), 7000 North Glenwood Avenue, 7

Lucky Platter ($), 845 Davis Street, Evanston, 173

Red Light ($$$), 820 West Randolph Street, 96

Tibet Cafe ($), 3911 North Sheridan Road, 179, 182, 183

ROMANTIC LODGINGS

Note: *Bed & Breakfast Chicago handles bookings for many B&B homes listed here. The company's policy is to give guests the B&B's address only after a reservation is made. We've therefore listed B&B Chicago properties by neighborhood but without addresses.*

Inexpensive

Bed & Breakfast Chicago, 14, 93, 139, 155, 221

  Edgewater, 5

  Maud Travels (Wicker Park/Bucktown), 155

Cheney House Bed and Breakfast, 520 North East Avenue, Oak Park, 104, 105

Gold Coast Guest House, 76

Moderate

Best Western Inn of Chicago, 162 East Ohio Street, 236–37

Best Western River North, 125 West Ohio Street, 237

City Suites, 933 West Belmont Avenue, 179, 180

Claridge Hotel, 1244 North Dearborn Street, 115

Inter-Continental Hotel, 505 North Michigan Avenue, 109

Marriott Suites, 6155 North River Road, Rosemont, 209, 210

Omni Orrington, 1710 Orrington Avenue, Evanston, 172, 174

Majestic Hotel, 528 West Brompton Place, 179–80

Ramada Hotel O'Hare, 6600 North Mannheim Road, Rosemont, 209, 210

Rosemont Suites Hotel, 5500 North River Road, Rosemont, 209–10

Windy City Inn, 139, 140

Indulgent

Drake Hotel, 140 East Walton Street, 52, 53, 137

Four Seasons Hotel, 120 East Delaware Place, 40–45, 137

Hilton Chicago, 720 South Michigan Avenue, 137–38

Omni Ambassador East, 1300 North State Parkway, 147, 148

Palmer House Hilton, 17 South State Street, 243, 244

Sheraton Chicago Hotel & Towers, 301 East North Water Street, 83–84

Swissotel, 323 East Wacker Drive, 32–34

W Chicago Lakeshore, 644 North Lake Shore Drive, 230–31

Wheeler Mansion, 2020 South Calumet Avenue, 24–25

DAYTIME DIVERSIONS

Museums and Historic Districts

Alta Vista Terrace, 186

Art Institute of Chicago, 126–28, 164, 165, 217, 239

Bronzeville, 47–48

Chicago Academy of Science Peggy Notebaert Nature Museum, 93, 95

Chicago Children's Museum, 196

Chicago Historical Society, 14, 22, 49, 164, 166

David and Alfred Smart Museum of Art, 30

Donald E. Stephens Museum of Hummels, 211

DuSable Museum of African-American History, 47, 49

Ernest Hemingway Museum, 108

Italian Cultural Center, 62–63

Mexican Fine Arts Center Museum, 244, 246

Museum of Broadcast Communications, 218

Museum of Contemporary Art, 155, 157

Museum of Science and Industry, 24, 26–27, 53, 164

National Heritage Corridor (cruise), 91

Prairie Avenue Historic District, 215, 216

Prairie School of Architecture National Historic District, 106

Swedish American Museum, 4, 7

Terra Museum of American Art, 239

First Dates

Auditorium Theatre, 112, 155, 159

Grant Park, 75

Lincoln Park Zoo, 92–95

Second City, 244, 247

Wrigley Field, 178, 179, 180–81, 185

Outdoor Activities

ballooning, 71

bird-watching, 6

canoeing, 72–73

golf, 6

hiking, 205
horseback riding, 242
kayaking, 72
paddleboating, 94
sailboarding, 74
swimming, 5

Day Trips

Brookfield Zoo, 93, 97
Chicago Botanic Garden, 76, 79,
    224–25
Evanston, 171–77
Mathiessen State Park, 206
Oak Park, 104, 106–7

EVENING DIVERSIONS

Dancing

Baby Doll Polka Club, 24, 26, 149
Cotton Club, 148, 150
Kustom, 148, 152
Pump Room, 148, 149
Wild Hare & Singing Armadillo Frog
    Sanctuary, 231, 234
Willowbrook Ballroom, 148, 149,
    152–53, 237

Dance Performance

Chicago Dance and Music
    Alliance (performance
    hotline), 147, 150
Hubbard Street Dance
    Theater, 149–50
Joffrey Ballet, 148, 151

Classical Music, Opera

Chicago Opera Theater, 138
Chicago Symphony
    Orchestra, 140, 145
Do-It-Yourself *Messiah*, 60
Grant Park Music
    Festival, 76, 135
Light Opera Works, 138
Lyric Opera, 132–34, 136
Ravinia Park, 80

Jazz and Blues Clubs

Andy's (jazz), 140, 222–23
Blue Chicago (blues), 223
B.L.U.E.S., 140, 142
Buddy Guy's Legends
    (blues), 127, 131

Checkerboard Lounge (blues), 142

Green Dolphin Street (jazz), 58–59

Green Mill Jazz Club, 115, 123, 144

House of Blues, 139

Jazz Showcase, 145–46

Kingston Mines, 142

Rosa's Blues Cruise, 145

Venues for Other Popular Music

Cubby Bear (rock, pop, eclectic), 182, 241

Double Door (rock, eclectic), 143

Empty Bottle (rock, eclectic), 96, 143–44

FitzGerald's (country, rock), 240–41

Martyrs (rock, eclectic), 144

Metro (rock), 140, 143, 181–82

Old Town School of Folk Music (folk, eclectic), 18, 140, 141–42

Park West (rock, pop, eclectic), 20

Schubas (country, rock), 241

Wild Hare & Singing Armadillo Frog Sanctuary (reggae), 231, 234

Theater

Arie Crown Theater, 215–16

Auditorium Theatre, 112, 155, 159

Chicago Shakespeare Theater, 130, 162

Court Theater, 24, 29, 158–59

eta Creative Arts Foundation, 47, 51

Festival Theater Shakespeare in the Park, 109

Goodman Theatre, 53, 58, 130

Griffin Theater, 9, 11

Live Bait Theater, 182

Lookingglass, 130

Marriott Theatre in Lincolnshire, 155–56

Neo-Futurarium, 9–10, 11

Northlight, 162

Organic Theater, 162

Pegasus Players, 162

Piven Theater, 162

Redmoon, 161

Steppenwolf Studio, 160–61

Teatro Vista, 161–62

Tony 'n' Tina's Wedding, 63, 64–65

Comedy Clubs

Improv Olympic, 179, 182

Second City, 244, 247

Zanies, 185

Movie Theaters

Brew & View at the Vic, 120

Davis Theater, 124

Documentary Films, 26

Facets Cinematheque, 65–66

Music Box Theater, 179, 183–84

900 North Michigan Cinemas, 43

Village Arts Theater, 22

Cocktail Lounges and Bars

Big, 35

Big Chicks, 7

Charlie's Ale House, 87

Ginger Man, 182

Hidden Cove Karaoke Bar, 223

Jilly's, 36

Jimmy's (Woodlawn Tap and Liquor Store), 29

Kitty O'Sheas, 138

Pepper Lounge, 185

Pops for Champagne, 215, 218–19

Red Lion Pub, 245

Cabaret and Piano Bars

Hotel Inter-Continental, 53, 54, 109

Metropole Lounge, 35

Palette's, 248

Redhead Piano Bar, The, 197

Evening Cruises

Chicago Supernatural Cruise, 89

Rosa's Blues Cruise, 145

Spirit of Chicago, 84, 88

Summer Sunset Cruise, 88

About the Author

SUSAN FIGLIULO IS A LIFELONG CHICAGOAN whose flirtations with Florence and other European cities have only deepened her love for her hometown. A former copy editor at the *Chicago Sun-Times*, she compiled the newspaper's entertainment listings for two years, and has written extensively for its entertainment, fashion, food, travel, and general features sections. She is the author of four books and the editor of five, and she teaches journalism at Northwestern University. She lives near Chicago's lakefront in a hip, '50s split-level house with her family.